MW00791738

The Book of Mormon:

MOSIAH,
Salvation Only
Through
Christ

RELIGIOUS STUDIES CENTER PUBLICATIONS

BOOK OF MORMON SYMPOSIUM SERIES

The Book of Mormon: The
Keystone Scripture
The Book of Mormon: First
Nephi, the Doctrinal
Foundation
The Book of Mormon: Second
Nephi, the Doctrinal Structure

The Book of Mormon: Jacob
Through Words of Mormon,
To Learn with Joy
The Book of Mormon: Mosiah,
Salvation Only Through Christ

MONOGRAPH SERIES

Nibley on the Timely and the
Timeless
Deity and Death
The Glory of God Is
Intelligence
Reflections on Mormonism
Literature of Belief
The Words of Joseph Smith
Book of Mormon Authorship
Mormons and Muslims
The Temple in Antiquity

Isaiah and the Prophets
Scriptures for the Modern World
The Joseph Smith Translation:
The Restoration of Plain and
Precious Things
Apocryphal Writings and the
Latter-day Saints
The Pearl of Great Price:
Revelations From God
The Lectures on Faith in
Historical Perspective

SPECIALIZED MONOGRAPH SERIES

Supporting Saints: Life Stories
of Nineteenth-Century
Mormons
The Call of Zion: The Story of
the First Welsh Mormon
Emigration
The Religion and Family
Connection: Social Science
Perspectives

Welsh Mormon Writings
from 1844 to 1862: A
Historical Bibliography
Peter and the Popes
John Lyon: The Life of a
Pioneer Poet
Latter-day Prophets
and the United States
Constitution

OCCASIONAL PAPERS SERIES

Excavations at Seila, Egypt

The Book of Mormon:

MOSIAH, Salvation Only Through Christ

Papers from the Fifth Annual Book of Mormon Symposium, 1989

Edited by
Monte S. Nyman and Charles D. Tate, Jr.

Religious Studies Center
Brigham Young University
Provo, Utah

Library of Congress Catalog Card Number: 91–76149
ISBN 0–88494–816–1

First Printing, 1991

Distributed by BOOKCRAFT, INC.
Salt Lake City, Utah

Printed in the United States of America

Contents

"The Children of Christ" 1

Elder Neal A. Maxwell

I want to congratulate BYU for its sponsorship of the Book of Mormon symposia that now stretch out over several years. It's a marvelous thing for a university to be concerned with a great book, and in this instance, one of the greatest, even the greatest, we yet have. The day will come, brothers and sisters, when we will have other books of scripture which will emerge to accompany the Holy Bible and the Book of Mormon and the Doctrine and Covenants and the Pearl of Great Price. Presently you and I carry our scriptures around in a "quad"; the day will come when you'll need a little red wagon. And this university by then will surely want to sponsor some other symposia.

As in the hymn so beautifully rendered ("When I Survey the Wondrous Cross" by Isaac Watts), I will attempt to "survey the wondrous cross" by focusing on the Christology in the book of Mosiah, using not only the words of king Benjamin, Mosiah, Abinadi, and Alma the Younger, but scriptures which lie in the suburbs of the book of Mosiah as well as other related scriptures, of course. The final focus will be on the requirements for our becoming what king Benjamin called "the children of Christ," which is my text (Mosiah 1:11; 5:7, 9; 26:18).

Left unexplored are other possibilities, such as those some of our Latter-day Saint scholars are reconnoitering. For instance, the Biblical term *mosiah*, was probably a political designation; it is also an honorific title in Hebrew meaning

Elder Neal A. Maxwell is a member of the Quorum of the Twelve Apostles of The Church of Jesus Christ of Latter-day Saints.

"savior" or "rescuer" ("What Was a 'Mosiah'"). Not bad for a bright but unschooled Joseph Smith who, while translating early on, reportedly wondered aloud to Emma if there were walls around Jerusalem (*History of the Reorganized Church* 4:447).

There is so much more in the Book of Mormon than we have yet discovered. The book's divine architecture and rich furnishings will increasingly unfold to our view, further qualifying it as "a marvelous work and a wonder" (Isa 29:14). As noted from this pulpit in 1986, the Book of Mormon is like a vast mansion with gardens, "towers, courtyards, and wings" (Maxwell 15). All the rooms in this mansion need to be explored, whether by valued traditional scholars or those at the cutting edge. Each plays his role, and one Latter-day Saint scholar cannot say to the other, "I have no need of thee" (1 Cor 12:21).

Professor Hugh Nibley has reconnoitered much of that mansion, showing how our new dispensation links with the Old World. There is not only that Nibley nexus, but also one between him and several generations of Latter-day Saint scholars.

The book of Mosiah begins with a father instructing his sons, as was done in ancient Israel (see Deut 6:7). Alma the Younger remembered at a critical point a Christ-centered prophecy of his father, you'll recall (Alma 36:17, 18). The book of Mosiah ends as the successor-son approaches death, having sought to "do according to that which his father [king Benjamin] had done in all things" (Mosiah 6:7). As a result, Mosiah's people "did esteem him more than any other man" (Mosiah 29:40). So did the Mulekites, who accepted him as their next king though he was an immigrant among them.

Within the book's 60-plus printed pages occur not only family and political drama, but some stunning verses of Christology concerning the role, mission, and deeds of Jesus Christ. The Christology of the Restoration, brothers and sisters, restructures our understanding of so many fundamental realities.

A significant portion of king Benjamin's towering sermon was given to him by an angel, and angels speak by the power of the Holy Ghost (2 Nephi 32:3; see also Mosiah 3:2). At its center is the masterful sermon about the exclusive means of salvation:

> There shall be no other name given nor any other way nor means whereby salvation can come unto the children of men, only in and through the name of Christ, the Lord Omnipotent. (Mosiah 3:17; see also Mosiah 4:7)

It is not only the divinity, however, but also the specificity of king Benjamin's sermon which marks it. Hence father Helaman, in sending his two sons, Lehi and Nephi, on a mission to the land of Nephi, exhorted them to "remember, remember, my sons, the words which king Benjamin spake unto his people" (Hel 5:9).

In Restoration scriptures, not only is salvation specific, but so is the identity of the Savior, as various scriptures foretell. A savior was to be provided in the meridian of time (Moses 5:57). His name was to be Jesus Christ (2 Nephi 25:19). Christ volunteered for that mission premortally (Abr 3:27). He was to be born of Mary, a Nazarene, but to be born in Bethlehem, a fact over which some stumbled in the meridian of time (John 7:40–43; see also Micah 5:2; Matt 2:23; Luke 2:4; 1 Nephi 11:13, 18; Alma 7:10). There would even be a new star celebrating his birth (Hel 14:5; 3 Nephi 1:21).

We also learn from holy scriptures that the sacrifice of the Father's Firstborn premortally, his Only Begotten Son in the flesh, was the sacrifice of a Creator-God. The Atoner was the Lord God Omnipotent, who created this and many other planets (D&C 76:24; see also Mosiah 3:5, 8–9; Moses 1:33). Therefore, unlike the sacrifice of a mortal, Christ's was an "infinite atonement" made possible, declared king Benjamin, by the infinite goodness and mercy of God (Mosiah 4:6; 2 Nephi 9:7; Mosiah 5:3; Alma 34:10, 12).

Ironically, the Mortal Messiah would be disregarded and crucified, said Benjamin and Nephi:

> And lo, he cometh unto his own, that salvation might come unto the children of men even through faith on his name; and even after all this they shall consider him a man, . . . and shall scourge him, and shall crucify him. (Mosiah 3:9)

> And the world, because of their iniquity, shall judge him to be a thing of naught; wherefore they scourge him, and he suffereth it; and they smite him, and he suffereth it. Yea, they spit upon him, and he suffereth it. [Why?] Because of his loving kindness and his long-suffering towards the children of men. (1 Nephi 19:9)

This pattern of denigrating Jesus which existed in the meridian of time has continued in our time as noted in this next quotation:

> The sweetly-attractive-human-Jesus is a product of 19th century scepticism, produced by people who were ceasing to believe in His divinity but wanted to keep as much Christianity as they could. (Lewis, *Letters of C. S. Lewis* 181)

However mortals regard him, there is no other saving and atoning name under Heaven! (Mosiah 3:17; Moses 6:52).

> O remember, remember, . . . that there is no other way nor means whereby man can be saved, only through the atoning blood of Jesus Christ, who shall come; yea, remember that he cometh to redeem the world. (Hel 5:9)

All other gods, brothers and sisters, will fail and fall, including the gods of this world. Just as currently we're seeing again how "Princes come, Princes go, An hour of pomp[, An hour of] show" (Wright 9).

The Christology of Restoration scriptures constitutes the answer to what Amulek called "the great question," which is, will there really be a redeeming Christ? (Alma 34:5). As Abinadi declared, if Christ were not risen as the first fruits with all mortals to follow, then life would end in hopelessness (Mosiah 16:6–7). But he is risen, and life has profound purpose and rich meaning! One day, said king Benjamin, such knowledge of the Savior would spread:

> The time shall come when the knowledge of a Savior shall spread throughout every nation, kindred, tongue, and people. (Mosiah 3:20)

This spreading is happening in our day at an accelerated rate, brothers and sisters. At a later day, divine disclosure will be total and remarkable:

> The day cometh that . . . all things shall be revealed unto the children of men which ever have been among the children of men, and which ever will be even unto the end of the earth. (2 Nephi 27:11)

There will be so much to disclose (hence my comment about the little red wagon), because all the prophets have testified of the coming of Jesus Christ (Mosiah 13:33). Jesus, the Lord of all the prophets, even called them all "my prophets" (3 Nephi 1:13). How could he, therefore, as some aver, merely be one of them? Worse still, some consider Jesus only as another "moral teacher." Pronouncements such as Abinadi's underscore Jesus' transcending triumph:

> And thus God breaketh the bands of death, having gained the victory over death; giving the Son power to make intercession for the children of men—Having ascended into heaven, having the bowels of mercy; being filled with compassion towards the children of men; standing betwixt them and justice; having broken the bands of death, taken upon himself their iniquity and their transgressions, having redeemed them, and satisfied the demands of justice. (Mosiah 15:8–9)

It is very significant, brothers and sisters, that thought-leaders and founders of other world religions make no such declarative claims of divinity for themselves, though millions venerate these leaders. No wonder the Book of Mormon was urgently needed for "the convincing of the Jew and Gentile that Jesus is the Christ" (BofM title page). Such testifying is the purpose of all scripture, as the Apostle John stated:

> But these are written that ye might believe that Jesus is the Christ, the Son of God; and that believing ye might have life through his name. (John 20:31)

Of the Christ-centered plan of salvation, Nephi declared, "How great the importance to make these things known unto the inhabitants of the earth" (2 Nephi 2:8).

Jesus is even described as the Father, because he is the Father-Creator of this and other worlds. Furthermore, he is the

Father of all who are born again spiritually (D&C 76:24). When we take upon ourselves his name and covenant to keep his commandments, we then become his sons and daughters, "the children of Christ" (Mosiah 5:3–7; 15:1–5; 27:24–29). Additionally, since he and the Father are one in attributes and in purpose, Jesus acts for the Father through divine investiture, sometimes speaking as the Father (D&C 93:3–5).

The world desperately needs such divine declarations and instructions concerning *why* we are here and *how* we should live—concerning what is right and what is wrong, what is true and what is false. Much needed, too, is the Restoration's verification of the reality of the Resurrection. Also needed is the Restoration's clarification of the nature of God and man. Likewise much needed is the Restoration's enunciation of the divinely determined purposes of this mortal existence.

The millions who have lived on this planet in the midst of the famine foreseen by Amos, one of hearing the word of God, have never known the taste and nourishment of whole grain gospel (Amos 8:11–12). Instead, they have subsisted on the fast foods of philosophy. When Jesus spoke of himself as the bread of life, it caused some to walk no more with him (John 6:66). No wonder Jesus said, "Blessed is he, whosoever shall not be offended in me" (Matt 11:6; see also John 6:61). To which I add, brothers and sisters, "Blessed is he who is not offended by the Restoration!"

The pages of the Restoration scriptures ripple and resound with so many essential truths! For example, through correct Christology we learn about Christ's premortal pinnacle as the Creator-God, and how, even so, only later did he receive a fulness (D&C 93:12–13, 16). The Lord has told us how important it is to understand not only *what* we worship but also *how* to worship (D&C 93:19; see also John 4:22). After all, real adoration of the Father and Jesus results in the emulation of them! How shall we become more like them if we do not know about their character and nature? Said king Benjamin, "How knoweth a man the master whom he has not served, and who is a stranger unto him, and is far from the thoughts and intents of his heart?" (Mosiah 5:13).

Furthermore, unless we understand how the schoolmaster law of Moses was a preparing and a foretelling type, we will not understand dispensationalism, including the place of meridian Christianity in the stream of religious history.

> It is expedient that ye should keep the law of Moses as yet; but I say unto you, that the time shall come when it shall no more be expedient. . . . [For] God himself should come down among the children of men, and take upon him the form of man, and go forth in mighty power upon the face of the earth. (Mosiah 13:27, 34; see also Gal 3:24; Mosiah 3:15; 13:29–35; 16:14)

For modernity, brothers and sisters, the relevancy of the message in Mosiah is especially real. For instance, we are clearly indebted to our English ancestors for our precious King James Bible, yet that nation subsequently suffered from a wave of irreligion. Your Academic Vice-President, Stan Albrecht, wrote of that wave of irreligion:

> The pattern of downturn in religious activity in British society . . . made "agnosticism respectable if not universal by the turn of the century." . . . By the early 1900s . . . "The intelligentsia has sat back, shrugged its shoulders, given a sigh of relief, and decreed tacitly or by plain statement: 'The affair is over and done with.'"
> . . . By the 1970s only about 5 percent of the adult population in the Church of England even attended Easter religious services, and the percentage continues to decline. (98)

This next mid-twentieth-century expression is from a candid dean of that beautiful St. Paul's cathedral in London, who reportedly said:

> All my life I have struggled to find the purpose of living. I have tried to answer three questions which always seemed to be fundamental: the problem of eternity; the problem of the human personality; and the problem of evil.
> I have failed. I have solved none of them and I know no more now than when I started. I believe no one will ever solve them.
> I know as much about after-life as you do—NOTHING. I do not even know there is one—in the same sense which the Church teaches it. I have no vision of Heaven or of a welcoming God. I do not know what I shall find. I must wait and see. (*Daily Express* 4)

I marvel with you at how the Restoration scriptures are repetitively able to inform us and to inspire us; they enthrall us again and again. Ordinary books contain comparative crumbs, whereas the bread of life provides a perpetual feast!

Through those scriptures we learn that salvation is specific, not vague; it includes individual resurrection and triumph over death. We each will stand before God, as individuals, kneeling and confessing (Alma 12:13–15, 34–35). The faithful will even sit down, as individuals, with the spiritual notables of ages past, for God has said he will

> land their souls, yea, their immortal souls, at the right hand of God in the kingdom of heaven, to sit down with Abraham, and Isaac, and with Jacob, and with all our holy fathers, to go no more out. (Hel 3:30; see also Matt 8:11; Alma 7:25; D&C 124:19)

Thus we will not be merged into some unremembering molecular mass. Nor will we be mere droplets in an ocean of consciousness. In one way or another, sooner or later, all mortals will plead, as Alma did at his turning point, "O Jesus, thou Son of God, have mercy on me" (Alma 36:18). Thus we are blessed with enlarged perspectives because

> through the infinite goodness of God, and the manifestations of his Spirit, [we] have great views of that which is to come. (Mosiah 5:3)

Many in the world today, of course, are like some among the Book of Mormon peoples who believed that "when a man was dead, that was the end thereof" (Alma 30:18). For others, there are certain "existential givens":

> There is no built-in scheme of meaning in the world. (Yalom 67)

> No deity will save us; we must save ourselves. ("Humanist Manifesto II" 641)

No wonder the Restoration is so relevant and so urgent, having come, as the Lord said, so "that faith also might increase in the earth" (D&C 1:21). Compared to the great, divine declarations being noted this evening, which are central to real faith, what else really matters? Illustratively, two Book of

Mormon prophets in referring to a lesser concern, death, used the phrases "it mattereth not" or "it matters not" (Ether 15:34; Mosiah 13:9). Happily the reality of the Atonement does not depend upon either our awareness of it or our acceptance of it! Immortality is a free gift to all, including to the presently unappreciative (2 Nephi 2:4).

Meanwhile, however, even the spiritually sensitive feel less than full joy because, said C. S. Lewis:

> Our lifelong nostalgia, our longing to be reunited with something in the universe from which we now feel cut off, to be on the inside of some door which we have always seen from the outside, is . . . the truest index of our real situation. (*A Mind Awake* 23)

In that sense, brothers and sisters, we are all prodigals! We, too, must come to ourselves, having determined, "I will arise and go to my father" (Luke 15:18). This reunion, this reconciliation, is actually possible. Because of the Atonement, we are not irrevocably cut off.

The Book of Mormon, and the book of Mosiah in particular, has so many other jewels, including what seem to me, as a political scientist, to be some marvelous principles of politics and leadership. As more and more people on this planet are currently reaching out for a greater voice in their affairs, how relevant and instructive are the words of king Mosiah:

> Now it is not common that the voice of the people desireth anything contrary to that which is right; but it is common for the lesser part of the people to desire that which is not right; therefore this shall ye observe and make it your law—to do your business by the voice of the people. (Mosiah 29:26)

However, a democracy devoid of spiritual purpose may remain only a process, one within which citizens are merely part of a "lonely crowd," feeling separated from the past and from their ancestors. In contrast, king Mosiah's people had spiritual purpose; they deeply admired his profound political leadership:

9

> And they did wax strong in love towards Mosiah; yea, they did esteem him more than any other man; . . . yea, exceedingly, beyond measure. (Mosiah 29:40)

Laboring with his own hands, he was a man of peace and freedom. He wanted the children of Christ to esteem their neighbors as themselves (see Mosiah 27:4). King Mosiah was deeply anxious that all the people have "an equal chance" (Mosiah 27:3; 29:38). Yet there would be no free rides, because, said he, "every man [would] bear his [own] part" (Mosiah 29:34).

King Benjamin wanted his people to be filled with the love of God, to grow in the knowledge of that which is just and true, to have no mind to injure another, to live peaceably, to teach their children to love and to serve one another, and especially to succor the needy, including beggars (see Mosiah 4:12–30).

Mosiah was certainly not without his personal trials, for Mosiah went through that special suffering known only to the parents of disobedient children. The wickedness of his sons, along with Alma the Younger, created much trouble. Only after "wading through much tribulation" did they finally do much good and repair much of the damage they had done (Mosiah 27:28). Even later, however, after his sons had repented, before they were to have an enlarged missionary role, Mosiah first consulted with the Lord (Mosiah 28:6).

Mosiah also faced the challenges of leading a multi-grouped society: Nephites, Zoramites, Mulekites, Nehorites, Limhites (in Gideon), as well as those covenanters in Alma's group. How varied these interest groups were, and yet how united in their love of their leader.

Ponder this indicator of how Mosiah was an especially open, disclosing, and teaching leader:

> And many more things did king Mosiah write unto them, unfolding unto them all the trials and troubles of a righteous king, yea, all the travails of soul for their people, and also all the murmurings of the people to their king; [and note this brothers and sisters,] *and he explained it all unto them.* (Mosiah 29:33; emphasis added)

The political leader as teacher of his people.

King Benjamin as well as king Mosiah are examples of the leader-servant; they followed the pattern of their Master, Jesus. Prophets and leaders like Benjamin and Mosiah were charged to "regulate all the affairs of the church" (Mosiah 26:37). They did so both with style and with substance. There was love, but also admonishing discipline—with the repentant numbered among the Church and the unrepentant having their names blotted out. Missionary work went well; many were received into the Church by baptism (Mosiah 26:6, 35–39; Alma 1:7). So it was that the people became the children of Christ.

The children of Christ in any dispensation willingly make the sacrifice of a broken heart and a contrite spirit (Ps 51:17; 3 Nephi 9:20; D&C 59:8). The children of Christ are meek and malleable; their hearts can be broken, changed, or made anew. The child of Christ can eventually mature to become the woman or "the man of Christ," to whom the Lord promises that he will

> lead . . . the man of Christ in a strait and narrow course across that everlasting gulf of misery. (Hel 3:29)

The children of Christ are described by king Benjamin as being "submissive, meek, humble, patient, full of love," and then this sobering line, "willing to submit to all things which the Lord seeth fit to inflict upon [them], even as a child doth submit to his father" (Mosiah 3:19). Significantly, twice in the ensuing book of Alma the very same recitation of these important qualities is made with several added: to be "gentle," "temperate," easily entreated, and "long-suffering" (Alma 7:23; 13:28).

These virtues, brothers and sisters, are cardinal; they are portable; and they are eternal. They reflect in each of us the seriousness of our discipleship. After all, true disciples will continue to grow spiritually because they have "faith unto repentance" (Alma 34:16, 17; see also Alma 13:10). It takes a lot of faith to repent; otherwise, why bother? These cardinal qualities will finally rise with us in the Resurrection.

Interesting, isn't it, in contemplating each of the qualities in this cluster, how they remind us of the need to tame our egos? Blessed is the person who is progressing in the taming of his or her egotistic self. King Benjamin, for instance, had not the least desire to boast of himself (Mosiah 2:16). He was unconcerned with projecting his political image because he had Christ's image in his countenance.

In these marvelous scriptures we are not only instructed in what we are to become, but we're also told what we are to avoid. Abinadi noted, for instance, how Jesus suffered temptation but yielded not (Mosiah 15:5). Unlike many of us, Christ gave no heed to temptations (D&C 20:22). This is yet another instructive example to us, his children, for even if you and I later evict temptations, we so often first entertain them at length.

The development of these cardinal virtues is central to God's plan for all of us. It was a lack of this perspective about God's plans that was the failure of Laman and Lemuel, of whom we read:

> And thus Laman and Lemuel . . . did murmur because they knew not the dealings of that God who had created them. (1 Nephi 2:12; see also Mosiah 10:14)

They didn't understand. They deeply resented difficulty.

Illustratively, we are advised that on occasion God will chasten his people and will try our patience and our faith (Mosiah 23:21). Whenever you and I, even inwardly, ask the question, "Why, O Lord?" we pose a question which goes to the heart of the further development of our faith amid tutoring. Similarly, the question, "How long, O Lord, how long?" is one which goes to the very heart of developing patience. Thus we see how interactive all these things are in the developmental dimensions of God's plan of salvation which culminates in eternal life.

Immortality comes to all by God's grace—it is unearned "after all we can do" (2 Nephi 25:23). Full salvation, however, eternal life, is God's greatest gift (D&C 6:13; 14:7). Unlike the blessing of immortality, eternal life is conditional. Eternal life, said king Benjamin, is more than endless existence; it is endless happiness (Mosiah 2:41). It was this which was promised to Alma the Younger:

Thou art my servant; and I covenant with thee that thou shalt have eternal life. (Mosiah 26:20)

Eternal life will feature the joys of "always rejoic[ing], and be[ing] filled with . . . love" (Mosiah 4:12), of growing in the knowledge of God's glory, of being in his presence, of being in eternal families and friendships forever (D&C 76:62; 130:2; 132:24, 55).

Eternal life also brings with it, brothers and sisters, the full bestowal of all the specific promises made to us in connection with the temple's initiatory ordinances and the holy endowment and temple sealing; then thereby God "may seal you his" (Mosiah 5:15). Additionally, all other blessings promised upon the keeping of God's commandments will likewise flow in the abundant Malachi measure, so many that "there shall not be room enough to receive [them]" (Mal 3:10). John declared that the faithful "shall inherit all things" (Rev 21:7). Modern scriptures confirm that the faithful will eventually receive "all that [the] Father hath" (D&C 84:38). Meanwhile, how much of that promised birthright will some of us sell and for what particular mess of pottage? Comparing the magnitude of all this, all the great gifts of God to us, our meager service to Him, said king Benjamin, makes us unprofitable servants (Mosiah 2:21; 4:19).

As we accept Christ and become his children, there begins to be a change—even a "mighty change" (Mosiah 5:2) in us. As we earnestly strive to become one with him and with his purposes, we come to resemble him, though in small degrees. Christ, who has saved us, thus becomes the father of our salvation, and we become the "children of Christ," having his image increasingly in our countenances and in our conduct (Mosiah 5:7).

The children of Christ will understand, for instance, the importance of feasting regularly on sacred records which testify of Jesus (see 2 Nephi 31:20; 32:3; Jacob 2:9; JS-M 1:37). Without such records, belief in him and in the glorious Resurrection can quickly wane:

> And at the time that Mosiah discovered them, . . . they had brought no records with them; and they denied the being of their Creator. (Omni 1:17)

> There were many of the rising generation that could not understand the words of king Benjamin, being little children at the time he spake unto his people; and they did not believe the tradition of their fathers. They did not believe what had been said concerning the resurrection of the dead, neither did they believe concerning the coming of Christ. (Mosiah 26:1–2)

For those either untaught or unheeding of the essential gospel truths, the lapse of faith in Christ is but one generation away!

So many scriptures point to the reality that Jesus is to be the specific example for the children of Christ. We really are to emulate him in our lives. Consider these examples:

> Be ye therefore perfect, even as your Father which is in heaven is perfect. (Matt 5:48)

> Therefore I would that ye should be perfect even as I, or your Father who is in heaven is perfect. (3 Nephi 12:48)

> Therefore, what manner of men ought ye to be? Verily I say unto you, even as I am. (3 Nephi 27:27)

> Ye shall be holy; for I am holy. (Lev 11:44)

> Be ye therefore merciful, as your Father also is merciful. (Luke 6:36)

> For I have given you an example, that ye should do as I have done to you. (John 13:15)

> Jesus Christ [shows] forth all long-suffering, for a pattern to them which should hereafter believe on him. (1 Tim 1:16)

> Christ also suffered for us, leaving us an example, that ye should follow his steps. (1 Peter 2:21)

> And again, it showeth unto the children of men the straitness of the path, and the narrowness of the gate, by which they should enter, he having set the example before them. (2 Nephi 31:9)

> Ye know the things that ye must do in my church; for the works which ye have seen me do that shall ye also do; for that which ye have seen me do even that shall ye do. (3 Nephi 27:21)

> Behold I am the light; I have set an example for you. (3 Nephi 18:16)

No wonder, in view of these and many other scriptures, that Joseph Smith taught, "If you wish to go where God is, you must be like God, . . . [drawing towards God in] the principles which God possesses" (*Teachings of the Prophet Joseph Smith* 216; hereafter *TPJS*).

The "loving kindness" of the Lord which Nephi spoke about (1 Nephi 19:9) is likewise noted in Exodus:

> And the Lord passed by . . . him, and proclaimed, The Lord, The Lord God, merciful and gracious, longsuffering, and abundant in goodness and truth. (Ex 34:6)

There is even more exemplifying seen in this soaring scriptural declaration: mercy and justice both make their rightful claims, but, even so, mercy "overpowereth justice" (Alma 34:15).

Since Jesus' qualities are to be understood and emulated by his children, it is, as the Prophet Joseph Smith taught us, vital for us to comprehend the character and personality of God, if we are to comprehend ourselves (*TPJS* 343).

However, as we begin to truly emulate Jesus' example, we will thereby encounter the costs of discipleship. Through our own micro-experiences, we will come to know what it is to suffer and to be reproached for taking upon ourselves the name of Christ (Luke 6:22; 1 Peter 4:14). Therefore, brothers and sisters, our fiery trials, said Peter, should not be thought of as "some strange thing" (1 Peter 4:12).

As the believing, trusting children of Christ become more and more Christlike, it will be evident in their daily lives, whether in their treatment of the poor or in the management of their civic affairs (see Mosiah 4:16). Ammon taught, for instance, that those who become the children of Christ will truly be of "great benefit to [their] fellow beings" (Mosiah 8:18). Alma, Mosiah's successor, learned from the Lord how the illuminated individual can actually evoke faith in other people by "his words alone" (Mosiah 26:15–16; see also 3 Nephi 11:2; D&C 46:13–14).

With his highly developed sense of proportion, king Benjamin said, "Even so I would that ye should . . . always retain in remembrance, the greatness of God, and your own nothingness, and his goodness and long-suffering towards you" (Mosiah 4:11; see also Moses 1:9–10). We who have the Restoration scriptures have further reasons to feel overwhelmed by the greatness of God. We are told that there is no space in which there is no kingdom (D&C 88:37). God's works are without end, and he has created worlds which are "innumerable . . . unto man" (Moses 1:4, 33, 35). The very heavens and the planets do witness that there is a Supreme Creator (Alma 30:44).

Mortal astrophysics confirms the awesome nature of the universe. Astronomers recently indicated they have discovered a collection of galaxies "so extensive that it defies explanation by any present theory." Dubbed "the great wall," these "galaxies form a sheet . . . 3,000 billion billion miles." One scientist said, "We keep being surprised that we keep seeing something bigger as we go out farther" (*Sacramento Union* 22).

> And as one earth shall pass away, and the heavens thereof even so shall another come; and there is no end to my works. (Moses 1:38)

At the Judgment Day, declared Mosiah's successor, everyone at that assemblage will "confess that [God] is God" (Mosiah 27:31). When one considers history's disbelieving notables who will be there, these lines are subduing:

> Then shall they confess, who live without God in the world, that the judgment of an everlasting punishment is just upon them; and they shall quake, and tremble, and shrink beneath the glance of his all-searching eye. (Mosiah 27:31; see also Mosiah 16:1; Alma 12:15)

However, the children of Christ, the faithful, "shall stand before him" and "see his face with pleasure" (Enos 1:27). His all-searching eyes will likewise emanate perfect, overwhelming love, a love which, alas, few will have reciprocated. Our sense of undeservingness will be deep and profound!

Thus we have a sense of the rendezvous which lies ahead. There is no end to his works. At that same Judgment Day, as they confess that God is God, there will be this sense of being enveloped, as indicated, in a love which we will not have reciprocated. It will be subduing beyond measure.

We do not know the details of how they who live without God in the world will confess, but they will acknowledge openly and publicly that his judgment is just, "and shrink beneath the glance of his all-searching eye" (Mosiah 27:31). I'm struck, as you must be, by how the faithful will see his face with pleasure. I am struck as well by Jesus' promise of ackowledgment for those who have been faithful, even though the faithful will not have reciprocated his love as it should have been reciprocated. Hence, this sense of undeservingness, and how deep and profound it will be. Restoration scriptures tell us who else will be there. Benjamin, Abinadi, Mosiah, and Moroni will be present at the day of judgment, and we will be judged out of their words (Moroni 10:27).

At the Judgment, we will not only have the prophesied "bright recollection" and "perfect remembrance" of our misdeeds, but of happy things as well (Alma 11:43). The joyous things will be preserved too (see Alma 5:18; D&C 93:33). (Most of you are too young to appreciate how those of us who are older feel as the sense of memory slips away. I can safely hide my own Easter eggs now.) Among "all things that will be restored" will be our memories (see Alma 11:43; 40:23), including eventually our premortal memories. What a flood of feeling and fact will come to us then, as a loving God deems wise, and it will increase our gratefulness for God's long-suffering and for Jesus' atonement. What joy upon being connected again with the memories of both the first and the second estates!

Meanwhile, however, during this life we will continue to experience the unwelcome sense "of having ended a chapter. One more portion of oneself slipping away into the past" (Lewis, *Letters of C. S. Lewis* 306). Mary Warnock wrote about how "anything that is *over* . . . is a lost *possession*. . . . The past is a paradise from which we are necessarily excluded" (Jacobson 52). Dan Jacobson, commenting on Thomas Hardy, wrote of Hardy's realization that past experiences once shared "are now his alone. . . . The past continually comes to him; but he knows that he can never go back to it" (52). But one day it will all come back!

The children of Christ know whose they are, whence they came, why they are here, and what manner of men and women they are to become (2 Peter 3:11; 3 Nephi 27:27). Still, the children of Christ, like Alma, will "long to be there" in the "royal courts on high" (Alma 36:22; "O My Father," *Hymns* #292). It is the only destination that really matters. Resplendent reunion awaits us! Brothers and sisters, what is more natural and more wonderful than children going home? Especially to a home where the past, the present, and the future form an everlasting and eternal now! (D&C 38:2; 130:7; *TPJS* 220).

Therefore, let us do as king Benjamin urged us:

> Believe in God; believe that he is, and that he created all things, both in heaven and in earth; believe that he has all wisdom, and all power, both in heaven and in earth; believe that man doth not comprehend all the things which the Lord can comprehend. (Mosiah 4:6, 9)

I ask you, as I ask myself as I prepare to close, as we think of the discipleship involved in becoming the children of Christ, brothers and sisters, how can there be refining fires without some heat? How can we develop greater patience without some instructive waiting? How can we develop more empathy without first bearing one another's burdens? Not only that their burdens may be lightened, but that we thereby may be enlightened through greater empathy. How can we have increased individual faith without some customized uncertainty in our lives? How can we learn to live in cheerful insecurity without some insecurity? How can there be the later magnification without some present deprivation?

Except we are thus tutored, how else shall we grow spiritually to become the men and women of Christ? In this brief mortality, therefore, there is so much to do; reveries, even deserved reveries, are often rudely elbowed aside by tutoring adversities. Meanwhile, as faithful children, the challenge is will we prove ourselves, in king Benjamin's phrase, "willing to submit" (Mosiah 3:19).

Finally, I should like to leave my own witness with you. In my life, whichever way I turn, brethren and sisters, there looms "Jesus! Name of Wondrous Love!" (*The Choirbook* 24–27). He is our fully atoning and our fully comprehending Savior. And in the words of scripture, there is none like unto him (see Ex 8:10; Ps 86:8; Jer 10:6–7).

Whether taught in the holy scriptures or in the holy temples, his gospel is remarkable. Whether it concerns the nature of God, the nature of man, the nature of the universe, the nature of this mortal experience, it is remarkable. His gospel is stunning in its interior consistency; it is breathtaking in its exterior expansiveness. Rather than being without the gospel in a mortal maze, "I Stand All Amazed" (*Hymns* #193) at the wonders of that gospel, that we should be privileged to be his children!

Whatever my experiences, the spiritual facts which have emerged from these encompass me. They encompass me and echo the words of king Benjamin about "the goodness of God, and his matchless power, and his wisdom, and his patience, and his long-suffering towards the children of men" (Mosiah 4:6).

Every one of God's virtues I have counted on, I count on now, I will count on again, whether it is his long-suffering, his matchless power, or his goodness, and so do you. Those are the very virtues that must come, in a measure, to be ours, brothers and sisters. This is the journey of discipleship. We must, like the prodigal son, arise and go to our Father and be prepared for that resplendent reunion. And we can hasten the journey only in so far as we hasten the process of becoming like him, as the children of Christ going home. For his help in my personal journey, I plead, and for his help for you. You are the leaven for mankind, and all the winds of political freedom that blow, that can bring great blessings with them, intrinsically carry within them the added prospects that the children of Christ will be able to reach out to more of their brothers and sisters on this planet with this wondrous message—as we "survey the wondrous cross."

May it be so, I humbly pray, in the name of Jesus Christ. Amen.

BIBLIOGRAPHY

Albrecht, Stan L. "The Consequential Dimension of Mormon Religiosity." *BYU Studies* (Spr 1989) 29:57–108.

The Choirbook. Salt Lake City: The Church of Jesus Christ of Latter-day Saints, 1982.

Daily Express (13 Jul 1958) 4.

The History of the Reorganized Church of Jesus Christ of Latter Day Saints. 8 vols. Independence, MO: Herald, 1896.

"Humanist Manifesto II." *The Encyclopedia of American Religions: Religious Creeds.* Ed. J. Gordon Melton. Detroit: Gale, 1988.

Hymns. Salt Lake City: The Church of Jesus Christ of Latter-day Saints, 1985.

Jacobson, Dan. "Of Time and Poetry." *Commentary* (Nov 1989) 88:48–53.

Lewis, C. S. *Letters of C. S. Lewis.* Ed. W. H. Lewis. New York: Harcourt, 1966.

————. *A Mind Awake: An Anthology of C. S. Lewis.* Ed. Clyde S. Kilby. New York: Harcourt, 1968.

Maxwell, Neal A. "The Book of Mormon: A Great Answer to 'The Great Question.'" *The Book of Mormon: First Nephi, The Doctrinal Foundation.* Salt Lake City: Bookcraft, 1988. 1–17.

Sacramento Union (19 Nov 1989) 22.

Teachings of the Prophet Joseph Smith. Comp. Joseph Fielding Smith. Salt Lake City: Deseret Book, 1976.

"What Was a 'Mosiah'?" F.A.R.M.S. Update. Provo, UT: F.A.R.M.S., 1989.

Wright, Robert and George Forrest. *Kismet: A Musical Arabian Night.* Boston: Frank, 1955.

Yalom, Irvin D. "Exploring Psychic Interiors." *U. S. News and World Report* (30 Oct 1989) 107:67.

What Parents Should Teach Their Children from the Book of Mosiah

2

Kenneth W. Anderson

Most parents want to be good parents, to prepare their children to live successful lives. The living prophets of the Lord and the scriptures have instructed parents to teach their children to learn and obey the decrees of God (Ether 2:11). One of the best ways to learn those decrees is from reading the Book of Mormon. In the April 1960 general conference of the Church, Elder Marion G. Romney, then of the Quorum of the Twelve Apostles, said the following:

> I feel certain that if, in our homes, parents will read from the Book of Mormon prayerfully and regularly, both by themselves and with their children, the spirit of that great book will come to permeate our homes and all who dwell therein. The spirit of reverence will increase, mutual respect and consideration for each other will grow. The spirit of contention will depart. Parents will counsel their children in greater love and wisdom. Children will be more responsive and submissive to that counsel. Righteousness will increase. Faith, hope, and charity—the true love of Christ—will abound in our homes and lives, bringing in their wake peace, joy, and happiness. (436)

When President Ezra Taft Benson gave his first conference address after he was sustained as the prophet and president of the Church, he quoted this part of Elder Romney's talk and seconded his teachings. Then in his concluding address to that conference, President Benson said:

Kenneth W. Anderson is director of Evening Classes at Brigham Young University.

> I bless you with increased discernment to judge between Christ and
> anti-Christ. I bless you with increased power to do good and resist
> evil. I bless you with increased *understanding* of the Book of Mor-
> mon. I promise you that from this moment forward, if we will daily
> sup from its pages and abide by its precepts, God will pour out upon
> each child of Zion and the Church a blessing hitherto unknown. ("A
> Sacred Responsibility" 78)

In light of this counsel to read and teach the Book of
Mormon in our homes, this paper will present five simple, yet
powerful scriptural lessons from the book of Mosiah that
parents can teach their children. It will also give practical
suggestions on how to make this teaching effective. If mothers
and fathers will teach their children these principles in the right
spirit, they will be better able to reach out to them in love as
they invite them to live by the light of the gospel.

Lesson 1: Teach Children to Love, Study, and Obey the Scriptures and the Living Prophets

King Benjamin taught his children the importance of
studying the word of God: "And it came to pass that he [king
Benjamin] had three sons; and he called their names Mosiah,
and Helorum, and Helaman. And he caused that they should
be taught in all the language of his fathers, that thereby they
might become men of understanding" (Mosiah 1:2). These
sons, as President Benson notes, "needed to understand and use
the language of holy writ. If they didn't know the right words,
they wouldn't know the plan" ("Worthy Fathers, Worthy Sons"
36). When parents use words like *Jesus Christ, Savior, Creation, Fall, Atonement, covenant, salvation, justice, mercy,* and
eternal life in the home, they familiarize their children with the
language of holy writ.

Having taught his children the language of the scriptures,
king Benjamin also ensured that they understood the importance of the word of God:

> My sons, I would that ye should remember that were it not for these
> plates . . . we must have suffered in ignorance, . . . not knowing the

> mysteries of God. For it were not possible that our father, Lehi, could have remembered all these things, to have taught them to his children, except it were for the help of these plates; . . . therefore he could read these engravings, and teach them to his children, that thereby they could teach them to their children, and so fulfilling the commandments of God. (Mosiah 1:3–4)

Verse 5 notes that had they not had "his commandments always before [their] eyes," they would have dwindled in unbelief as the Lamanites had. For us today to "have his commandments always before our [children's] eyes" means that we need to encourage them to read the scriptures, especially the Book of Mormon.

Children may require assistance as they read the Book of Mormon the first time. Some children need nothing but the idea and some encouragement. Others, at an early age, need help to read even a line. Some progress through the Book of Mormon only by taking turns reading a verse with a parent. Over the years, they will begin reading on their own. Although we don't know how much children understand the Book of Mormon the first time they read it, when they complete the book they experience a change in their hearts. The Church becomes their Church. They belong. Confidence floods through their souls and sweeps away bridges of disbelief and obstacles of doubt.

There is another important lesson to learn from king Benjamin's example. In Mosiah 1:6–7, king Benjamin tenderly bears his testimony to his sons, saying, "O my sons, I would that ye should remember that these sayings are true, and also that these records are true. . . . Remember to search them diligently, that ye may profit thereby." The Prophet Joseph Smith testified of the importance of parents' bearing testimony to their children when he said:

> We have also seen that it was human testimony, and human testimony only, that excited this inquiry [after a knowledge of the glory of God] in their minds in the first instance. It was the credence they gave to the testimony of their fathers, it having aroused their minds to inquire after the knowledge of God. That inquiry frequently terminated, indeed always terminated when rightly pursued, in the most glorious discoveries and eternal certainty. (*Lectures on Faith* 2:56)

Another way to teach children to love, study, and obey the word of God is to tell them bedtime stories from the scriptures followed by personal, human testimony rather than the fables and creations of men and women. Children then fall asleep with the stories of God's servants resting upon their minds.

In addition to teaching children to love, study, and obey the word of God as found in the scriptures, we also need to teach them to love, study, and obey the living prophets. Alma stresses the importance of the living prophets in Mosiah 18:19, where he commands the people "that they should teach nothing save it were the things which he had taught, and which had been spoken by the mouth of the holy prophets."

One can regularly record general conference on videotape and use these talks as a basis for family home evening to teach children to love, study, and obey the living prophets. When children give talks at church they will then tend to teach "none other things than that which the prophets and apostles have written" (D&C 52:9).

Elder James E. Faust stated at a recent general conference: "We have been promised that the President of the Church will receive guidance for all of us as the revelator for the Church. Our safety lies in paying heed to that which he says and following his counsel" (10). As Elder Faust suggests, parents need to set an example for children by supporting Church leadership.

In summary, here are five suggestions of how we can teach our children to love, study, and obey the scriptures and the living prophets:

1. Speak with them in the language of holy writ.

2. Help them read the Book of Mormon from their earliest years.

3. Bear personal, human testimony to them.

4. Tell them bedtime scripture stories so that these stories rest upon their minds.

5. Let them see your example of upholding and sustaining Church leaders.

Having positive experiences with the scriptures and the words of the living prophets is essential for each child. Such experiences need to be repeated over and over, day after day and year after year, with such regularity that gospel lessons become fixed in their minds. President Benson said: "Teaching is done by precept and example, and by word and deed. A good model is the best teacher. Therefore, a father's [or mother's] first responsibility is to set the proper example" ("Worthy Fathers, Worthy Sons" 35). Testimony and instruction without a living model may not be sufficient to instill the desire to believe within each child.

Lesson 2: Teach Children That the Lord Has Come to Teach Us How to Obtain Eternal Life

President Benson stated:

What did the righteous fathers of the Book of Mormon teach their sons? They taught them many things, but the overarching message was "the great plan of the Eternal God"—the Fall, rebirth, Atonement, Resurrection, Judgment, eternal life. (See Alma 34:9.) . . .

Those in the Book of Mormon who were taught nothing concerning the Lord but only concerning worldly knowledge became a cunning and wicked people. (See Mosiah 24:5, 7.) ("Worthy Fathers, Worthy Sons" 36)

How can parents use the book of Mosiah to teach "the great plan of the Eternal God"? Here is one example. Through brief discussion each child can perceive three main problems inherent in mortal life: (1) not knowing how to get back to our Heavenly Father's home (attaining eternal life) is a problem for every person; (2) everyone is going to die; (3) no one is perfect, and everyone will commit some sin.

The book of Mosiah is rich in doctrinal statements that can help children find the answers the Lord has given to these three problems of mortality. Consider the following scriptural statements as examples of the many points of doctrine that can be learned and taught from the book of Mosiah.

> For behold, the time cometh, and is not far distant, that with power, the Lord Omnipotent who reigneth, who was, and is from all eternity to all eternity, shall come down from heaven among the children of men, and shall dwell in a tabernacle of clay. (Mosiah 3:5)

> And he shall be called Jesus Christ, the Son of God, the Father of heaven and earth, the Creator of all things from the beginning; and his mother shall be called Mary. (Mosiah 3:8)

> He should take upon him the image of man, and it should be the image after which man was created in the beginning; or in other words, . . . man was created after the image of God. (Mosiah 7:27)

> [Christ] shall go forth amongst men, working mighty miracles, such as healing the sick, raising the dead, causing the lame to walk, the blind to receive their sight, and the deaf to hear, and curing all manner of diseases. And he shall cast out devils, or the evil spirits which dwell in the hearts of the children of men. (Mosiah 3:5–6)

> And lo, he cometh unto his own, that salvation might come unto the children of men even through faith on his name; and even after all this they shall consider him a man, and say that he hath a devil, and shall scourge him, and shall crucify him. (Mosiah 3:9)

> And lo, he shall suffer temptations, and pain of body, hunger, thirst, and fatigue, even more than man can suffer, except it be unto death; for behold, blood cometh from every pore, so great shall be his anguish for the wickedness and the abominations of his people. (Mosiah 3:7)

> For behold, . . . his blood atoneth for the sins of those who have fallen by the transgression of Adam, who have died not knowing the will of God concerning them, or who have ignorantly sinned. But wo, wo unto him who knoweth that he rebelleth against God! For salvation cometh to none such except it be through repentance and faith on the Lord Jesus Christ. (Mosiah 3:11–12)

> He shall rise the third day from the dead. (Mosiah 3:10)

> The bands of death shall be broken, and the Son reigneth, and hath power over the dead; therefore, he bringeth to pass the resurrection of the dead. (Mosiah 15:20)

> And behold, he standeth to judge the world; and behold, all these things are done that a righteous judgment might come upon the children of men. (Mosiah 3:10)

I say unto you, if you have come to a knowledge of the goodness of God, and his matchless power . . . and also, the atonement which has been prepared from the foundation of the world, that thereby salvation might come to him that should put his trust in the Lord, and should be diligent in keeping his commandments, and continue in the faith even unto the end of his life, I mean the life of the mortal body—I say, this is the man who receiveth salvation. (Mosiah 4:6, 7)

These and other scriptural statements can help parents teach their children how Heavenly Father's plan overcomes the problems of ignorance, death, and sin. The "knowledge of the goodness of God" has eliminated ignorance; Christ's "matchless power" has broken the bands of death so that each person will be resurrected; and the Atonement has paid for the sins of those who repent and continue to keep the commandments until they die.

President Benson has said: "All truths are not of the same value. The saving truths of salvation are of greatest worth. These truths the fathers taught plainly, frequently, and fervently. Are we fathers doing likewise?" ("Worthy Fathers, Worthy Sons" 36). The book of Mosiah is certainly a rich source of these "saving truths," which parents today can teach their children.

Lesson 3: Teach Children the Difference Between the Man of Christ and the Natural Man

"When king Benjamin made an end of speaking the words which had been delivered to him by the angel of the Lord, [his people] cried aloud with one voice, saying: O have mercy, and apply the atoning blood of Christ that we may receive forgiveness of our sins, and our hearts may be purified; for we believe in Jesus Christ, the Son of God." King Benjamin's people had put off "the natural man" (Mosiah 3:19), and the spirit of the Lord had come upon them. They received a remission of their sins and peace of conscience because of their faith in Jesus Christ (Mosiah 4:1–3).

Just like the people of king Benjamin, believers today can obtain a forgiveness of sins, receive the Holy Ghost, and have peace of conscience. However, once a person is baptized and has obtained an initial remission of sins, the challenge lies in retaining that remission of sins. Parents can help their children understand how to retain a remission of sins by teaching them the difference between the man of Christ and the natural man (see Hel 3:29; Mosiah 3:19). This can be done by contrasting some of the qualities of each type of person as described by king Benjamin in Mosiah 4.

TABLE 1 *The Man of Christ vs. the Natural Man*

The Man of Christ A Friend to God	The Natural Man An Enemy to God
Has no mind to injure others (4:13).	Has more concern for himself than for others.
Does not suffer children to go hungry or naked (4:14).	Neglects his children.
Does not transgress the laws of God (4:14).	Transgresses the laws of God.
Does not fight, quarrel, or serve the devil (4:14).	Fights and quarrels; serves the devil.
Loves others (4:15).	Shows hatred to others.
Serves others (4:15).	Serves himself.
Visits the sick and imparts to the poor (4:16, 26).	Neglects the sick and the poor.
Uses the wisdom of God; does not run faster than he has strength; is orderly and reliable (4:27).	Follows the wisdom of the world; often runs faster than he has strength; not dependable in all things.
Watches himself—his thoughts, words, and deeds (4:30).	Not in control of his thoughts, words, and deeds.
Keeps the commandments (4:30).	Does not keep the commandments.

Because examples of both these attitudes are all around us, parents need to teach their children the many differences between the natural man and the man of Christ so their children will be able to recognize the differences on their own. If parents do not help them do this, the powerful messages from their peers and the media will set their minds for them. Children can distinguish the man of Christ from the natural man if parents teach them how.

The best way to teach children how to be a person of Christ is by example, yet parents sometimes fail to act as men and women of Christ. This is especially true in the family and home setting. Elder Neal A. Maxwell has stated:

> Life in a family means we are known as we are, that our frailties are exposed and, hopefully, we then correct them.
>
> The affection and thoughtfulness required in the home are no abstract exercises in love, no mere rhetoric concerning some distant human cause. Family life is an encounter with raw selfishness, with the need for civility, of taking turns, of being hurt and yet forgiving, and of being at the mercy of others' moods.
>
> Family life is a constant challenge, not a periodic performance we can render on a stage and then run for the privacy of a dressing room to be alone with ourselves. The home gives us our greatest chance, however, to align our public and private behavior, to reduce the hypocrisy in our lives—to be more congruent with Christ. (3)

Parents themselves need to learn to be more congruent with Christ so that their children can learn from their examples what men and women of Christ are like.

Lesson 4: Teach Children to Make Covenants with Christ and Obtain Power to Become Like Him

Before we can become a man or woman of Christ we must make covenants. Parents must teach their children what covenants are and why they are important. Victor L. Ludlow explains:

> The word *covenant* comes from the Hebrew word *b'rith*, which has at least two probable Semitic roots. The Akkadian root *biritu* means to "bind or fetter," while the Hebrew root *barah* means "to eat bread with." The meanings of both roots contribute to an accurate comprehension of covenant concepts as taught in the Old Testament. In the scriptures, although covenant-making is serious and solemn, it is

not something harsh, like adversaries binding and carefully obligating themselves as they sign a compact; but it is something gentle, like two friends (especially a father with his children) sitting and eating bread together, externally symbolizing an internal commitment to each other. (Ludlow 4)

In the book of Mosiah, king Benjamin and Alma both teach about the baptismal covenant. It is an agreement in which the one baptized promises to do the following:

1.   Be baptized, do God's will, and keep his commandments (Mosiah 5:5)
2.   Bear one another's burdens (Mosiah 18:8)
3.   Mourn with those that mourn (Mosiah 18:9)
4.   Comfort those in need of comfort (Mosiah 18:9)
5.   Stand as a witness of God in all things until we die (Mosiah 18:9)
6.   Serve Christ and keep his commandments (Mosiah 18:10)

Then Christ promises to do the following for the one baptized:

1.   Give those baptized a spiritual rebirth (Mosiah 5:7, 9)
2.   Become their new father (Mosiah 5:7)
3.   Make them free under his head, his direction (Mosiah 5:8)
4.   Give them a new name, the name of Christ (Mosiah 5:9)
5.   Give them a new voice, the voice of the Spirit (Mosiah 5:12; 18:10)
6.   Give them eternal life (Mosiah 18:9)

Parents should teach their children that this baptismal covenant is renewable every week through the ordinance of the sacrament. Partaking of the sacrament worthily is like being baptized again. It is an external symbol of "an internal commitment to each other" (Ludlow 4). Those who partake of the sacrament take upon themselves the name of Christ, remembering him in all that they do. Then as they keep his commandments he gives them the Holy Spirit and the hope of eternal life. The power to become like Christ comes from obedience and worthy participation in the sacred ordinances (D&C 84:20). Because of Jesus Christ and his atoning sacrifice, when we sin we may repent (see D&C 58:43), return to obedience, and become clean again.

Children, especially teenagers, ask, "When will my parents ever think I am mature enough to act for myself?" When children are willing not only to take upon themselves this covenant but also to live it, to do God's will and keep his commandments all of their days, then parents should be willing to give them increasing freedom. When they covenant to follow Christ, they will begin to govern themselves through increased obedience. Parents should teach their children that making and keeping baptismal covenants and renewing them through the ordinance of the sacrament will enable them to become more like Christ.

Lesson 5: Teach Children That God Made Humankind in His Own Image

For a number of years, the real reason the prophet Abinadi was slain was a mystery to me. Why would wicked king Noah and those worldly priests slay a man for saying "that Christ was the God, the Father of all things, and . . . that he should take upon him the image of man" (Mosiah 7:27)?

Then one evening, a lecturer solved the mystery for me. He simply quoted all of Mosiah 7:27 and part of verse 28:

> And because he said unto them that Christ was the God, the Father of all things, and said that he should take upon him the image of man, and it should be the image after which man was created in the beginning; or in other words, he said that man was created after the image of God, and that God should come down among the children of men, and take upon him flesh and blood, and go forth upon the face of the earth—And now, because he said this, they did put him to death.

It became clear that if God the Son, Jesus Christ, took upon him a body, just as humankind has, and still lived a sinless life, then this knowledge would force a terrible self-imposed indictment on the unrepentant and immoral. They would be cut to the core "with guilt, and pain, and anguish, which is like an unquenchable fire" (Mosiah 2:38). We need not wonder why king Noah and his priests put Abinadi to death. Being in a body "that was created after the image of God" is life's test. Because of their licentious lifestyle, they could not tolerate Abinadi's voice of truth and silenced him with a fiery death.

When parents understand and teach the full implications of our being clothed in a body "created after the image of God" (Mosiah 7:27), they can provide their children with a basis for a moral life. Regarding the nature of God the Prophet Joseph Smith taught:

> If we start right, it is easy to go right all the time; but if we start wrong, we may go wrong, and it be a hard matter to get right. . . .
> . . . If men do not comprehend the character of God, they do not comprehend themselves. . . .
> *God himself was once as we are now, and is an exalted man, and sits enthroned in yonder heavens! That is the great secret.* . . .
> . . . he was once a man like us; yea, . . . God himself, the Father of us all, dwelt on an earth, the same as Jesus Christ himself. (*Teachings of the Prophet Joseph Smith* 343, 345–46)

If children are taught in their earliest years that God has a body and that they were created in his image; and if in their adolescent years, when their bodies are maturing, they could see their bodies as "clothing" in a likeness of their Heavenly Father's or Heavenly Mother's bodies; and if they understand that this body puts them "in the image of God" and serves as a testing vehicle for their mortal life; if they can conceive these eternal truths and hold them in their minds through all of their mortal life, these truths will provide them a basis for moral conduct. And when an untoward generation teaches them the mechanics of procreation without the morals of godliness, the children who already understand the full implications of being "created after the image of God" will not accept the errors of the world. Further, when they become completely mature men and women and are tempted, as all are, they will have both reason and power to flee from sin as did Joseph of old (Gen 39:12).

Nothing is more sacred than for a loving parent to sit down with a child in private and discuss in tenderness the sacred powers of procreation. This type of teaching, with regular follow-up interviews for support, can be the firm basis for a child's holding to correct moral values and conduct throughout life.[1]

Parents who teach these truths allow their children to see themselves clothed in the image of God. Understanding this concept can mean life to a questioning or tempted child. When it comes to children understanding their bodies, Jesus Christ is their only light in the darkened world. For "he was conceived by the power of God" (Mosiah 15:3) and "dwelleth in flesh" (Mosiah 15:2), but "having subjected the flesh to the will of the Father" (Mosiah 15:2), he did suffer temptation and did not yield (Mosiah 15:5).

Conclusion

The book of Mosiah contains several lessons which parents should teach their children. I have presented five possible lessons in this paper, but there are many more which could be taught. If parents teach their children from their earliest years to love, study, and obey the word of God as found in the scriptures and the words of the living prophets, then their children will learn from the Lord how to obtain eternal life. They will learn that there is a difference between the man of

---

[1] Three excellent references parents should use to teach their children these principles are *To Young Men Only* by Elder Boyd K. Packer (N.p.: The Church of Jesus Christ of Latter-day Saints, 1976); *A Parent's Guide* (Salt Lake City: The Church of Jesus Christ of Latter-day Saints, 1985); and "Teaching Children About Human Intimacy," *Follow Me: Relief Society Personal Study Guide 1989* (Salt Lake City: The Church of Jesus Christ of Latter-day Saints, 1988) 184-92. Each of these booklets teaches that parents are responsible to teach their children wholesome attitudes and a sound understanding of their bodies and of the law of chastity.

Christ and the natural man, that by making and keeping covenants with Christ they will have power to become like him, and that God made man and woman in his own image. Then they will avoid "suffering in ignorance," as President Benson has said so many do today.

I began this paper by quoting Elder Romney's and President Benson's admonitions to teach children to read from the Book of Mormon to lead them to eternal life. It is my prayer that parents will accept their responsibility to teach their sons and daughters individually and as a family, that they may bless their lives with the light of the gospel.

BIBLIOGRAPHY

Benson, Ezra Taft. "A Sacred Responsibility." *Ensign* (May 1986) 16:77–78; also in *Conference Report* (Apr 1986) 98–100.

———. "Worthy Fathers, Worthy Sons." *Ensign* (Nov 1985) 15:35–37; also in *Conference Report* (Oct 1985) 46–49.

Faust, James E. "Continuous Revelation." *Ensign* (Nov 1989) 19:8–11; also in *Conference Report* (Oct 1989) 8–12.

The Lectures on Faith in Historical Perspective. Ed. Larry E. Dahl and Charles D. Tate, Jr. Salt Lake City: Bookcraft, 1990.

Ludlow, Victor L. "Unlocking the Covenant Teachings in the Scriptures." *Religious Studies Center Newsletter* (Jan 1990) 4:2, 4.

Maxwell, Neal A. *That My Family Should Partake.* Salt Lake City: Deseret Book, 1974.

Romney, Marion G. "Drink Deeply from the Divine Fountain." *Improvement Era* (Jun 1960) 63:435–36; also in *Conference Report* (Apr 1960) 110–13.

Teachings of the Prophet Joseph Smith. Comp. Joseph Fielding Smith. Salt Lake City: Deseret Book, 1976.

King Benjamin: In the Service of Your God

3

Susan Easton Black

Many years ago, Moses declared to gathered Israel, "Love the Lord your God, and . . . serve him with all your heart and with all your soul" (Deut 11:13). Since this declaration, rulers of the house of Israel have vacillated in their love of and service to the Lord. Yet there was one Israelite king who obediently lived this ancient command. His name was Benjamin, king over the land of Zarahemla in ancient America in the second century BC. Unfortunately, we know little about king Benjamin's reign, except the last part which is recorded in the book of Mosiah. That part radiates with the brightness, hope, and love of a righteous, Christian king. His example is an ensign to rulers and a beacon to all disciples of Christ. My purpose in this paper is to share understanding and insight into the significance king Benjamin placed on the mysteries of God and on service, and to show how these concepts are interrelated.

King Benjamin, like prophets before him, wanted his people to share in the knowledge of revealed truth which he had obtained by prophecy, revelation, and the ministration of an angel. His love for his people had grown as he defended them against both external and internal forces of destruction. Near the end of his life, king Benjamin wanted to give his people one last sermon, "that [he] might go down in peace, and

Susan Easton Black is associate professor of Church History and Doctrine at Brigham Young University.

[his] immortal spirit may join the choirs above in singing the praises of a just God" (Mosiah 2:28, 30).

In an outpouring of love, this elderly king desired to share with his people his most precious pearl of great price, the great mysteries that he had extracted from eternal realms. He did not merely inform subordinate heads of the government so they, in turn, could disseminate the mysteries. Rather he considered his revelation, prophecy, and visit by an angel so precious that he wanted to personally tell everyone his message at the same time. All were invited to come to the heart of the kingdom, the city of Zarahemla, to hear it.

Mosiah, Benjamin's oldest son, gathered the people so they could hear their prophetic king. King Benjamin stated that the purpose of this gathering was for him to

> proclaim unto this my people out of mine own mouth that thou [Mosiah] art a king and a ruler over this people, whom the Lord our God hath given us. And moreover, I shall give this people a name, that thereby they may be distinguished above all the people which the Lord God hath brought out of the land of Jerusalem. (Mosiah 1:10–11)

The place for gathering was not the king's residence, his palace, or government offices. It was the temple, the house of the Lord. The time was appointed and a nation responded.

The people of Zarahemla and the people of Mosiah all gathered at the temple. Their cultural distinction, readily apparent by name usage alone, had existed since Mosiah I and his followers first discovered the people of Zarahemla. These "people of Zarahemla" were the inhabitants of Zarahemla who traced their heritage to Mulek, the son of Zedekiah, while the "people of Mosiah" (Mosiah 1:10) were the descendants of those who followed Mosiah I, Benjamin's father, when he escaped from a wicked Nephite culture and found Zarahemla. Benjamin desired to unite these two distinct peoples with one name and one purpose, with a name that would "never . . . be blotted out, except it be through transgression" (Mosiah 1:12).

This he knew would bring them abundant joy and rejoicing throughout time and all eternity.

Benjamin's Speech Combines Mysteries of God with Service to Humanity

Benjamin delivered his long-awaited message in a series of three orations on different topics. The first is contained in Mosiah 2:9–41, the second in Mosiah 3:1–27, and the third in Mosiah 4:4–30. These three topics were separate and distinct from each other and echoed the three areas of service that king Benjamin had performed in his reign. In the first section Benjamin spoke as a king reporting his royal stewardship, recalling how he had provided them temporal and spiritual peace. For his second topic he spoke as a prophet, once again teaching his people how to avoid spiritual chaos and unrest. In this phase of his speech he spoke the words of an angel, words which emphasized Christ's service to others, including a portrayal of Christ's atoning sacrifice. For his third and final topic the prophet Benjamin spoke of how service can extend the knowledge of the glory, truth, and justice of God beyond a spiritual awakening, thus fulfilling his final act of service by bringing his people spiritual salvation.

The common element in each section was the hope-filled message of service to God through service to humanity. The first two messages were examples of service from Benjamin's and Christ's lives. The third message was a discourse on how the people could retain a remission of their sins by implementing these examples of service.

Benjamin's Example of Service

After a lifetime of service, king Benjamin's final act of service was to help his people understand and live in abiding love. To illustrate abiding love he used an example that all the people recognized—that of himself and his own actions. He reminded them first of his actions in the realm of civil government during times of peace, not of his earlier military role in the beginning of his reign. He pointed out his caring and responsible civil actions, such as not allowing confinement in dungeons, murder, plundering, stealing, or adultery (Mosiah 2:13). He did not use harsh disciplinary measures or tyrannical or arbitrary means to stop depredations in his kingdom. Instead he emphasized obedience to the commandments of God and avoidance of wickedness. He governed his people through this Christian approach and through his own frugality and simplicity in living. As he spoke, remembering the implementation of these governing principles, he humbly stated, "I have only been in the service of God" (Mosiah 2:16).

Following this gospel-based review of his royal stewardship, king Benjamin proclaimed to his people, "I can answer [with] a clear conscience before God this day" (Mosiah 2:15). Service for Benjamin had become a sign of pure love. By establishing a civil government based on the commandments of God, king Benjamin manifested his love to his subjects. He had clearly embarked "in the service of God" as he began his reign, "and had serve[d] him with all [his] heart, might, mind and strength" (D&C 4:2). He now stood on a tower at the end of that reign, blameless before God and before his people.

King Benjamin did not review his royal service "to boast" (Mosiah 2:16). He stated, "I tell you these things that ye may learn wisdom," which he defined by saying, "When ye are in the service of your fellow beings ye are only in the service of your God" (Mosiah 2:17). Like Jesus Christ in his ministry, king Benjamin gave selfless service. Benjamin knew by revelation and experience the great mystery that Christ would later teach during his earthly ministry: "Inasmuch as ye have done it unto one of the least of these my brethren, ye have done it unto me" (Matt 25:40).

King Benjamin also knew his own life was merely a type and shadow of Christ. He knew each person listening must turn his or her own heart, might, mind, and strength to God. Like the prophets before him, Benjamin realized that "in every work that [one] began in the service of the house of God, and in the law, and in the commandments, to seek his God, he did it with all his heart" (2 Chr 31:21). With a humble appeal, he pled with his people, "If I, whom ye call your king, do labor to serve you, then ought not ye to labor to serve one another? . . . If I . . . do merit any thanks from you, O how you ought to thank your heavenly King!" (Mosiah 2:18–19).

King Benjamin taught that the combination of service and gratitude was higher than sacrificing the firstlings of the flocks. It was to "render all the thanks and praise which your whole soul has power to possess" (Mosiah 2:20). Yet, even if you achieved this height of gratitude, "ye would be unprofitable servants" (Mosiah 2:21). What the Lord required of his sons and his daughters was that they keep the commandments. If they kept the commandments, they would be blessed. These blessings included prosperity in the land and protection from enemies (Mosiah 2:31).

Christ's Example of Service

After commenting on his own service, Benjamin began to prophesy, saying, "I have things to tell you concerning that which is to come" (Mosiah 3:1). The prophetic message he expressed during the second phase of his speech was made known to him by an angel. Because of his prayers and personal righteousness, the angel told Benjamin what the shepherds were to learn over 120 years later: "I am come to declare unto you the glad tidings of great joy" (Mosiah 3:3; see Luke 2:10). These glad tidings were of the birth of Jesus in Bethlehem and his ministry among the Jews.

Christ's ministry had not been revealed to Benjamin as a series of mere verbal sermons, preachings, or admonitions; rather, it was revealed as a continuous series of examples of service. These acts included "healing the sick, raising the dead, causing the lame to walk, the blind to receive their sight and the deaf to hear, and curing all manner of diseases" (Mosiah 3:5).

After these scenes, Benjamin was shown Christ's greatest service—the Atonement:

> And lo, he shall suffer temptations, and pain of body, hunger, thirst, and fatigue, even more than man can suffer, except it be unto death; for behold, blood cometh from every pore, so great shall be his anguish for the wickedness and the abominations of his people. (Mosiah 3:7)

The atoning sacrifice had been symbolically declared by earlier prophets (see Isa 53:6; Moses 5:7). Yet, only when the prophet Benjamin spoke of Mary and the atonement, death, and resurrection of Christ did an entire nation hear the glorious good news in fulness and in power. Previous prophets alluded to the same message, but their people were "stiffnecked" (Mosiah 3:14; compare Ex 32:9; Isa 48:4). Of necessity, types and shadows replaced clear revealed light, and the law of Moses replaced the fulness of the joyous news of the redemption. But for the people gathered to hear Benjamin the prophet, there was no symbolic replacement, no delaying substitution, no alternative name. There was "no other name given nor any other way nor means whereby salvation [could] come unto the children of men, only in and through the name of Christ, the Lord Omnipotent" (Mosiah 3:17).

King Benjamin delivered his message in plainness because those gathered had come prepared to learn of Christ. They had before them a benevolent prophet whose example had taught them preparatory to their receiving these angelic words. They had listened and had already begun to put off the natural man and become saints. They had learned from his actions and words the need to demonstrate in their sacrificial offerings a spirit of rejoicing and thanksgiving to God. They were becoming like children, "submissive, meek, humble, patient, full of love, willing to submit to all things which the Lord [saw] fit to inflict upon [them]" (Mosiah 3:19).

In solemn unity they cried, "O have mercy, and apply the atoning blood of Christ that we may receive forgiveness of our sins, and our hearts may be purified" (Mosiah 4:2). They further pled, "We believe in Jesus Christ, the Son of God, who created heaven and earth, and all things; who shall come down among the children of men" (Mosiah 4:2).

Retaining a Remission of Sins Through Service

In an attitude of loving tenderness, king Benjamin expressed his knowledge that what his people now felt was a beginning. It was an awakening, not a fulfillment. His people had been in spiritual darkness and in a state of slumber. Just as the angel told Benjamin to "awake," Benjamin now called upon his people to "awake" (Mosiah 3:2; 4:5). They were to arise from slumbering in the types and shadows of the law of Moses to find the gospel of Christ and Christian service.

Benjamin recognized that his people had tasted of the goodness, power, wisdom, love, and glory of God. Obtaining a remission of sins had brought "exceedingly great joy in your souls," proclaimed Benjamin (Mosiah 4:11). Yet to this noble prophet, remembrance and retention of this joy was vital as well. There is a marked difference between having a taste of food and enjoying a continuing feast. King Benjamin desired that his people feast spiritually on and endure in the word of God. This feasting and enduring comes by remembering and retaining the knowledge of the greatness of God and your own nothingness. It is renewed by, "even in the depths of humility, calling on the name of the Lord daily, and standing steadfastly in the faith of that which is to come" (Mosiah 4:11). As the climax of his third message Benjamin promised in surety, "If ye do this ye shall always rejoice, and be filled with the love of God, and always retain a remission of your sins" (Mosiah 4:12). In other words, they would not just taste but feast as they grew in the knowledge of glory, truth, and justice.

He promised them that this glory or love would produce peaceful coexistence in the kingdom and that this unity would be lasting because it would be upheld and sustained by righteousness. A righteous people would have no desire "to injure one another," but would desire "to render to every man according to that which is his due" (Mosiah 4:13). That which was due to every man, woman, and child, according to the prophet Benjamin, was Christlike service.

Benjamin taught that service should commence with family members. Husbands, wives, sons, and daughters were to give and receive Christian service. The prophet Benjamin focused on specific service needed by children:

> And ye will not suffer your children that they go hungry, or naked; neither will ye suffer that they transgress the laws of God, and fight and quarrel one with another, and serve the devil, who is the master of sin, or who is the evil spirit which hath been spoken of by our fathers, he being an enemy to all righteousness. But ye will teach them to walk in the ways of truth and soberness; ye will teach them to love one another, and to serve one another. (Mosiah 4:14–15)

Through the specific service outlined for parents to give to their children, the great eternal mystery of peace and happiness passes from one generation to another.

With service within the family as a foundation, the Lord counseled that service be extended to those outside the family who stand in need of succor. The Prophet Joseph Smith stated, "A man filled with the love of God, is not content with blessing his family alone, but ranges through the whole world, anxious to bless the whole human race" (*Teachings of the Prophet Joseph Smith* 174). The "whole human race" includes those who "stand in need of your succor" or substance, the beggar, and even "the man [who] has brought upon himself his misery" (Mosiah 4:16–17). For in actuality, all are beggars unto the Lord.

Therefore, "impart of the substance that ye have one to another" (Mosiah 4:21). If you are poor as to earthly means, Benjamin counseled, "Say in your hearts that: I give not because I have not, but if I had I would give" (Mosiah 4:24). It is apparent that Benjamin was appealing to the gathered people to give Christlike service and develop a consecrated Zion society. Each person present was to emulate more than a type and shadow of a benevolent king; each was to emulate the Savior in his earthly ministry. Benjamin commanded the people:

> Impart of your substance to the poor, every man according to that which he hath, such as feeding the hungry, clothing the naked, visiting the sick and administering to their relief, both spiritually and temporally, according to their wants. (Mosiah 4:26)

As they administered their charitable service, they were to do so "in wisdom and order; for it is not requisite that a man should run faster than he has strength" (Mosiah 4:27).

Reaction of the Nation to Benjamin's Speech

When king Benjamin finished his speech, he desired to know whether his people believed the words he had spoken. Did they believe the great mysteries he had shared? The people cried with one voice saying, "Yea, we believe all the words which thou hast spoken unto us" (Mosiah 5:2). They had followed the admonition of king Benjamin and had opened their ears that they might hear, their hearts that they might understand, and their minds to accept the mysteries of God.

Through the confirmation of the Holy Ghost they attested to the truthfulness of Benjamin's words. Because of their receptivity, each had experienced a mighty change of heart. All who read or heard Benjamin's words were changed. "We have no more disposition to do evil, but to do good continually," proclaimed the people (Mosiah 5:2). They "could prophecy of all things" if it were expedient (Mosiah 5:3).

A nation changed. All of the people, excepting their little children, expressed their commitment and willingness to enter into a covenant. They had partaken of the "infinite goodness of God, and the manifestations of his Spirit" and were willing to make a binding promise between themselves and God (Mosiah 5:3). This covenant was "to do his will, and to be obedient to his commandments in all things that he shall command us, all the remainder of our days" (Mosiah 5:5). Benjamin achieved his desire to unite his people in purpose by uniting them in Christian service.

Because they were united in purpose, they could now be united in name. They would be known throughout the land and throughout centuries to come as the children of Christ (Mosiah 5:7). This name would distinguish them from all other people. It would be a sign to the Lamanites, the Zoramites, and every other "-ite" that this people in 124 BC served the Lord and kept his commandments.

In conclusion, Benjamin warned that transgression was the only way to lose the bonding name. Benjamin did not want his people to be divided again. He counseled, "Be steadfast and immovable, always abounding in good works, that Christ, the Lord God Omnipotent, may seal you his, that you may be brought to heaven, that ye may have everlasting salvation and eternal life" (Mosiah 5:15).

Conclusion

As the speech ended, the names of all the people were recorded, and a church of Christ was established in Zarahemla. This scene of becoming a covenant people, to be known as the children of Christ, would be repeated again and again through the centuries that followed. In our dispensation the Lord, through holy prophets, has again organized a covenant people known as the children of Christ.

We are privileged to read the abridged words of king Benjamin, which are some of the most divine and glorious ever uttered by a prophet. The truths revealed by this ancient sovereign-prophet illuminate the path leading to God. Our responsibility, as we read these words and listen to modern prophets, parallels the responsibility of earlier Christians in

124 BC. We, too, are to "succor the weak, lift up the hands which hang down, and strengthen the feeble knees" (D&C 81:5). We, too, are to "be anxiously engaged in a good cause, and do many things of [our] own free will, and bring to pass much righteousness" (D&C 58:27). Service is our covenant obligation as members of Christ's church in this dispensation.

Nothing is more exalting to the soul than selfless service. For as Benjamin expressed it, "When ye are in the service of your fellow beings ye are only in the service of your God" (Mosiah 2:17). The person who renders anonymous, loving service may be unknown to us, but the gift and the giver are known to God. As this service is rendered we should remember the Savior's counsel, "Do not your alms before men, to be seen of them" (Matt 6:1). Instead, we must be careful that we "let not [our] left hand know what [our] right hand doeth" (Matt 6:3). And when our service eases the burden of another, we must "tell no man" (Matt 8:4).

Christlike service has overtones of the Atonement. By giving service we are promised that we can retain "a remission of [our] sins from day to day" (Mosiah 4:26). As all are in need of our service, all may benefit by it. Only when we lift another's burden will God lift our own cares. It is a holy paradox. The disciples who stagger and even fall because their burdens are too heavy can lighten their burdens by carrying the weight of another's burden. By so doing their hearts will be lighter, their lives brighter, and their souls greater.

Hopefully, we look upward as we move forward in service to God and to humanity.

> Then shall the King say unto them on his right hand, Come, ye blessed of my Father, inherit the kingdom prepared for you from the foundation of the world: For I was an hungred, and ye gave me meat: I was thirsty, and ye gave me drink: I was a stranger, and ye took me in: Naked, and ye clothed me: I was sick, and ye visited me: I was in prison, and ye came unto me. . . . Verily I say unto you, Inasmuch as ye have done it unto one of the least of these my brethren, ye have done it unto me. (Matt 25:34–36, 40)

BIBLIOGRAPHY

Teachings of the Prophet Joseph Smith. Comp. Joseph Fielding Smith. Salt
Lake City: Deseret Book, 1976.

Benjamin and Noah: The Principle of Dominion

4

Lee L. Donaldson

The book of Mosiah's penetrating look into the characters of king Benjamin and king Noah illustrates a lesson on righteous and unrighteous uses of power and authority. The scriptural term for power is *dominion* (see Gen 1:26; D&C 121:39, 46), which Noah Webster's 1828 *American Dictionary* defines as "sovereign or supreme authority: the power of governing and controlling. . . . [The] right of governing." Dominion is not limited to the realm of civil government. Whenever any individual makes decisions that affect the lives of other people, be it through family, church, or municipal government, that person exercises dominion.

In the waning moments of his life, king Mosiah II gathered his people together to propose a change in the structure of their government. He warned them of the risks of unrighteous dominion in a monarchy and illustrated his point by summoning up the two most prominent examples of kingship from Nephite political history, king Benjamin and king Noah:

> If it were possible that you could have just men to be your kings, who would establish the laws of God, and judge this people according to his commandments, . . . I say unto you, if this could always be the case then it would be expedient that ye should always have kings to rule over you. . . . Now I say unto you, that because all men are not

Lee L. Donaldson is a coordinator in the Church Educational System, Chicago, Illinois.

just it is not expedient that ye should have a king or kings to rule over you. For behold, how much iniquity doth one wicked king cause to be committed, yea, and what great destruction! (Mosiah 29:13, 16–17)

Contrast Between Two Kings

A close look at the book of Mosiah makes it obvious why Mosiah II would have selected these two kings to make his point: Benjamin is the type of a righteous king, Noah the model of a wicked one. King Benjamin's purpose was to bring his people to Christ, while Noah led his people away from Christ. The "great joy" of Benjamin's people came from the teachings of their righteous king (Mosiah 5:4), whereas the "sore afflictions" of Noah's reign were the fruits of his evil leadership (Mosiah 12:4).

The book of Mosiah contrasts the characters of Benjamin and Noah on at least seven points: their treatment of and attitude toward temples; their handling of conflicts with the Lamanites; their methods of succession; their use of and reaction to sermons; and their attitudes toward physical labor and service, the written word, and the living prophets. These contrasts give life to our understanding of the principle of dominion.

Temples

The temple is placed in the center of Israel both literally and symbolically. For ancient Israel, the entire camp was laid out in relationship to the tabernacle, or temple. The temple was located in the center of the camp, and each tribe was responsible for guarding a certain portion of it (Num 2–3). For modern Israel, the temple is where we are prepared in all things to enter the presence of the Lord. It is at the center of our spiritual lives. Elder Boyd K. Packer also places the temple in the administrative center of modern Israel. He writes, "We would do well to see that in administering the organizations of the Church, all roads lead to the temple" (Packer).

The temple is a sacred place where God makes himself and his plan known to his people. This plan is an eternal pattern or template. The words *temple* and *template* (possibly) both derive from the same Latin word, *templum* (*Oxford English Dictionary*, s.vv. "template," "temple").[1] A template is "a gauge, pattern, or mold . . . used as a guide to the form of a piece being made" (*Webster's Ninth New Collegiate Dictionary*). One can learn much about a people by their use of sacred places. In the book of Mosiah, Mormon points out striking differences in temple worship between the peoples of Benjamin and Noah.

The purpose of Benjamin's temple is clear. The temple was where Benjamin's people "took of the firstlings of their flocks, that they might offer sacrifice and burnt offerings . . . that they might give thanks to the Lord their God" (Mosiah 2:3–4). It was also where they gathered to have "the mysteries of God . . . unfolded to [their] view" (Mosiah 2:9). While they were gathered at the temple, Benjamin's people "enter[ed] into a covenant" to obey the commandments of God and do his will (Mosiah 5:5). Mormon never gives the reader a physical description of Benjamin's temple, perhaps to show that temples are to help us understand things beyond the physical realm.

Like ancient Israel, Benjamin's people " pitched their tents round about the temple, every man having his tent with the door thereof towards the temple" (Mosiah 2:6). As the word *tent* can also mean household, or people (*Interpreter's Dictionary of the Bible* 4:572), in a very real sense the families of Benjamin's colony turned toward the temple.

Noah's temple, on the other hand, symbolizes the degenerate nature of his reign. Mormon describes that temple as having

---

[1] Hugh Nibley also covers several other possible origins for the word *temple* in *Mormonism and Early Christianity* (Salt Lake: Deseret Book, 1987) 358.

all manner of fine work within the walls of the temple, of fine wood, and of copper, and of brass. And the seats which were set apart for the high priests, which were above all the other seats, he did ornament with pure gold; and he caused a breastwork to be built before them, that they might rest their bodies and their arms upon while they should speak lying and vain words to his people. (Mosiah 11:10–11)

Mormon here reduces Noah's temple to an empty expression of worldliness; reference to true temple worship is conspicuously absent. The temple, for Noah, appears to have been a symbol of the ruling class's authority rather than a place of honest worship.

Conflicts with the Lamanites

Another point of comparison between Benjamin and Noah is their reaction to combat. In wartime Benjamin gathered together "his armies, and he did stand against [the Lamanites]; and he did fight with the strength of his own arm, with the sword of Laban. And in the strength of the Lord they did contend against their enemies" (WofM 1:13–14). Benjamin's courage and faith in God helped him drive the Lamanites "out of all the lands of [the Nephites'] inheritance" (WofM 1:14) and establish peace in the land.

King Noah's response was completely different. His tyrannical reign brought about the collapse of his kingdom. In the final moments of his rule, he spinelessly fled to the false security of his tower to escape being slain by Gideon. He cried out for Gideon's mercy, avoiding death only by alerting Gideon to the surprise invasion of a Lamanite army. Noah then "commanded the people that they should flee before the Lamanites, and he himself did go before them, and they did flee into the wilderness" (Mosiah 19:5–9).

Then, in one of the most appalling acts in the Book of Mormon, Noah "commanded them that all the men should leave their wives and their children, and flee before the Lamanites" (Mosiah 19:11). Although the marriage union was constituted by the covenants of the patriarchal order of the priesthood, Noah commanded his followers to flee for their own lives and follow him into the wilderness. This final act of cowardice and evil was too much for many of his people. They refused to leave their families and were captured by the Lamanites. Those who followed Noah deeper into the wilderness finally mutinied and took his life (Mosiah 19:12–15).

Succession

Another striking contrast between the two kings is seen in the transfer of royal authority from monarch to successor. Righteous leaders like Adam, Joseph, and Moses gathered their people together to leave them a blessing and to ensure the peaceful passing of authority (Gen 48:8–20; JST Gen 50:24–38; Deut 33; 34:9; 2 Nephi 3:5–21; 4:2; D&C 107:53). Benjamin followed this pattern while Noah did not.

King Benjamin had legitimate claim to the throne. His own father had not sought the Nephite monarchy but had been called to it by the Lord (Omni 1:12). King Benjamin's personal actions show that he viewed the authority to govern as a divine stewardship and treated succession to the throne as a sacred obligation. For instance, when Benjamin realized that "he must very soon go the way of all the earth," he selected his oldest son, Mosiah II, to be the next king (Mosiah 1:9–10). He passed on the records, the sword of Laban, and the Liahona (Mosiah 1:16), which, according to Gordon C. Thomasson, were the three tokens of Nephite kingship (3–4). Benjamin also gathered his people together to prepare them for a change in leadership. There is no record of any contention or power struggle between his sons.

Noah, on the other hand, did not provide for succession to his throne. Instead, his son Limhi was appointed king by the people after his father's kingdom had collapsed (Mosiah 19:26). There is no record of Noah's ever having taught Limhi about royal responsibilities. Ironically, Limhi's first official act of government was to indenture his people to the Lamanites.

Noah's reign brought about his people's bondage and landed his son in a political quagmire, while Benjamin's son ruled without conflict.

Sermons

Another vivid contrast between the two kings is seen in the context of the two greatest sermons found in the book of Mosiah: Benjamin's tower discourse and Abinadi's moving testimony. The common theme of these two sermons is the Atonement. Each king, however, took a different role in the two sermons. Benjamin delivered the first one himself, while Noah heard and rejected the second one.

The audiences of both sermons and their reactions also differ. King Benjamin had his son Mosiah send "a proclamation throughout all the land," after which "the people gathered themselves together throughout all the land, that they might go up to the temple to hear the words which king Benjamin should speak unto them" (Mosiah 2:1). The people responded to their beloved king and gathered to the holy place to hear the word of the Lord. His prophetic description of the suffering Messiah who would take upon him the sins of his people caused a mighty change in the hearts of the people: they had "no more disposition to do evil, but to do good continually" (Mosiah 5:2). Benjamin had the names of those who entered into a covenant with the Lord recorded. He also "appointed priests to teach the people, that thereby they might hear and know the commandments of God, and to stir them up in remembrance of the oath which they had made" (Mosiah 6:3).

Noah not only failed to gather his people to hear the word of the Lord, but he also imprisoned the very messenger who brought it. Abinadi delivered his sermon not from a tower but in chains. His audience, Noah and Noah's priests, hardened their hearts against his sermon, and the priests flaunted the hardness of their hearts by condemning Abinadi to death. The wicked king wavered for a moment out of fear, but then agreed to the atrocious sentence of his priests. Abinadi's sermon had no effect on Noah's disposition to do evil; instead, Noah forced Alma, the only one of his priests who believed Abinadi, to flee for his life.

The two kings' reactions to the message of the gospel typified their individual reigns. One directed his power to proclaim the gospel, while the other used his authority to prevent its spread.

Physical Labor and Service

Another striking contrast between the two kings is their different attitudes toward physical labor and service. King Benjamin labored with his own hands among his people, a fact which he used as a model of service during his farewell address. He stated, "I . . . have labored with mine own hands that I might serve you, and that ye should not be laden with taxes" (Mosiah 2:14). He then told the people they should learn to serve one another.

Conversely, Noah would not labor with his own hands. Instead, he spent his time "in riotous living" (Mosiah 11:14). "He laid a tax of one fifth part of all [his people] possessed. . . . And all this did he take to support himself, and his wives and his concubines; . . . and thus they were supported in their laziness" (Mosiah 11:3–6). Noah used his position to avoid physical labor and service. His indolent lifestyle reflected his reliance on the things of this world.

The Written Word

Another interesting difference between the two kings is their attitude toward the written word. Benjamin was careful to teach his sons to read the sacred records: "And he caused that they should be taught in all the language of his fathers, that thereby they might become men of understanding; and that they might know concerning the prophecies which had been spoken" (Mosiah 1:2). He taught that knowing the written word is knowing the commandments and mysteries of God (Mosiah 1:5). Benjamin's sons shared his reverence for the written word.

The priests under Noah's direction developed a completely different attitude toward the written word. For them it was a skill to be used for profit. After Noah's death, his priests taught the Lamanites the written word:

> And thus the language of Nephi began to be taught among all the people of the Lamanites. And they were a people friendly one with another; nevertheless they knew not God; neither did the brethren of Amulon teach them anything concerning the Lord their God, neither the law of Moses; nor did they teach them the words of Abinadi; But they taught them that they should keep their record, and that they might write one to another. And thus the Lamanites began to increase in riches, and began to trade one with another and wax great, and began to be a cunning and a wise people, as to the wisdom of the world. (Mosiah 24:4–7)

Noah's priests secularized the written word.

Living Prophets

Benjamin made good use of the prophets, while Noah abused them. Benjamin put down "false prophets, and false preachers and teachers among the people . . . with the assistance of the holy prophets who were among his people" (WofM 1:16). Benjamin carefully cultivated feelings of respect for the Lord's chosen messengers. But there was no reverence for prophets in the court of wicked king Noah. Noah sought the lives of both Abinadi and Alma. Thus Mormon's skillful juxtaposition of Benjamin's and Noah's reactions to the Lord's prophets highlights the differences between the two kings.

Conclusion

For the ancients, character and personality were best seen in a person's deeds. Mormon followed this ancient philosophy in portraying the deeds of the two Nephite kings, Benjamin and

Noah. But the deaths of the two monarchs also characterized their lives. Benjamin peacefully passed the kingdom to his son, retired from the kingship, and spent the last three years of mortality in peace. His obedience secured him a place in God's kingdom. On the other hand, Noah, who spent his life on the lusts and desires of the flesh, pronounced a death sentence on the one messenger who could have saved him from destruction. His cruel treatment of Abinadi became his own death sentence, though his desire for power and dominion consumed his soul long before the physical flames ever touched his body. How fitting it is that Noah was consumed in flames of his own making.

Mormon's graphic account of the two contrasting leaders makes the book of Mosiah vital reading for anyone who would aspire to lead others or who is called to lead others in the latter days. Mosiah II also recognized the great value of studying these two kings and concluded the book of Mosiah with a one-chapter summary of the lessons we should learn from them. Those who have dominion either follow the Messianic model of leadership by service (exemplified by Benjamin) or the satanic model of leadership by domination (exemplified by Noah). Leadership by service builds Zion, while leadership by domination builds Babylon.

BIBLIOGRAPHY

The Interpreter's Dictionary of the Bible: An Illustrated Encyclopedia. Ed. Arthur Buttrick. 4 vols. New York: Abingdon, 1962.

The Oxford English Dictionary. 2nd ed. 1989.

Packer, Boyd K. Address delivered at Regional Representatives' Seminar, 3 Apr 1987. Copy in possession of the author.

Thomasson, Gordon C. "Mosiah: The Complex Symbolism and the Symbolic Complex of Kingship in the Book of Mormon." Working Paper. TSN-82. Provo, UT: F.A.R.M.S., 1982.

Webster's Ninth New Collegiate Dictionary. 1990 ed.

Webster's 1828 American Dictionary. Facsimile. San Francisco: Foundation for American Christian Education, 1967.

Lessons from the Zarahemla Churches

5

Dennis L. Largey

In the October 1986 general conference, President Ezra Taft Benson said:

> We must make the Book of Mormon a center focus of our study [because] it was written for our day. The Nephites never had the book; neither did the Lamanites of ancient times. It was meant for us. . . . Under the inspiration of God, who sees all things from the beginning, [Mormon] abridged centuries of records, choosing the stories, speeches, and events that would be most helpful to us. . . .
>
> If they [the Book of Mormon writers] saw our day and chose those things which would be of greatest worth to us, is not that how we should study the Book of Mormon? We should constantly ask ourselves, "Why did the Lord inspire Mormon (or Moroni or Alma) to include that in his record? What lesson can I learn from that to help me live in this day and age?" ("The Book of Mormon" 6)

Why did the Lord inspire Mormon to include Mosiah 25–27 for our day? These chapters inform us of the state of the Church in Zarahemla from about 120 to 92 years before the birth of Jesus Christ. Mosiah 25 records the reaction of the people of Zarahemla as they listened to the accounts of Zeniff and his people "from the time they left the land of Zarahemla until they returned again" (Mosiah 25:5) and that of Alma and his people and the afflictions they suffered. Chapter 25 also recounts Alma's labors in establishing the Church in Zarahemla. Mosiah 26 describes the difficulties encountered by the Church

Dennis L. Largey is assistant professor of Ancient Scripture at Brigham Young University.

because of the unbelief of the rising generation, as well as Alma's struggle to handle the transgression of Church members properly. Chapter 27 tells the story of the conversion of Alma the Younger and the four sons of king Mosiah and the beginning of their labors for the Church.

What, then, can members of The Church of Jesus Christ of Latter-day Saints learn from the "stories, speeches, and events" which comprise this portion of Nephite history? I believe that an examination of the operation of the churches in Zarahemla, as well as events associated with the Church, offers at least three invaluable lessons for our day. First, the doctrines contained in Mosiah 25–27 provide a standard of truth to a darkened latter-day world. Second, these chapters show how the Nephites dealt with four challenges that face the Church in our own day: the challenges of flattery, teaching the rising generation, persecution, and transgression in the Church. And third, the example of the rebirth of Alma the Younger and the four sons of Mosiah is a message of hope to those troubled by sins in our own day.

Mosiah 25–27: A Standard of Truth

Nephi prophesied that the Book of Mormon would come forth in a day when churches would be "built up, [but] not unto the Lord" (2 Nephi 28:3). He also saw that latter-day churches would "contend one with another," each proclaiming to be the Lord's church, and that they would "teach with their learning, and deny the Holy Ghost" (2 Nephi 28:3, 4).

Belief in the Book of Mormon as a divine record settles many issues that have been debated for centuries in the Christian world. The Book of Mormon confounds false churches and the precepts of humankind. A standard of judgment is thus established, and by comparing other churches with this standard, error can be discerned and eliminated.

For example, just within Mosiah 25–27 are the following doctrinal truths: (1) Jesus is the head of the Church (Mosiah

26:22); (2) Jesus directs his Church through revelation to his prophet (Mosiah 26:13–32); (3) baptism must be by total immersion (Mosiah 18:14; 25:18); (4) Church members who sin must be admonished by the Church (Mosiah 26:6); (5) the Church may have many congregations, yet there is only one Church—all branches teach the same doctrine as directed by the living prophet (Mosiah 25:21–22); and (6) baptism is necessary to take upon oneself the name of Jesus Christ and to enter into his Church (Mosiah 25:18, 23). The functioning of the Church in Zarahemla is a reflection of the operation of the true Church of Jesus Christ in any age. By having this blueprint, readers are strengthened in their belief that "God is the same yesterday, today, and forever" (Mormon 9:9).

Some Christians have criticized members of The Church of Jesus Christ of Latter-day Saints for being church-centered instead of Christ-centered in worship. Perhaps this belief comes from repeated testimonies of members that the *Church* is true, attempting to bear witness of the truth of the Restoration. Chapters 25–27 of Mosiah reveal the true relationship between Christ and his Church. One must come to Christ through faith and repentance of all sin, and then receive the ordinances of salvation provided by the Church (Mosiah 25:15–18).

Four Challenges to the Church

Perhaps another reason why the Lord included Mosiah 25–27 is that the Lord knew it would benefit us to study how the Nephite church handled challenges that we face in our day. At the point in Nephite history discussed in Mosiah 25–27, members fell prey to the deception of flattery; parents had the challenge of effectively teaching the rising generation; many suffered persecution; and priesthood leaders had to learn how to handle transgression in the Church.

The Challenge of Flattery

Many members of the Church in Zarahemla became victims of sin by believing the flattering words of unbelievers. Mormon wrote, "They did deceive many with their flattering words, who were in the church, and did cause them to commit many sins" (Mosiah 26:6). One of the prominent unbelievers of this period was Alma the Younger:

> He being called Alma, after his father; nevertheless, he became a very wicked and an idolatrous man. And he was a man of many words, and did speak much flattery to the people; therefore he led many of the people to do after the manner of his iniquities. (Mosiah 27:8)

Flattery, as it is used in the Book of Mormon, is associated with deception, vanity, idolatry, false prophecy, apostasy, bringing souls to destruction, and persuasive speech attributed to the power of the devil. Flattery is portrayed not as a coercive measure but as a deceptive skill that enables one to lead others in a desired direction (see Mosiah 27:8; Alma 46:5). Alma's motive in using flattery was to lead others to do "after the manner of his iniquities" (Mosiah 27:8). False shepherds can also carry the message, "Come follow me." Their success in gaining followers becomes an investment in their own deception, as in the case of Korihor (see Alma 30:53).

President Joseph F. Smith foresaw that flattery would be one of three temptations that the latter-day Church would face: "There are at least three dangers that threaten the Church within, and the authorities need to awaken to the fact that the people should be warned unceasingly against them. As I see these, they are flattery of prominent men in the world, false educational ideas, and sexual impurity" (312–13).

It is imperative that we be careful about whom we allow to influence us. There are prominent hirelings in many fields who do not care for the Lord's sheep or for his teachings. President Benson, reflecting upon the words of President Smith, said:

> Seeking the applause of the world, we like to be honored by the men whom the world honors. But therein lies real danger, for ofttimes, in order to receive those honors, we must join forces with and follow those same devilish influences and policies that brought some of those men to positions of prominence.
>
> More and more the honors of this world are being promoted by the wicked for the wicked. We see this in publicity and awards that are given in movies, literature, art, journalism, etc. (*God, Family, Country* 235)

Jesus warned, "Woe unto you, when all men shall speak well of you! for so did their fathers to the false prophets" (Luke 6:26). President Heber J. Grant was known to have said many times: "When certain men start to praise me or applaud me or speak well of me, I say to myself: 'Heber Grant, you must not be doing your duty or such men would not praise you'" (Lee 14).

Flattery appeals to pride, vain ambition, and excessive appetite for approval, acceptance, or praise. Apostatizing for power or position in the world is tantamount to exchanging one's birthright for the temporary satisfaction of a mess of pottage. Jesus cautioned, "If ye were of the world, the world would love his own: but because ye are not of the world, but I have chosen you out of the world, therefore the world hateth you" (John 15:19). As that is true, perhaps people can gauge their closeness to the kingdom by their distance from the world.

The Challenge of Teaching the Rising Generation

Many of the rising Nephite generation rejected the faith of their fathers. They refused baptism, would not pray, and chose to remain "in their carnal and sinful state" (Mosiah 26:4). Mormon wrote, "And now because of their unbelief they could not understand the word of God; and their hearts were hardened" (Mosiah 26:3). Together, unbelief and sin create a barrier, or shield, which prevents people from feeling the spiritual influence that enlightens the mind. Nephi told his brothers:

> Ye are swift to do iniquity but slow to remember the Lord your God. Ye have seen an angel, and he spake unto you; yea, ye have heard his voice from time to time; and he hath spoken unto you in a still small voice, but ye were past feeling, that ye could not feel his words. (1 Nephi 17:45)

Unbelief and sin are inversely related to the first principles of the gospel: faith in Jesus Christ removes unbelief, and repentance removes sin. Unimpaired by these handicaps, a person can then begin to understand and obey the word of God. Mormon noted that in this same time period "there was nothing preached in all the churches except it were repentance and faith in God" (Mosiah 25:22). The preaching of these two pre-requisites to baptism served anciently as an antidote to the problems of unbelief and sin. Parents of the rising generation today are likewise under strict command to teach these first principles to their children (D&C 68:25).

The Challenge of Persecution

During this time of unbelief, persecution against the Church in Zarahemla became so great that king Mosiah sent out a proclamation forbidding the persecution of Church members (Mosiah 27:1–2). In an epistle to Timothy, the Apostle Paul wrote, "All that will live godly in Christ Jesus shall suffer persecution" (2 Tim 3:12). This truth spans dispensations and continents and will be true of members of the Church of Jesus Christ until the millennial day. The Prophet Joseph Smith taught, "The enemies of this people will never get weary of their persecution against the Church, until they are overcome" (*Teachings of the Prophet Joseph Smith* 259). Although elements of our modern society may have altered the form of the attack, the challenges are still basically the same. Perhaps the day of mass martyrdom is over, but Lucifer's goal has never been exclusively the death of the body. A live body, dead to Christ, is more important to him than a martyr awaiting celestial glory. Jesus cautioned his disciples: "Be not afraid of them that kill the body, and after that have no more that they can do.

But I will forewarn you whom ye shall fear: Fear him, which after he hath killed hath power to cast into hell; yea, I say unto you, Fear him" (Luke 12:4–5). The Church today faces a sophisticated and in some cases organized force of unbelievers who have at their disposal the communication technology to spread their war of words against the Saints.

In a First Presidency message entitled "Keep the Faith," Elder Gordon B. Hinckley wrote:

> There is another group presently receiving wide publicity across the nation. They are poking into all the crevices of our history, ferreting out little things of small import and magnifying them into great issues of public discussion, working the media in an effort to give credibility to their efforts.
>
> None of this is new, of course. From the day that Joseph Smith walked out of the grove in the year 1820, critics and enemies— generation after generation of them—have worked and reworked the same old materials. . . . Early in this fishing expedition, one of them gathered affidavits from neighbors and associates in an effort to undermine the character of Joseph Smith. This old bale of straw has been dished up again and again as if it were something new. They have raked over every available word that he spoke or wrote, and they then in turn have written long tomes and delivered long lectures trying to explain the mystery of his character and his work. (4)

The story of the efforts of Alma the Younger and the four sons of Mosiah to destroy the Church sends a message to those who would pursue a similar course today. The Lord's words in the preface to the Doctrine and Covenants are applicable:

> What I the Lord have spoken, I have spoken, and I excuse not myself; and though the heavens and the earth pass away, my word shall not pass away, but shall all be fulfilled, whether by mine own voice or the voice of my servants, it is the same. (D&C 1:38)

The message to modern-day persecutors is the same as it has always been, whether the warning voice comes personally from the mouth of an angel, or vicariously through the voice of scripture: "Go thy way, and seek to destroy the church no more, . . . and this even if thou wilt of thyself be cast off" (Mosiah 27:16).

The Challenge of Handling Transgression in the Church

Alma anguished in spirit because as chief high priest he had to sit in judgment over those who had sinned in the church. What he learned is significant to Latter-day Saints. Alma's tribulation and the revelation that followed are a guide for modern priesthood leaders who, by virtue of their callings, must make similar decisions.

Mormon recorded, "It became expedient that those who committed sin, that were in the church, should be admonished by the church" (Mosiah 26:6). The Church as a light to the world cannot be allowed to dim through tolerance of sin. Neither the Lord nor his Church can "look upon sin with the least degree of allowance" (Alma 45:16). The Lord told Alma the conditions that would qualify one to be found on the right hand of God following judgment:

> For it is I that taketh upon me the sins of the world; for it is I that hath created them; and it is I that granteth unto *him that believeth unto the end* a place at my right hand. For behold, in my name are they called; and *if they know me* they shall come forth, and shall have a place eternally at my right hand. And it shall come to pass that when the second trump shall sound then shall they that never knew me come forth and shall stand before me. . . . And then I will confess unto them that I never knew them; and they shall depart into everlasting fire prepared for the devil and his angels. (Mosiah 26:23–25, 27; emphasis added)

Ironically, at the judgment day those who chose not to know Jesus during their mortal lives will receive from him the pronouncement "I never knew you" (3 Nephi 14:23; compare Mosiah 26:25–27). This judgment includes those who refuse to enter into a covenant relationship with the Lord, as did the rising generation in Alma's day, and those who break their covenants and refuse to repent. Sheep who know and reject the true shepherd in order to graze in other pastures will not be numbered or known in the fold, but will lose their inheritance. King Benjamin taught:

I would that ye should take upon you the name of Christ, all you that have entered into the covenant with God that ye should be obedient unto the end of your lives. And it shall come to pass that whosoever doeth this shall be found at the right hand of God, for he shall know the name by which he is called; for he shall be called by the name of Christ. And now it shall come to pass, that whosoever shall not take upon him the name of Christ must be called by some other name; therefore, he findeth himself on the left hand of God. (Mosiah 5:8–10)

The Lord then taught Alma that the same criteria for the separation of the wicked from the righteous at the judgment day should be applied within the Church, with the stipulation that one could change course through confession of sin and sincere repentance:

Therefore I say unto you, that he that will not hear my voice, the same shall ye not receive into my church, for him I will not receive at the last day. Therefore I say unto you, Go; and whosoever transgresseth against me, him shall ye judge according to the sins which he has committed; and if he confess his sins before thee and me, and repenteth in the sincerity of his heart, him shall ye forgive, and I will forgive him also. . . . Now I say unto you, Go; and whosoever will not repent of his sins the same shall not be numbered among my people; and this shall be observed from this time forward. (Mosiah 26:28–29, 32)

The Lord's words "if he confess his sins before *thee* and *me*" are instructive for individuals seeking to repent. It is necessary to confess certain sins to bishops as well as to the Lord.

This story also reveals an important pattern concerning revelation in the Church. First, the unbelievers were leading people to sin, and it became necessary for Alma to deal with the transgressors (Mosiah 26:9, 10). Second, the prophet inquired of the Lord for a solution, and the Lord responded by revealing his will to Alma concerning those who had transgressed (Mosiah 26:13–32). Finally, the prophet recorded the Lord's word, and the revelation then became a standard in the Church for judgment (Mosiah 26:33). Many of the revelations in the Doctrine and Covenants were received in much the same manner.

The Rebirth of Alma the Younger
and the Four Sons of Mosiah

The transition from the world to the kingdom of God was a painful process for Alma and the four sons of king Mosiah. Alma's testimony confirms this: "After wading through much tribulation, repenting nigh unto death, the Lord in mercy hath seen fit to snatch me out of an everlasting burning, and I am born of God" (Mosiah 27:28).

Despite the pain involved, the conversion stories in Mosiah chapter 27 send a message of hope to those today who have deeply sinned and desire to repent. The scriptures describe Alma the Younger as a wicked and an idolatrous man (Mosiah 27:8) and the sons of Mosiah as "the very vilest of sinners" (Mosiah 28:4). Church members today who despair because they perceive their sinful past as a barrier to positive growth or opportunities to serve in the Church can receive assurance from the experience of Alma the Younger and the sons of Mosiah that the repentant can become great in the sight of God.

One precept discussed in the text of Mosiah 27 is that the prayers of faithful parents can help bring about the repentance of their rebellious children. The angel told Alma the Younger, "For this purpose have I come to convince thee of the power and authority of God, that the prayers of his servants might be answered according to their faith" (Mosiah 27:14). Parents today often pray with great faith for their rebellious sons and daughters, yet they do not always receive the same results. Alma the Elder's gospel is the same gospel that we have today; why then are there not more angels and more thunderous and transforming experiences? Mortal parents who make their own best efforts to reach their children can invoke divine assistance through prayer, for all scriptures unite in testifying that God answers prayers. Perhaps the Lord *does* send angels, but angels of a different sort. Inspired teachers, friends, bishops, home teachers, scout leaders, and others can serve the same function as angels from above. These embodied angels, inspired by the Holy Ghost, are sent by the Lord to assist and to love.

Evidently there were factors in Alma the Younger's circumstance that necessitated his peculiar experience. President Wilford Woodruff taught: "The Lord never did nor ever will send an angel to anyone merely to gratify the desire of the individual to see an angel. If the Lord sends an angel to anyone, He sends him to perform a work that cannot be performed only by the administration of an angel" (Ludlow 191).

Although Alma's transformation was initiated by an angel, Alma still needed to exercise his agency and choose for himself. Later verses about his life reveal steps that all who achieve conversion must follow. In a sermon to the people of Zarahemla, Alma the Younger said:

> Behold, I testify unto you that I do know that these things whereof I have spoken are true. And how do ye suppose that I know of their surety? Behold, I say unto you they are made known unto me by the Holy Spirit of God. Behold, I have fasted and prayed many days that I might know these things of myself. And now I do know of myself that they are true; for the Lord God hath made them manifest unto me by his Holy Spirit. (Alma 5:45–46)

Alma revealed even more details about his experience to his son Helaman. His emphasis to Helaman was not upon his experience with the angel, but upon his deliverance through Christ from the pain and bitterness of sin (see Alma 36:16–20). Alma's story, together with other conversion stories in the Book of Mormon, teaches the process one can follow to come to know the Savior. One of the great truths revealed in Alma's conversion story pertains to the doctrine of rebirth. Alma recounted that after he had repented "nigh unto death" (Mosiah 27:28) he was born of God. Concerning his experience with the Lord he said:

> And the Lord said unto me: Marvel not that all mankind, yea, men and women, all nations, kindreds, tongues and people, must be born again; yea, born of God, changed from their carnal and fallen state, to a state of righteousness, being redeemed of God, becoming his sons and daughters; And thus they become new creatures; and unless

they do this, they can in nowise inherit the kingdom of God. (Mosiah 27:25–26)

Alma's experience exemplifies this change from the carnal to the spiritual. Recognition gives way to remorse and then to forgiveness and a mighty change of heart. Spiritual rebirth then leads to the desire to preach the gospel so others might receive this same joy.

Conclusion

In making his abridgment of the sacred records of the Nephites, Lamanites, and Jaredites, Mormon wrote, "I cannot write the hundredth part of the things of my people" (WofM 1:5). So, as President Benson has reminded us, Mormon chose to record "the stories, speeches, and events that would be most helpful to us" ("The Book of Mormon" 6).

Mosiah 25–27 has special relevance for members of The Church of Jesus Christ of Latter-day Saints. It testifies of Christ and restores plain and precious truths about the true gospel and church of Christ. It counsels us on how to handle the challenges that we face in our own day, including flattery, teaching the rising generation, persecution, and transgression in the Church. It also teaches us, through the story of the conversion of Alma the Younger and the sons of Mosiah, that although repentance can be painful, even those who have sinned deeply can become tools in the Lord's hands to bless others' lives, if they will repent of their sins.

BIBLIOGRAPHY

Benson, Ezra Taft. "The Book of Mormon—Keystone of Our Religion." *Ensign* (Nov 1986) 16:4–7; also in *Conference Report* (Oct 1986) 3–7.

————. *God, Family, Country: Our Three Great Loyalties*. Salt Lake City: Deseret Book, 1974.

Hinckley, Gordon B. "Keep the Faith." *Ensign* (Sep 1985) 15:3–6.

Lee, Harold B. *Ye Are the Light of the World*. Salt Lake City: Deseret Book, 1974.

Ludlow, Daniel H. *A Companion to Your Study of the Book of Mormon*. Salt Lake City: Deseret Book, 1976.

Smith, Joseph F. *Gospel Doctrine*. Salt Lake City: Deseret Book, 1968.

Teachings of the Prophet Joseph Smith. Comp. Joseph Fielding Smith. Salt Lake City: Deseret Book, 1976.

Divine Indebtedness and the Atonement 6

Gerald N. Lund

The title for this paper was first suggested to me when I was invited to participate in this symposium. At first it seemed odd, a curious juxtaposition of important but unrelated ideas. As I began to reread the magnificent closing sermon of the great and righteous king Benjamin, I wondered what in those chapters had caused the committee to choose this title. After carefully reading and examining king Benjamin's closing sermon, I could not think of a title that better summarized the message of this Nephite king to his people. Because of that experience, I will use an approach similar to the one I used in my own study to present this paper, hoping to share with you what I have learned about the relationship between divine indebtedness and the Atonement. I shall examine the message of king Benjamin, look at its antecedents, outline its structure, note relationships within that structure, watch for patterns in the words and phrases he chose to use, and explore some of the implications of his address for us today. I shall let this great sermon speak for itself on the relationship between divine indebtedness and the atonement of Jesus Christ.

To understand the full impact of Benjamin's address, we must consider the setting in which it was given. Mormon, writing some four centuries after the fact, informs us about king Benjamin and the circumstances leading to his last great

Gerald N. Lund is a zone administrator in the Church Educational System, Salt Lake City, Utah.

sermon (WofM 1:12–18; Mosiah 1:1–2:8). Benjamin did not inherit a comfortable situation when he became king of the Nephite nation; it was a time of war. The armies of the Lamanites came down against the Nephites, and king Benjamin led his people in battle, wielding the sword of Laban with his own hand. Thousands were killed, and eventually the Lamanites were driven out of the land (WofM 1:13–14). But this external threat to the society was not the only problem. Mormon says that the wars with the Lamanites were in addition to "contentions among [king Benjamin's] own people." He also explains that there were false Christs, false prophets, false preachers, and false teachers among the people. There was also "much contention and many dissensions," and the people were described as stiffnecked (WofM 1:12, 15–17).

But Benjamin was not content with that state of affairs. With the assistance of holy prophets and through his own personal righteousness, king Benjamin brought about a complete change of heart in his people. In one single sentence Mormon summarizes Benjamin's greatness: "King Benjamin, by laboring with all the might of his body and the faculty of his whole soul . . . did once more establish peace in the land" (WofM 1:18). By peace, Mormon almost certainly means more than the absence of war.

The ultimate proof of Benjamin's success is evident at the end of his sermon, when all of the people

> had fallen to the earth, for the fear of the Lord had come upon them. And they had viewed themselves in their own carnal state, even less than the dust of the earth. And they all cried aloud with one voice, saying: O have mercy, and apply the atoning blood of Christ that we may receive forgiveness of our sins, and our hearts may be purified; for we believe in Jesus Christ, the Son of God, who created heaven and earth, and all things; who shall come down among the children of men. (Mosiah 4:1–2)

This is the context in which we must examine king Benjamin's last address to his people, asking ourselves why he would choose the theme of indebtedness to God.

A Stewardship Report (Mosiah 2:9–17)

There must have been a tremendous outpouring of love and gratitude toward king Benjamin when the people learned that he was turning the kingdom over to his son and that this would possibly be the last speech of their beloved king. Even king Benjamin seemed unprepared for the huge multitude that responded to his proclamation to come hear him. When the multitude spilled out beyond the temple courtyard, a tower was built. But even that was not sufficient; the address had to be written and distributed among the people as well (Mosiah 2:8).

As the throngs came, Benjamin surely would have been inundated with people seeking to thank him for all he had done. Praise and thanks for his goodness and greatness must have been showered upon him like a tropical downpour. Many people might be tempted in the face of such praise to say in their hearts, "Yes, you are right; I have done well." But Benjamin would not let the credit and praise rest with himself. He epitomized the counsel of the Apostle Paul that a man ought "not to think of himself more highly than he ought to think" (Rom 12:3). To God went the glory. These were his opening thoughts as he spoke to his people:

> I have not commanded you to come up hither that ye should fear me, or that ye should think that I of myself am more than a mortal man. But I am like as yourselves, subject to all manner of infirmities in body and mind; yet I have been chosen by this people, and consecrated by my father, and was suffered by the hand of the Lord that I should be a ruler and a king over this people; and have been kept and preserved by his matchless power, to serve you with all the might, mind and strength which the Lord hath granted unto me. (Mosiah 2:10–11)

Next, he gave what might be termed a brief "stewardship report" to the people whom he had served. And what a report that was. By his own admission we learn that king Benjamin was a man of honor and justice. He did not suffer his people to be placed in prisons or to practice slavery. He saw that criminals and sinners were punished. He labored with his own hands so that his people would not have to pay burdensome taxes (Mosiah 2:12–14). How his people must have loved him! Peace, security, honesty, justice, prosperity, and righteousness were the legacies which he left them. The long and tragic history of the world's monarchies clearly testifies that few other kings could have given similar stewardship reports at the ends of their earthly reigns.

Hastily, lest he be misunderstood, king Benjamin noted that this report was not an attempt to boast of his accomplishments, but only an acknowledgement that his service to the people was an extension of his desire to serve God (Mosiah 2:16). And then, in what is surely one of the finest, most beautiful, and most succinct lessons on Christian service ever given, he commented on the exemplary lesson of his own righteous life. If you learn anything from me, he said, learn this one lesson: "When ye are in the service of your fellow beings ye are only in the service of your God" (Mosiah 2:17).

Our Indebtedness to Our Heavenly King
(Mosiah 2:18–26)

King Benjamin's stewardship report and the resulting lesson on service led him naturally to the concept of divine indebtedness. He had already noted that any success he had enjoyed had come only through the grace and sustaining power of God; therefore, their praise of him was misdirected. "If I, whom ye call your king," he said, "do merit any thanks from you, O how you ought to thank your heavenly King!" (Mosiah 2:19). This provides the basis for king Benjamin's concept of divine indebtedness. It is a lesson as applicable today as when it was given to the Nephites gathered in their tents in the land of Zarahemla.

A careful look at verses 20 through 25 of chapter 2 reveals the logic of king Benjamin's thoughts about our indebtedness to God. A capsulization of it into outline form looks like this:

A. God has
   1. Created us (v 20)
   2. Kept and preserved us (v 20)
   3. Caused us to rejoice (v 20)
   4. Granted that we should have peace (v 20)
B. He continues to
   1. Preserve us day to day by giving us breath (v 21)
   2. Allow us to live and move and do as we will (v 21)
   3. Support us from one moment to the next (v 21)
   4. Grant unto us our lives (v 23)
C. We would still be unprofitable servants even if we should
   1. Render all the thanks and praise our souls possess (v 20)
   2. Serve him with our whole souls (v 21)
D. All he requires is that we keep his commandments (v 22)
E. Which if we do, he immediately blesses us (v 22)
F. Conclusions
   1. We are indebted to God because
      a. He created us and grants us life (v 23)
      b. When we keep his commandments he blesses us more,
         which only increases our indebtedness (v 24)
   2. We cannot boast of anything (v 24)
   3. We are not even as much as the dust of the earth (v 25)

What God Has Done for His Children

In his address, king Benjamin emphasizes various aspects of God's graciousness to his children. One aspect is the fact that God created us. King Benjamin seems to mean far more than simply the creation of our bodies; rather he seems to mean that God is responsible for the whole of creation—the heavens, the earth, and everything in them. This simple fact alone should be reason enough for our unending gratitude.

When we create something through our own labor—a work of art, a building, a piece of furniture, great music—we say it is ours. We believe we have claim upon it, stewardship over it, and the right to do with it as we wish. By this same logic we should acknowledge that because all we see and know comes from the labor of God's hands, everything is his. Therefore, whatever we have, take, use, or enjoy automatically places us in God's debt. In a revelation to the Prophet

Joseph Smith, the Lord clearly stated that this is indeed the case:

> For it is expedient that I, the Lord, should make every man accountable, as a steward over earthly blessings, which I have made and prepared for my creatures. I, the Lord, stretched out the heavens, and built the earth, my very handiwork; and all things therein are mine. (D&C 104:13–14)

Note the possessive phrases used in those verses: "which I have made," "my very handiwork," "all things therein are mine." As the Psalmist said, "The earth is the Lord's, and the fulness thereof; the world, and they that dwell therein" (Ps 24:1).

Think for a moment how that simple concept would alter our thinking if we would really accept it. We clutch things to our bosoms and say, "These are mine." People rob, cheat, steal, manipulate, and maneuver so they can claim things as their own. The rich ignore the desperate sufferings of the poor because they somehow think that what they have belongs solely to them. Nations go to war over land which they did nothing to create.

If we truly believed that God owns all things and that we only use and borrow what is already his, it would vastly alter the way we approach life. A classic illustration of this principle is found in the life of Job. After facing devastating losses of family, property, and health, he states simply, "Naked came I out of my mother's womb, and naked shall I return thither: the Lord gave, and the Lord hath taken away; blessed be the name of the Lord" (Job 1:21).

Bishop Henry B. Eyring spoke of the natural human tendency to forget all that God has done for us:

> We so easily forget that we came into life with nothing. Whatever we get soon seems our natural right, not a gift. And we forget the giver. Then our gaze shifts from what we have been given to what we don't have yet.... The remembrance urged upon us by king Benjamin can be ours. Remembrance is the seed of gratitude. (12–13)

We accept daily miracles as commonplace precisely because they are daily experiences—the birth of an infant, the coming of spring, the glory of a forested mountain range, the healing processes within the human body, the never ending procession of glorious sunrises and sunsets, the infinite variety and incredible beauty of something as simple as snow flakes showering down upon the earth in countless billions. Those who try to duplicate nature in the laboratory stand in awe as they see how short they fall. The author of a December 1989 *National Geographic* article on the development of new high-tech materials discusses such mind-boggling advances as ceramic ball bearings so tough they leave dimples on an anvil when hammered by a blacksmith, yet they do not break; a metal that actually hardens as its temperature rises; cement sheets so thin and light that they are used in hang-glider fabric; plastics so flexible they can be stretched as much as 1,000 percent and grow stronger in the process! After quoting a scientist who said his goal was to develop materials which respond as nature does, the author of the article concludes: "[Their goal is to be] like nature. For materials scientists, the perfection of a tree, a bone, a spiderweb remains the distant goal" (Canby 781).

Numerous scriptures state clearly our obligation of feeling and expressing gratitude to God. Two will suffice to illustrate. In language similar to that of the Ten Commandments, the Lord says in the Doctrine and Covenants, "Thou shalt thank the Lord thy God in all things" (59:7). And then a few verses later he comments, "And in nothing doth man offend God, or against none is his wrath kindled, save those who confess not his hand in all things, and obey not his commandments" (59:21). In section 78 of the Doctrine and Covenants, the Lord ties gratitude to both spiritual and temporal results: "And he who receiveth all things with thankfulness shall be made glorious; and the things of this earth shall be added unto him, even an hundred fold, yea, more" (v 19).

When we consider the richness of God's creation, the inestimable abundance he gives to us so freely, his life-sustaining power, and the continual outpouring of his blessings when we are obedient, it is not difficult to understand why king Benjamin describes our state as one of being indebted to our Heavenly Father.

Now we come to two statements in king Benjamin's address which some Latter-day Saints may find a little troubling. Unlike Calvinism and many other Christian faiths, we do not view humanity as inherently evil. A strong central concept in our theology is that we are literally the spirit children of our Heavenly Father. We speak positively about the need for self-esteem and self-reliance. We speak of our potential to become gods, a concept so bold and daring that it causes many Christians to recoil. So how do we reconcile these ideas with king Benjamin's powerful *if* statements? He says that even *if* we should render all of the praise and thanks to God of which our souls are capable, and even *if* we should serve him with our whole souls, we would still be "unprofitable servants" (Mosiah 2:20–21). Even more pointed (some might say more devastating) is his answer to his own rhetorical question, "Can you say aught of yourselves?" He replies, "Ye cannot say that ye are even as much as the dust of the earth" (Mosiah 2:25). Let's examine these two points one at a time, for they are pivotal to our understanding of the connection between divine indebtedness and the Atonement.

Unprofitable Servants

The phrase "unprofitable servants" was used by the Savior in a short parable he taught to the disciples in response to their plea, "Increase our faith" (Luke 17:5):

> But which of you, having a servant plowing or feeding cattle, will say unto him by and by, when he is come from the field, Go and sit down to meat? And will not rather say unto him, Make ready wherewith I may sup, and gird thyself, and serve me, till I have eaten and drunken; and afterward thou shalt eat and drink? Doth he thank that servant because he did the things that were commanded him? I trow not. So likewise ye, when ye shall have done all those things

which are commanded you, say, We are unprofitable servants: we have done that which was our duty to do. (Luke 17:7–10)

In some ways, this parable is no less troublesome than king Benjamin's statement. But to better understand the concept of unprofitable servants, we must focus on the word *profit*. Profit means an increase in personal assets, status, or benefits. That is the crux of the concept of our being unprofitable servants. God is perfect in his knowledge, power, influence, and attributes. He is the Creator of all things! What could any of us—or all of us collectively—do that would bring profit (that is, an increase in assets, status, or benefits) to God?

A nineteenth-century scholar, commenting on this parable, eloquently noted that people cannot

> work righteousness, in the smallest degree, beyond those powers which God has given them; and justice and equity require that they should exert those powers to the uttermost in the service of their *Maker*; and, after having acted thus, it may be justly said, *They have done only what it was their duty to do.* The nature of God is illimitable, and all the attributes of that nature are infinitely glorious: they cannot be *lessened* by the *transgressions* of his creatures, nor can they be *increased* by the uninterrupted, eternal *obedience*, and unceasing *hallelujahs*, of all the intelligent creatures that people the whole vortex of nature. When ages, beyond the power of arithmetic to sum up, have elapsed, it may be said of the most pure and perfect creatures, "Ye are unprofitable servants." Ye have derived your being from the infinite fountain of life: ye are upheld by the continued energy of the Almighty: his glories are infinite and eternal, and your obedience and services, however excellent in themselves, and profitable to *you*, have added nothing, and can add nothing, to the absolute excellencies and glories of your God. (Clarke 5:468)

That we are his children and that he loves us is undeniable. But we must rid ourselves of the notion that we can bring personal profit to God through our own actions. That would make God indebted to us, and that is unthinkable. This explains king Benjamin's ringing *ifs*: even if we were to serve him with all the power of our souls, even if we should render thanks with that same power (which very few of us, if any, ever do), we would still be unprofitable servants.

Less Than the Dust of the Earth

The comment that we are even less than the dust of the earth may, on the surface, seem a little more difficult to resolve. Have we no worth at all, as this statement implies? Before answering, let us note an interesting parallel to king Benjamin's thinking. Benjamin concluded that humans are less than the dust of the earth immediately after he noted that God is the creator and sustainer of humanity. About 1,000 years earlier, the prophet Moses was caught up in heavenly vision and was shown the creation of "the world . . . and all the children of men" (Moses 1:8). Then the heavenly power withdrew and Moses was left to himself. When he recovered from the experience, his first words were, "Now, for this cause I know that man is nothing, which thing I never had supposed" (Moses 1:10).

Something about the majesty and infinite awesomeness of the Creation reminds both king Benjamin and Moses of humanity's puny and finite nature. But are we really less than the dust of earth? It is this "less than" concept that stings particularly. The nothingness of which Moses speaks is one thing; the worthlessness implied in Benjamin's phrase, "ye cannot say ye are even as much as the dust of the earth" (Mosiah 2:25), is quite another. Let us examine Benjamin's phrase and its subsequent uses for clues that may aid our understanding.

First of all, "dust of the earth" is a scriptural phrase that seems to imply far more than mere dirt particles. We are told, "The Lord God formed man of the dust of the ground" (Gen 2:7). Perhaps another word that would come close to the metaphorical meaning of *dust* would be *elements*. God certainly did not pull together a pile of mud, form it into the shape of a human being, and breathe life into it. But he did create our bodies from the elements of the earth.

King Benjamin makes a second point immediately following his "less than" statement. He reminds us that we are created of the dust of the earth, but then adds, "But behold, it belongeth to him who created you" (Mosiah 2:25). This is a simple, but profound line of reasoning:

1. God created all things, including the dust (or elements) of the earth
2. We are made of those elements
3. Therefore, our bodies belong to God

Yet this still doesn't completely clarify king Benjamin's comment that we are not "even as much as the dust of the earth." We can easily acknowledge that we are made of earthly elements, but king Benjamin says far more than that. He says we are not "even as much as" those elements. Why? Are we truly so worthless? Mormon gives us the clues that help us better understand king Benjamin's statement. We will examine two of Mormon's statements, one made immediately following king Benjamin's address, and one made later in the Book of Mormon.

King Benjamin's words, as well as the angel's message which the king delivered, had such a powerful effect on the people that they fell to the ground. Regarding the people's reaction, Mormon comments, "And they had viewed themselves in their own carnal state, even less than the dust of the earth" (Mosiah 4:2). What a significant clue! It is the carnal or natural man that is less than the dust of the earth. Thus, one of the first things Benjamin says as he continues his address is that the people had been awakened to a sense of "[their] own nothingness, and [their] worthless and fallen state" (Mosiah 4:5). Again, our worthlessness is mentioned in connection with our fallen state.

Interestingly, king Benjamin says a lack of humility (or not remembering our own nothingness) leads us to a state of being called "the natural man," a state in which one becomes "an enemy to God" (Mosiah 2:37; 3:19). In a similar vein, President Benson defines pride as enmity toward God:

The central feature of pride is enmity—enmity toward God and enmity toward our fellowmen. Enmity means "hatred toward,

83

hostility to, or a state of opposition." It is the power by which Satan wishes to reign over us. Pride is essentially competitive in nature. We pit our will against God's. ("Beware of Pride" 4)

This leads us to Mormon's later explanation of why we are less than the dust of the earth:

> Yea, how quick [are people] to be lifted up in pride; yea, how quick to boast, and do all manner of that which is iniquity; and how slow are they to remember the Lord their God, and to give ear unto his counsels, yea, how slow to walk in wisdom's paths! Behold, they do not desire that the Lord their God, who hath created them, should rule and reign over them; notwithstanding his great goodness and his mercy towards them, they do set at naught his counsels, and they will not that he should be their guide. O how great is the nothingness of the children of men; yea, even they are less than the dust of the earth. For behold, the dust of the earth moveth hither and thither, to the dividing asunder, at the command of our great and everlasting God. (Hel 12:5–8)

This is the key. King Benjamin said that all God asks of us as payment for our debt to him is our obedience. But natural or fallen individuals are by nature disobedient. Even the elements of the earth respond to God's voice, but fallen individuals do not. They persist in their sinful ways, ignoring God's goodness to them and their own indebted state, and, therefore, are even less than the dust of the earth.

Indebtedness and the Atonement (Mosiah 2:26–3:27)

I began this paper by noting that the juxtaposition of indebtedness and the Atonement seemed a little odd at first. Having examined the concept of our nothingness and our being less than the dust of the earth, we can now see how Benjamin makes indebtedness and the Atonement interdependent.

Earlier, I outlined the logical organization of king Benjamin's comments on divine indebtedness. I will now summarize that portion of his address in one sentence (A) and then continue the outline to show how indebtedness relates to the Atonement.

A. King Benjamin asserts that humanity alone is nothing; therefore, we are indebted to God, though all God requires for payment of our indebtedness is our obedience (2:19–25)
B. King Benjamin discharges his obligation and warns against disobedience (2:26–41)
  1. He gives a charge to keep the commandments under the new king (2:31)
  2. He commands us to avoid obeying evil spirits (2:32–35)
    a. Those who sin and die in their sins are damned, a just wage for transgressing knowingly (2:33)
    b. All have been taught how to avoid evil by the prophets and the scriptures—yet another reason for our indebtedness to God (2:34–35)
  3. He states that those who knowingly transgress (2:36–39)
    a. Withdraw from the Spirit (2:36)
    b. Receive no guidance on life's path (2:36)
    c. Become enemies to God—that is, natural men (2:37)
    d. Have no place for the Lord (2:37)
    e. Will experience guilt, shame, pain, and torment unless they repent (2:38–39)
  4. He calls on all to consider the two choices (2:40–41)
    a. The awful state of those who transgress (2:40)
    b. The blessed and happy state (temporal and spiritual) of the obedient (2:41)
C. King Benjamin delivers the angel's message (3:1–27)
  1. He prophesies of Christ (3:1–11)
    a. God will come to the earth and minister to humanity (3:5–8)
    b. He will be crucified and resurrected (3:9–10)
    c. His blood will atone for those who ignorantly sin (3:11)
    d. His blood will not atone for those who knowingly sin and remain unrepentant (3:12–13)
  2. He teaches the relationship between the law of Moses and the Atonement (3:14–15)
    a. The law of Moses was given because of the hardness of Israel's hearts (3:14)
    b. The law of Moses pointed to Christ (3:15)
    c. The law of Moses had no power to save without the Atonement (3:15)
  3. He teaches and testifies of Christ and the Atonement (3:16–23)
    a. Little children are saved unconditionally through the Atonement (3:16)

    b. There are no other means of salvation but through
       Christ (3:17)

    c. People are damned unless they become as children
       and believe in Christ (3:18)

    d. The natural man is an enemy to God and will be unless
       he (3:19)

      i. Yields to the enticings of the Holy Spirit

      ii. Puts off the natural man

      iii. Becomes a saint through the Atonement

      iv. Becomes as a child

4. He teaches consequences of the Atonement (3:20–27)

    a. When knowledge of the Atonement spreads, none
       will be blameless but children (3:20–21)

    b. Those who reject Christ's words are damned, and their
       punishments are just (3:23–27)

With this outline we clearly see that once Benjamin establishes the concept of divine indebtedness, he moves immediately to disobedience (the ultimate proof of our ingratitude) and its consequences. From there he logically turns to the only cure for those consequences—the Atonement.

The Atonement of Christ

Benjamin's discussion of our indebtedness and worthlessness naturally leads him directly to a discussion of the Atonement and of the concept of grace, though king Benjamin never uses the word *grace* itself. The LDS Bible Dictionary defines *grace* as the "divine means of help or strength given through the bounteous mercy and love of Jesus Christ. . . . This grace is an enabling power that allows men and women to lay hold on eternal life and exaltation after they have expended their own best efforts."

Note that last phrase. It is another way of saying exactly what king Benjamin was saying, namely, that even if we thank God with all our souls, even if we serve him our whole lives (another way to describe "best efforts") we would still be unprofitable servants. There must be a source of help, some "enabling power" that lifts us out of our utter helplessness and helps us overcome our carnal and fallen nature so that we may become the sons and daughters of God.

As the angel explained to Benjamin, without Christ and his saving power we are damned: we are destined to remain in our fallen, natural state as enemies to God. But through God's grace, his enabling power, we can put off the natural man and become saints, sanctified and holy, and thus return to God's presence. Thus the concepts of indebtedness and atonement are inextricably interwoven in king Benjamin's thinking. The Atonement is both another reason for our indebtedness and the means by which we escape from its effects.

Obtaining and Retaining a Remission of Sins (Mosiah 4:1–30)

The concepts of indebtedness and atonement are in some ways one. And, as taught by king Benjamin, they had a tremendous impact on the people. They cried for mercy and asked that the atoning blood of Christ be applied in their behalf so their sins could be forgiven (v 2). Their request was granted, and Mormon tells us that they received a remission of their sins (v 3).

Filled with joy at his people's repentance, king Benjamin returned to his initial theme and taught them how to retain the remission of sins they had just experienced. And here, as in the first part of his address, the concept of indebtedness still heavily flavors his thinking. Note his reasoning:

1. The knowledge of God has awakened you to a sense of your nothingness and your fallen state (v 5)
2. A knowledge of God's goodness and of the Atonement brings salvation to those who (v 6)
   a. Trust in God
   b. Are diligent in keeping the commandments
   c. Continue in faith to the end
3. These are they who receive salvation (v 7)
4. There is no other way to receive salvation (v 8)
5. We retain a remission of sins by remembering God's goodness and our own nothingness and unworthiness (v 11)

6. This remembrance will influence all we do and lead us to eternal life (vv 12–30)

Thus the key to the whole process of salvation is remembering, and the primary focus of our remembrance is (1) God's goodness and greatness, (2) our own nothingness, and (3) God's greatest gift, Jesus Christ, through whom we can be saved.

Conclusion: Remembrance, the Key to Salvation

President Ezra Taft Benson has said:

> The Prophet Joseph said at one time that one of the greatest sins of which the Latter-day Saints would be guilty is the sin of ingratitude. I presume most of us have not thought of that as a great sin. There is a great tendency for us in our prayers and in our pleadings with the Lord to ask for additional blessings. But sometimes I feel we need to devote more of our prayers to expressions of gratitude and thanksgiving for blessings already received. We enjoy so much. Of course we need daily blessings of the Lord, but if we sin in the matter of prayer, I think it is in the lack of our expressions of thanksgiving, for blessings that we receive daily. (*God, Family, Country* 199)

Gratitude is a simple thing; perhaps that is why so many easily overlook it. But in the matchless address of the humble, righteous king Benjamin we are taught that profound consequences can result from gratitude or the lack of it. It was not a sense of hopelessness king Benjamin sought to invoke when he noted that we are less than the dust of the earth. It was a sense of humility, and more especially, a sense of our utter and total dependence upon God for all that we have, all that we are, and all that we can be—a sense of the relationship between divine indebtedness and the Atonement.

BIBLIOGRAPHY

Benson, Ezra Taft. "Beware of Pride." *Ensign* (May 1989) 19:4–7; also in *Conference Report* (Apr 1989) 3–7.

————. *God, Family, Country: Our Three Great Loyalties.* Salt Lake City: Deseret Book, 1974.

Canby, Thomas Y. "Reshaping Our Lives: Advanced Materials." *National Geographic* (Dec 1989) 176:746–81.

Clarke, Adam. *Clarke's Bible Commentary.* 6 vols. Nashville: Abingdon, n.d.

Eyring, Henry B. "Remembrance and Gratitude." *Ensign* (Nov 1989) 25:11-13; also in *Conference Report* (Oct 1989) 12–16.

Abinadi: The Prophet and Martyr

Robert J. Matthews

The Nephite prophet Abinadi holds a singular place in the Book of Mormon. He is the first Nephite of whom we have record to die as a martyr. His doctrinal teachings are some of the most valuable in the Book of Mormon, clarifying the purpose of the law of Moses, identifying who the Redeemer would be, and declaring some facts about the Resurrection not previously mentioned in the Book of Mormon. He was capable of exquisitely colorful language sparked with fiery metaphor, yet at times was plain-spoken to the point of bluntness.

Abinadi confronted the wicked establishment—in the person of king Noah and his priests—single-handedly. The record gives no hint of any other prophet being present with whom he could share the burden of his ministry. So far as we know, he converted but one man; yet that one man, Alma, became the progenitor of a posterity that kept the sacred records and served the Nephites as their ecclesiastical leaders (and sometimes their political leaders) for the remainder of their history, a period of well over 400 years. (This is seen in the lineage of Alma[1], Alma[2], Helaman[2], Shiblon, Helaman[3], Nephi[2], Nephi[3], Amos[1], Amos[2] and Ammoron. We do not know if Mormon was also a descendant of Alma, since the abridged record that we have does not give Mormon's lineage, other than to say he was a descendant of Lehi [3 Nephi 5:20] and of Nephi [Mormon

---

Robert J. Matthews is professor of Ancient Scripture and former dean of Religious Education at Brigham Young University.

1:5].) Abinadi's history and teachings were preserved in the writings of his one convert, Alma, and Alma's posterity kept the records down to the time of the prophet Mormon, thus making the remainder of the Book of Mormon possible. Abinadi's ministry influenced the entire second half of Nephite history. Because Abinadi's story is in the Book of Mormon, it has already influenced millions of readers in this dispensation and will yet influence billions more.

Several documentary sources have enabled me to prepare this paper. The basic source is the Book of Mormon itself, primarily Mosiah chapters 11 to 18. At least four LDS writers have produced valuable commentaries. These are, in sequence of publication, Elder George Reynolds' "Abinadi," in his *Dictionary of the Book of Mormon*, which is now out of print; Elder Mark E. Petersen's *Alma and Abinadi*; John W. Welch's "Judicial Process in the Trial of Abinadi"; and Rodney Turner's "Two Prophets: Abinadi and Alma" in *Studies in Scripture: 1 Nephi to Alma 29*. Each of these commentaries provides valuable and unique insights. With so many useful works already in print, one might wonder what was still left to be said. However, I found enough things in the text of the book of Mosiah that these commentators either had not noticed, treated only lightly, or chose not to mention, probably for want of space, that seemed to justify yet another paper about Abinadi.

In this paper I will deal with two general subjects. First, I will discuss the historical and circumstantial record of the man Abinadi—his life, ministry, and death. Second, I will discuss his doctrinal teachings. As we review these things, I invite you to think of the prophet Mormon, at the end of his nation's struggles in the fourth century AD, searching what must have been by that time a wagonload of the large plates of Nephi and selecting those things of greatest worth to include in his abridged and summarized record. Mormon was not a freelance writer, but was called of God to prepare a record of his people. He was divinely appointed to be the editor and compiler of a sacred record that would deliver a specific message. We can be grateful that he was inspired to include the story and the teachings of the prophet Abinadi. The Book of Mormon would lack continuity, and a major part of its message would be missing, without the Abinadi portion.

The Man Abinadi

We first hear of Abinadi's teachings and martyrdom in Mosiah 7:26–28. His name is not mentioned, but the fact that he was a prophet and had been slain for his teachings is stated in these verses by king Limhi, son of king Noah. Limhi was a good man, and he was sorry for the wicked things his father Noah had done which had resulted in the death of this prophet. Said Limhi:

> And a prophet of the Lord have they slain; yea, a chosen man of God, who told them of their wickedness and abominations, and prophesied of many things which are to come, yea, even the coming of Christ. And because he said unto them that Christ was the God, the Father of all things, and said that he should take upon him the image of man, and it should be the image after which man was created in the beginning; or in other words, he said that man was created after the image of God, and that God should come down among the children of men, and take upon him flesh and blood, and go forth upon the face of the earth—And now, because he said this, they did put him to death; and many more things did they do which brought down the wrath of God upon them. Therefore, who wondereth that they are in bondage, and that they are smitten with sore afflictions? (Mosiah 7:26–28)

We do not know of Abinadi's parentage or early life. The popular artist Arnold Friberg has given us an outstanding painting that depicts Abinadi as an old man, thin and weather-beaten. And it may very well be so. But I find nothing in the record to indicate whether he was old or young, large or small. Of his physical characteristics we know but little. However, the content of his teachings and his mannerisms when confronting the priests of Noah—baiting them, challenging their knowledge, and questioning their behavior—tells us quite a bit about his courage, his agile mind, his knowledge of the gospel, and his strength of character.

Abinadi reminds me of the Old Testament prophet Amos who predated him by 600 years. The biblical record does not tell us of Amos' death, but commentators have concluded that anyone who issued such fiery and sharp condemnations as did Amos would probably be martyred by those who were stung by the cutting truth of his words. One writer, Rodney Turner, sees a parallel between Abinadi and the New Testament prophet John the Baptist: both were lone preachers of righteousness; both encountered wicked kings; both spoke of the sinful practices of the king and his people; both testified of the coming of Christ; and both were martyred as victims of priestcraft (240).

Abinadi ministered to the people of Zeniff, a group of Nephites who left the land of Zarahemla and settled in the land of Lehi-Nephi and Shilom (Omni 1:27; Mosiah 7:1, 21) in about 200 BC. It appears that Zeniff reigned as king of his people in Lehi-Nephi (under the Lamanite king of the land) at the same time that Mosiah and king Benjamin reigned in Zarahemla. Zeniff was a good man, although he identifies himself as "over-zealous" (Mosiah 9:3). His son and successor was Noah, a very wicked man, as explained in Mosiah 11. Under Noah's reign both the government and the people moved rapidly into wickedness—idolatry, unchastity, materialism, secularism, pride, and extensive consumption of wine. These conditions were characterized by excessively elaborate buildings, love of riches, boasting in their own strength, and self-justification. Such a lifestyle is expensive, and, as is usually the case, it was supported by very high taxes. As a result of a military victory of Noah's army over the Lamanites, Noah's people were lifted up in the pride of their hearts, and delighted in the shedding of blood—all because of the wickedness of the king and his priests (Mosiah 11:19).

Several times in Mosiah 11 the point is made that the bad example of the leaders led the people into wrong-doing (vv 2,

6–7, 15, 19). Pointing out this cause-and-effect relationship is a major contribution of the story: people have a tendency to follow their leaders, and corrupt leaders corrupt the whole kingdom.

As defined in the record, the people's catalog of sins included the following (Mosiah 11:1–19):

1. having many wives and concubines
2. doing all manner of wickedness
3. levying heavy taxes, with which they supported their opulence and luxury
4. consecrating priests who were lifted up in pride
5. being lazy
6. worshiping idols
7. enjoying whoredoms
8. speaking lying and vain words
9. placing their hearts upon riches
10. spending their time in riotous living
11. becoming winebibbers
12. boasting of their own strength
13. delighting in the shedding of blood

As noted earlier, these were at first the sins of only Noah and his priests, but the iniquity spread until it became general among the people.

With this setting, Abinadi is introduced with these few words:

> And it came to pass that there was a man among them whose name was Abinadi; and he went forth among them, and began to prophesy, saying: Behold, thus saith the Lord, and thus hath he commanded me, saying, Go forth, and say unto this people, thus saith the Lord— Wo be unto this people, for I have seen their abominations, and their wickedness, and their whoredoms; and except they repent I will visit them in mine anger. (Mosiah 11:20)

Abinadi's warning consisted of the following (see Mosiah 11:20–25): Unless you repent, thus saith the Lord, (1) I will bring the entire people into bondage; (2) they will be afflicted by their enemies; (3) they will cry unto me (the Lord) for help, and "I will be slow to hear"; (4) I will allow them to be smitten;

and (5) they will be in such difficulty that only I will be able to deliver them.

Please note that although Abinadi was careful to say he was speaking for the Lord, he spoke in the first person singular. The Lord had told him what to say. The people also noticed Abinadi's first-person language and didn't like it. They were angry with Abinadi and with the Lord and endeavored to slay Abinadi, but the Lord enabled him to escape from them out of the city of Lehi-Nephi. King Noah said, "Who is Abinadi, that I and my people should be judged of him, or who is the Lord, that shall bring upon my people such great affliction?" (Mosiah 11:27). But neither the people, nor the priests, nor king Noah repented of their evil doings.

After two years Abinadi came back to the city in disguise and again publicly preached repentance. Where he had been these two years the record does not say. His first-person message this time was even more pointed, direct, specific, and descriptive than before. A summation is as follows:

> You have not repented or heeded the warning, therefore God has sent me to say that you shall be visited of the Lord in his fierce anger, that "this generation, because of their iniquities, shall be brought into bondage"; you "shall be smitten on the cheek, . . . and shall be driven by men, and shall be slain." The vultures, the dogs, and the wild beasts shall devour your flesh. "The life of king Noah shall be valued as a garment in a hot furnace. . . . He [Noah] shall know that I am the Lord." Noah shall be "as a dry stalk of the field, which is run over by beasts and trodden under foot." He [Noah] shall be as a fully ripe thistle, blown in the wind. "I [the Lord] will smite this my people with sore afflictions," and with famine and pestilence; they "will have burdens lashed upon their backs. . . . They shall be driven . . . like a dumb ass"; I will send hail to smite them; the east wind shall smite them; "insects shall pester their land also and devour their grain"; "they shall howl all the day long." "Except they repent I will utterly destroy them from off the face of the earth." (See Mosiah 12:1–12)

Abinadi's Colorful Language

As can be quickly perceived from the foregoing, Abinadi was an effective communicator. It would be difficult to misunderstand him. His sentences (at least as they now appear in English) are full of high-intensity verbs, descriptive adjectives, and colorful nouns. His discourse has a poetic and lyric element to it.

Abinadi Confronts the Priests of Noah

Abinadi was taken by the people, bound, and brought before the king. After telling the king of Abinadi's prophecies against the people, his captors elaborated on his pronouncements against the king (Mosiah 12:9). Their self-justification reads something like this (Mosiah 12:12–16):

1. He [Abinadi] pretendeth the Lord hath spoken. . . .
2. And he saith all this shall come upon thee except thou repent. . . .
3. O king, what great evil hast thou done,
4. Or what great sins have thy people committed,
5. That we should be condemned of God
6. Or judged of this man?
7. We are guiltless,
8. And thou, O king, hast not sinned; . . .
9. This man has lied . . . and he has prophesied in vain. . . .
10. We are strong, we shall not . . . be taken captive. . . .
11. Thou hast prospered in the land, and thou shalt also [continue] to prosper.

Noah ordered Abinadi cast into prison and called the priests together as a council to decide what to do with him (Mosiah 12:17). The priests asked that Abinadi be brought before them, that they might question him and "cross him" and find a charge on which to formally accuse him (Mosiah 12:18). The record says they began to question him, "But he answered them boldly, and withstood all their questions, yea, to their astonishment; for he did withstand them in all their questions, and did confound them in all their words" (Mosiah 12:19). Abinadi's "defense" before the priests was not defensive. He was aggressive, confident, forward, and marvelous.

When one of the priests asked Abinadi the meaning of the words of Isaiah that say, "How beautiful upon the mountains are the feet of him that bringeth good tidings, . . . that saith unto Zion, Thy God reigneth! . . . And all the ends of the earth shall see the salvation of our God" (Isa 52:7–10), Abinadi did not immediately explain the meaning of the scripture. Instead, he became the questioner. To the request for enlightenment on a scripture, he asked:

Are you priests, and pretend to teach . . . and to understand the spirit of prophesying, and yet desire . . . of me what these things mean?

Noting their perversion of the ways of the Lord, he asked:

What teach ye this people?

When they said they taught the law of Moses, he asked:

If ye teach the law of Moses, why do ye not keep it? Why do ye set your hearts upon riches? Why do ye commit whoredoms and spend your strength with harlots, . . . and cause this people to commit sin?

Then to test their knowledge of the purpose of the law of Moses, he asked:

What know ye concerning the law of Moses? Doth salvation come by the law of Moses? . . . What say ye? (Mosiah 12:25–31)

When they answered "that salvation did come by the law of Moses," Abinadi refuted their answer explaining that salvation comes only through Christ, and that the law alone cannot save (Mosiah 12:32). He then quoted the first two of the Ten Commandments given to Moses: "Thou shalt have no other God before me," and "Thou shalt not make unto thee any graven image." He then asked the priests if they had obeyed these commandments or taught the people to obey them, and then answered for them that they had not (Mosiah 12:37).

When Noah heard Abinadi's thunder-and-lightning words, he ordered him to be put to death, for "he is mad" (Mosiah 13:1). To proclaim Abinadi "mad" provided Noah and his priests with a legal excuse to kill him, since a madman was a threat to the community. As the priests attempted to take him, Abinadi withstood them and said:

> Touch me not, for God shall smite you if ye lay your hands upon me, for I have not delivered the message which the Lord sent me to deliver; neither have I told you that which ye requested that I should tell; therefore, God will not suffer that I shall be destroyed at this time.
>
> But I must fulfil the commandments wherewith God has commanded me; and because I have told you the truth ye are angry with me. And again, because I have spoken the word of God ye have judged me that I am mad.
>
> . . . And his face shone with exceeding luster, even as Moses' did while in the mount of Sinai, while speaking with the Lord.
>
> And he spake with power and authority from God; and he continued his words, saying:
>
> Ye see that ye have not power to slay me, therefore I finish my message. . . .
>
> Yea, and my words fill you with wonder and amazement, and with anger.
>
> But I finish my message; and then it matters not whither I go, if it so be that I am saved.
>
> But this much I tell you, what you do with me, after this, shall be as a type and a shadow of things which are to come. (Mosiah 13:3–10)

Abinadi then read to them the remainder of the Ten Commandments. Very likely he could have quoted them from memory, but it appears that he had an object lesson in mind when he read from a written text. Here are his words: "And now I read unto you the remainder of the commandments of God, for I perceive that they are not written in your hearts; I perceive that ye have studied and taught iniquity the most part of your lives" (Mosiah 13:11).

Having read the Ten Commandments, he asked the priests again, "Have ye taught this people [to obey] these things?" (Mosiah 13:25). He answered his question himself by saying, "If ye had, the Lord would not have caused me to come forth and to prophesy evil concerning this people" (Mosiah 13:26).

Abinadi then delivered the remainder of his message, that which he said he must deliver, which consists of a prophecy and explanation of the coming of Christ to redeem humankind, and also his answer to the question the priests had asked him about a passage from Isaiah (Mosiah 14–16). His teachings at this juncture constitute five and one-half pages of material in our present Book of Mormon. He cites Moses and Isaiah particularly, and all of the prophets generally, as having taught that God himself would come down from heaven and dwell in the form of a man on the earth and redeem humankind from the Fall. He speaks at length of Christ's mission and of his power to redeem humankind from sin and from the grave.

True Prophets Testify of Jesus Christ

There is a very significant point to be made here. Abinadi, with all the thunder and power characteristic of any Old Testament prophet, preached repentance and inveighed against the sins of king, priests, and populace alike. But he showed that forgiveness and redemption were not available to them merely by change and reformation, but also by repentance and faith in the coming of Jesus Christ, the Messiah. And he explained with great clarity and emphasis that it would be the God of Israel himself who would come down from heaven and be the Son of God in the flesh.

This point is often lacking in our present Old Testament text. As the Old Testament now reads, the prophets were great reformers, champions of social justice, and preachers of righteousness. They were spokesmen for God. But our present Old Testament frequently does not make it clear that the God they worshiped would become the Redeemer on earth, the future Jesus Christ. Nor does it make it clear that these prophets taught the gospel of Jesus Christ, with its ordinances and ceremonies, such as baptism and the laying on of hands. We know from latter-day revelation that the ancient Old Testament prophets knew of Christ, taught his gospel, and worshiped him, but their records have not come to us in plainness and clarity as have the Book of Mormon records, and therefore these important concepts are not clear from the Old Testament alone.

Abinadi says that all of the ancient prophets taught that the God of Israel would come to earth as the Redeemer:

> And now, did they [the people] understand the law? I say unto you, Nay, they did not all understand the law; and this because of the hardness of their hearts; for they understood not that there could not any man be saved except it were through the redemption of God. For behold, did not Moses prophesy unto them concerning the coming of the Messiah, and that God should redeem his people? Yea, and even all the prophets who have prophesied ever since the world began—have they not spoken more or less concerning these things? Have they not said that God himself should come down among the children of men, and take upon him the form of man, and go forth in mighty power upon the face of the earth? Yea, and have they not said also that he should bring to pass the resurrection of the dead, and that he, himself, should be oppressed and afflicted? (Mosiah 13:32–35)

In summation, Abinadi said to the priests:

> And now, ought ye not to tremble and repent of your sins, and remember that only in and through Christ ye can be saved? Therefore, if ye teach the law of Moses, also teach that it is a shadow of those things which are to come—Teach them that redemption cometh through Christ the Lord, who is the very Eternal Father. Amen. (Mosiah 16:13–15)

Trial and Conviction of Abinadi

After Abinadi had finished his "sayings," king Noah sent him back to prison and counseled again with his priests (Mosiah 17:5). After three days Noah sent for Abinadi and informed him that they had found a charge against him, and he was "worthy of death" (Mosiah 17:7). The accusation was that Abinadi had said that "God himself should come down among the children of men" (Mosiah 17:8). This accusation was apparently a charge of blasphemy rather than a charge of a crime against the state.

King Noah offered to rescind the penalty of death if Abinadi would take back all that he had said against him and against the people. Abinadi refused and declared that he would suffer even to death to prove the truth of his words. He also warned the king that he would have to answer for his deeds at the last day, and if the king caused Abinadi's death (Abinadi being an innocent man), the king would also have to answer for that at the last day.

Noah was about to release Abinadi, for he feared the judgments of God. But the priests, seeing that the king began to waver, knew how to appeal to the king's vanity and raised their voices to accuse Abinadi, saying, "He has reviled the king" (Mosiah 17:12). Reviling the king may have been a crime against the state, a type of sedition. At any rate, the king regained his selfish courage, was stirred to anger again, and delivered Abinadi to be slain.

Keeping Abinadi in hold for three days before formally accusing him may reflect the difficulty Noah and the priests had in finding a capital charge against him. Or it may have been a psychological maneuver to give him time to think about and to fear his punishment and thereby break his spirit. Whatever the cause of the delay, Abinadi was condemned to die.

The Death of Abinadi

We generally say that Abinadi was burned at the stake—and that may be true, although technically it might not be the whole story. The scripture does not say he was "burned at the stake"; it says he "suffered death by fire" (Mosiah 17:20). A statement in Mosiah 17:13 catches our attention: "And it came to pass that they took him and bound him, and scourged his skin with faggots, yea, even unto death." Three words in the foregoing sentence should be noted. The first is that they *bound* him. That seems self-explanatory. The second is that they *scourged* him. To scourge means to whip, flail, or beat. The third term is *faggots*: "He was scourged with faggots, yea, even unto death." A faggot is a bundle of sticks or twigs, used for fuel. This passage seems to say that Abinadi's tormentors took burning torches and poked him with these, burning his skin until he died. And then, says the record, "He fell, having suffered death by fire; . . . having sealed the truth of his words by his death" (Mosiah 17:20).

If Abinadi was actually burned at the stake, the scene would have been somewhat different. I've never seen anyone burned at the stake, but my conception of it is that a person is tied to the stake, and wood or other combustible material is placed at the feet, and perhaps piled waist-high, and then lighted. The victim suffers from the flames and from smoke inhalation. It is a terrible way to die.

Several accounts in the Book of Mormon speak of death by fire, and at least one account in the Bible tells of an attempted execution by fire, but in no case does either record say anything about a stake. Two examples of death by fire from the Book of Mormon are, of course, Abinadi and king Noah (Mosiah 19:20). Others are the Lamanites who were killed by the descendants of the priests of Noah (Alma 25:5–11). Later, those same descendants of the priests of Noah were themselves hunted and burned (Mosiah 17:18; Alma 25:12). The converts of Alma and Amulek in Ammonihah also suffered death by fire, evidently by being thrown into a burning pit (Alma 14:8). In the Bible we read that the three friends of Daniel were cast into a fiery furnace, though they received no harm (Dan 3:20–27).

In my mind I see Abinadi bound, possibly supported by something, and his fiendish executioners (probably the priests) gathered about him with burning torches (faggots) in their hands, jabbing him and rubbing him with these until they caused him to die. They actively, eagerly, and physically caused his death; they were not merely passive, interested bystanders watching a bonfire. I can imagine them dancing and cavorting about Abinadi, and hear them shouting, exulting, and gloating over what they were doing. And during it all, Abinadi was pronouncing prophecies of God's vengeance upon them— prophecies that were literally fulfilled. The noise, the din, the stench would be awful! Wickedness and righteousness, life and death, are real, and Abinadi's martyrdom really did happen. It was necessary that it happen so the righteous might be justified and the wicked might be condemned. Sadly, we read that "Abinadi was [only] the first [among the Nephites] that suffered death by fire because of his belief in God" (Alma 25:11).

Alma Writes the Words of Abinadi

A young man named Alma, one of Noah's priests, had felt the truth of Abinadi's words and had defended him before the king. For this act of bravery the king caused that Alma should be cast out of the palace and the kingdom, and then sent servants to slay him. Alma escaped and hid himself for many days, and "did write all the words which Abinadi had spoken" (Mosiah 17:1–4). We can be very grateful to Alma for doing this and making Abinadi's story and words available to us.

Although Alma wrote all of Abinadi's words, that does not necessarily mean that Mormon included all of them in the abridged account given to us in the book of Mosiah. There are at least four clues that we do not have a complete transcript of Abinadi's debates with the priests, nor a full account of his teachings. For example, in Mosiah 7:26–28 (which was cited earlier) Limhi speaks of Abinadi's death and explains for what teachings he was slain. Limhi states that Abinadi said the following:

> [1] Christ was the God, the Father of all things; [2] . . . that he should take upon him the image of man, and [3] it should be the image after which man was created in the beginning; or in other words, [4] he [Abinadi] said that man was created after the image of God, and [5] that God should come down among the children of men, and [6] take upon him flesh and blood, and [7] go forth upon the face of the earth. (Mosiah 7:27)

The teachings of Abinadi that are given us in the book of Mosiah chapters 11 through 17 cover each of these seven items except numbers three and four. Since Limhi makes a point of saying that these are the teachings for which Abinadi was slain, we naturally conclude that Abinadi had said something about each one of them. Either Limhi overstated the situation or else he had a more complete transcript than we have. Of course he could have had access to the original, while we have only Mormon's abridgment.

A second clue that we may not have the entire conversation is found in Mosiah 12:8, which says, "And many things did Abinadi prophesy against this people." We can't tell from the record whether or not all of these "many things" are included in the present text.

A third clue is found in Mosiah 12:18–19:

> And it came to pass that they [the priests] said unto the king: Bring him hither that we may question him; and the king commanded that he should be brought before them. And they began to question him, that they might cross him, that thereby they might have wherewith to accuse him; but he answered them boldly, and withstood all their questions, yea, to their astonishment; for he did withstand them in all their questions, and did confound them in all their words.

In our record, the one and only question that the priests ask and that Abinadi answers is a question about Isaiah 52:7–10, whereas the text above says that he answered "all their questions" and "did confound them in all their words." It appears that we have but a sampling of the great debate between Abinadi and the priests. How we wish we had it all!

A fourth clue is found in Mormon 1:19, where Mormon speaks of the "sorceries, and witchcrafts, and magics" in the land, "even unto the fulfilling of all the words of Abinadi." Our record contains no such prophecy of Abinadi. Obviously Mormon had a more complete record of Abinadi's words than we have. No doubt future readers will be privileged to find the much fuller account on the large plates themselves, and not be limited to the shortened version in the Book of Mormon.

Abinadi's Doctrinal Teachings

In my opening statement I said that Abinadi's doctrinal teachings are some of the most valuable in the Book of Mormon because they clarify the purpose of the law of Moses, identify who the Redeemer would be, and declare some facts about the Resurrection for the first time in the Book of Mormon. Elder George Reynolds rated Abinadi's words as "some of the most precious gospel teachings" and "important . . . doctrinal portions" of the Book of Mormon (10, 18). He identified the subject matter as "the principle of the atonement and other laws of God" (9). Elder Mark E. Petersen wrote that "Abinadi built on Nephi's foundation. [He] explained the Atonement in detail, stressed the resurrection of the dead, and made it clear that while all who die will be raised from their graves, salvation from sin will come only to those who accept and obey the gospel" (1). Elder Petersen further said that "Abinadi's . . . teachings concerning the Savior and the resurrection are an inspiration and great comfort to all" (20).

I will briefly review some major points of Abinadi's teachings, first about the law of Moses. Abinadi characterized the law of Moses as "a very strict law; . . . a law of performances and of ordinances, a law which they were to observe strictly from day to day, to keep them in remembrance of God and their duty towards him" (Mosiah 13:29–30). He further said that the things of the law were "types of things to come" (Mosiah 13:31), and that the day would come when it would no longer be expedient to obey the law of Moses. He also said that the ancients did not all understand the law, and did not comprehend that the law was completely unable to save anyone without the "redemption" and the "atonement, which God himself shall make for the sins and iniquities of his people" (Mosiah 13:28, 32).

I have found that it is not only ancient Israel that has misunderstood the law. There is a great deal of misunderstanding today about what the law was and why it was given. This misunderstanding is found both among Christian and Jewish denominations, and even among teachers in the Church. It takes a great deal of time and effort to examine what is given us about the law of Moses in the Old and New Testaments, the

Book of Mormon, the Doctrine and Covenants, the Joseph
Smith Translation of the Bible, the teachings of the Prophet
Joseph Smith, and the writings of other latter-day prophets.
Therefore I have found Abinadi's concise, summary-like state-
ments about the purpose and place of the law very enlightening.

A second major point of Abinadi's teachings is that "God
himself" will make the atonement that will redeem humankind.
Abinadi leaves no doubt in his teaching that the God of Israel
himself will be the Redeemer who will come to earth as the
Son of God. He is not the first in the Book of Mormon to teach
this doctrine, but he gives it more emphasis than those who
precede him in the record. Nephi had said that the Messiah,
who would come in 600 years, would be "the very God of Israel
. . . the God of Abraham, and of Isaac, and the God of Jacob"
(1 Nephi 19:7–10). Nephi also had shown that such identification of the Messiah as the God of Israel was likewise the
teaching of the earlier prophets Zenock, Neum, and Zenos
(1 Nephi 19:10). Jacob taught the same doctrine, saying that
the "great Creator" would come to earth and would be called
"Christ," and the people would "crucify him" (2 Nephi 9:5;
10:3). King Benjamin also taught that the "Lord Omnipotent,"
who reigns in the heavens for all eternity, would come to earth
by being born of Mary, would "dwell in a tabernacle of clay,"
and would go among the people. He would be called Jesus
Christ; he would be crucified and then rise from the dead
(Mosiah 3:5–10). King Benjamin's discourse was given 20 or
so years after Abinadi's death, but because of the structure of
the Book of Mormon it is placed before the story of Abinadi,
and thus the reader encounters it first.

Though Abinadi was not the first in the Book of Mormon
to identify the Savior as the God of ancient Israel, he gives the
topic such intensive and extensive coverage that if readers
hadn't picked up on the concept earlier, they could scarcely
miss it in the teachings of Abinadi. Abinadi mentions at least
eleven times that "God himself" will be the Messiah. These are
found in the following verses: Mosiah 13:28, 32, 33, 34–35;

15:1, 2–4, 5–7, 8, 23; 16:4, 15. A quick delineation of what Abinadi says in these verses is as follows:

1. "Were it not for the atonement, which God himself shall make, . . . they [all humankind] must unavoidably perish" (13:28).

2. "There could not any man be saved except it were through the redemption of God" (13:32).

3. Moses said that God should redeem his people. All the prophets ever since the world began have spoken concerning this same thing (13:33).

4. The prophets have said that "God himself should come down among men, and take upon him the form of man" and "bring to pass the resurrection" (13:34–35).

5. "I would that ye should understand that God himself shall come down among . . . men, and redeem his people" (15:1).

6. In Christ the attributes of mortal man and Eternal God are both in one person because he was conceived in the flesh by the power of God (15:2–4).

7. Although the Messiah has the attributes and will of the Father, he suffers temptation, but does not yield to the temptation. He is finally crucified and slain, "the will of the Son being swallowed up in the will of the Father" (15:5–7).

8. Thus God, being victorious over death, "breaketh the bands of death . . . for the children of men" (15:8).

9. The righteous will rise in the Resurrection "to dwell with God who has redeemed them" (15:23).

10. Because of the fall of our first parents, all humankind were "endlessly lost were it not that God redeemed his people" (16:4).

11. "Teach them that redemption cometh through Christ the Lord, who is the very Eternal Father" (16:15).

Abinadi was evidently effective in making his point, for the formal charge brought against him by Noah and the priests was, "Thou art worthy of death. For thou hast said that God himself should come down among the children of men" (Mosiah 17:7–8).

A third major contribution of Abinadi's teachings is his clarification about the resurrection of the dead. Others had mentioned the Resurrection, but Abinadi is the first in the Book of Mormon to describe and use the phrase *first resurrection.* We would suppose that earlier prophets such as Lehi, Nephi, and Jacob knew the details of the first and subsequent resurrections, but in our present Book of Mormon record Abinadi is the first to speak of a first resurrection or to discuss the Resurrection in detail. His discourse on the subject begins in Mosiah 15:20 and extends through Mosiah 16:11, a total of two complete pages, or the equivalent of 22 column inches of material.

A quick summary of what Abinadi says about resurrection, especially the first resurrection, is as follows:

1. "The Son [of God] . . . hath power over the dead; therefore, he bringeth to pass the resurrection of the dead" (Mosiah 15:20).

2. There is a first resurrection, consisting of those who have been, who are, and who shall be from the beginning down to the time of Christ. This means "all the prophets, and all those that have believed in their words, or all those that have kept the commandments"—they are the first resurrection (15:21–23).

3. Those who died in ignorance, before Christ came, to whom the plan of salvation was never declared, shall have part in the first resurrection (15:24).

4. "Little children [who die as little children] also have eternal life," which in the context of Abinadi's discourse means that they will be in the first resurrection (15:25).

5. If Christ had not broken the bands of death so that the grave could have no victory, there could have been no resurrection—but he did break the bands of death, and there is a resurrection, and "the grave hath no victory, and the sting of death is swallowed up in Christ" (16:6–8).

6. Resurrection means that "this mortal shall put on immortality," "that there can be no more death." The final judgment comes after the Resurrection (16:9–10).

7. The righteous shall be resurrected to a happy state; the wicked shall be resurrected to a state of damnation (16:11).

Abinadi's teachings are in harmony with the expanded knowledge we now have of the Resurrection through the revelations given to the Prophet Joseph Smith. However, Abinadi's record does not tell it all. For example, Abinadi says that those who die in ignorance, "not having salvation declared unto them," will have "a part in the first resurrection, or have eternal life" (Mosiah 15:24). Abinadi's use of the phrase "eternal life" is not as precise as we have come to use it today; in the context of his discourse he was pointing out that those who die in ignorance, who never had a chance, are not overlooked or neglected by a merciful, all-wise, and powerful God. A more detailed discussion would point out that "all who have died without a knowledge of this gospel, who would have received it if they had been permitted to tarry, shall be heirs of the celestial kingdom of God" (D&C 137:7). We have to conclude that Abinadi included this particular group of people when he spoke of the righteous. On the other hand, there would likely be some who would not have received the gospel with all their hearts, even if it had been offered. Among them would have been a number of good people who were not converted, and other people who were converted but not diligent. We learn from D&C 76:76–80 that many of these will inherit the terrestrial glory, which is also part of the first resurrection. Furthermore, we learn from D&C 45:54 that "the heathen nations" and "they that knew no law shall have part in the first resurrection."

What Abinadi did not say, at least in the record we have of his teachings, is that those who die after the time of Christ, who are righteous, will also be in the first resurrection. The first resurrection that Abinadi spoke of consists of the righteous who lived from the time of Adam to the time of Christ. We who live after the time of Christ know of a "second session" of the first resurrection, one stretching from Jesus' time to his second coming and then on through the Millennium. Abinadi spoke from his perspective; we speak from ours.

An interesting note is that in speaking of the righteous who have the gospel and obey it in mortal life, Abinadi says, "They *are* the first resurrection" (Mosiah 15:22; emphasis added). Whereas, in speaking of those who did not have the gospel and who died in an ignorance not of their own making, he says, "They have *a part* in the first resurrection" (Mosiah 15:24; emphasis added). There is a distinction in the diction used here, but I am not certain what we can make of it.

There are other great things in Abinadi's teachings, such as an identification of the "seed of Christ" and his marvelous use of Isaiah chapters 52 and 53, but these are dealt with by other participants in this symposium.

Ever present in Abinadi's ministry is his awareness that he was a witness for the Lord Jesus Christ. First, he spoke in great plainness and with much energy and total commitment. Second, his words were fulfilled to the letter (Mosiah 20:21; Alma 25:9–12; Mormon 1:19). Third, Abinadi was fierce and strong, a terror to evil-doers. There is a significant lesson to be learned here. If he had not been so blunt and so obvious, the people might not have thought he meant what he said, nor would they have thought what he said was so important. His energy no doubt helped Alma to have the strength to repent. As in all good teaching, Abinadi communicated well, and was by his own person and his own words the greatest of object lessons. He needed no additional audio-visual aids. In Abinadi the Lord had just the right kind of person he needed for the situation.

BIBLIOGRAPHY

Petersen, Mark E. *Alma and Abinadi.* Salt Lake City: Deseret Book, 1983.

Reynolds, George. *A Dictionary of the Book of Mormon.* Salt Lake City: Joseph Hyrum Parry, 1891.

Turner, Rodney. "Two Prophets: Abinadi and Alma." *1 Nephi to Alma* 29. Studies in Scripture, vol 7. Ed. Kent P. Jackson. Salt Lake City: Deseret Book, 1987. 240-59.

Welch, John W. "Judicial Process in the Trial of Abinadi." Preliminary Report. WEL-81. Provo, UT: F.A.R.M.S., 1985.

Government by the *Voice* of the People: A Witness and a Warning

8

Byron R. Merrill

Chapter 29 of the book of Mosiah furnishes insight into and prophetic warning from a pivotal transition in Nephite experience—a transition from kingship to government by the voice of the people. It briefly outlines the meaning, purpose, and consequences of a people's answering for their own sins—both moral and political. In so doing, Mosiah 29 speaks from the dust to the people of the latter days, helping us understand how this change in Nephite affairs affected their later history. More significantly, it bears witness of the love of Jesus Christ for his people and of his concern for and involvement in their earthly affairs. In conjunction with this witness it also issues a stern warning about the fragility of freedom by the "voice of the people," speaks of the need for constant vigilance to preserve this freedom, and foreshadows the certain destruction which will follow its iniquitous misuse. While the message of Mosiah 29 is pertinent to all who receive this sacred volume, it has special relevance to those people who inhabitant the "mighty nation among the Gentiles" which the prophet Nephi foretold would be established by the Lord "upon the face of this land" (1 Nephi 22:7).

Byron R. Merrill is assistant professor of Ancient Scripture at Brigham Young University.

The Tradition of Kingship Among the Nephites

The family of Lehi was accustomed to the tradition of kingship from their heritage at Jerusalem. However, from the time the colony first wandered into the wilderness to the time Nephi and his followers separated themselves from Laman and Lemuel, they followed Lehi under a patriarchal order, even though some, like Laman and Lemuel, followed reluctantly.

The reign of kings among the Nephites began when Nephi was asked by his people to be their king, and he agreed to do those things for them which were in his power to do (2 Nephi 5:18). He thereupon became known as "a king or a protector" (2 Nephi 6:2), and those who reigned after his death "were called by the people, second Nephi, third Nephi, and so forth, according to the reigns of the kings" (Jacob 1:11).

The only four kings over the main body of Nephites of whom we have any particular knowledge are Nephi, at the very beginning of the monarchy, and Mosiah I, Benjamin, and Mosiah II, the last three kings before the reign of the judges ended the tradition of kingship among the Nephites. These men were prophets as well as civic leaders, largely providing for their own needs instead of burdening the people, and thus serving God by serving his children (2 Nephi 5:14–18; Mosiah 2:12–14; 6:7; 29:14, 40). That other men of similar spiritual stature served as kings during the period between the reigns of Nephi and Mosiah I, a span of over 200 years, is indicated by Jarom's comment: "Our kings and our leaders were mighty men in the faith of the Lord" (Jarom 1:7). With that heritage, it is easy to understand why the two contemporaries Mosiah II and Alma both counseled that if it were possible to always have just men as kings, it would be well to have a king (Mosiah 23:8; 29:13).

Mosiah Sets Forth His Proposal

In Mosiah 29, king Mosiah II proposes that the people replace their monarchy with a system of judges installed "by the voice of the people" (v 26). He makes this proposal after an initial inquiry among his people showed that they wanted his son Aaron, then serving a mission among the Lamanites, to succeed him as king (Mosiah 29:2). What followed must have been an intense period of struggle for Mosiah as he wrestled, first with what direction to proceed, and then, once the charted course had been revealed to him (Hel 4:22), with how to present it to his people. Mormon records only a part of the proclamation Mosiah sent among his people (Mosiah 29:33), but it is enough to indicate that Mosiah used all his powers of reason and persuasion to convince them that the government needed the change which he proposed. His introduction to the proposal places the people on an equal standing with him: "Behold, O ye my people, or my brethren, for I esteem you as such, I desire that ye should consider the cause which ye are called to consider" (Mosiah 29:5). Here is no hint of condescending royalty, but more the tone of the Lord's offer to Isaiah, "Come now, and let us reason together" (Isa 1:18).

Mosiah explains that Aaron had declined the honor of being king, but warns them that if they were to choose someone else, Aaron might change his mind, return, and foment rebellion and bloodshed (Mosiah 29:7), thereby causing himself and the people to commit sin (vv 8–9). After consenting to continue his reign for the remainder of his days, Mosiah suggests that the people appoint judges to judge the people according to the laws of God. He then comments on the perfection of God's judgments as opposed to those of human beings (vv 11–13), and he extols his father, Benjamin, as the epitome of a righteous king, declaring that if the people could always have such righteous kings "it would be expedient that ye should always have kings to rule over you" (v 13). In a display of humility, Mosiah, who in the role of seer had translated the Jaredite record, refers to his father as a great king and says that he has done his best to follow his example. All of this was said with the understanding that no righteous prince awaited to take his place.

Having already mentioned the idea of choosing judges, Mosiah then states that since "all men are not just it is not expedient that ye should have a king or kings to rule over you" (v 16). (Many of the people were probably surprised, thinking Mosiah had only suggested judges as a way of removing some of his own burden, not of replacing him entirely. But he now left no doubt about the breadth of his proposal.) He then reminds them of the wickedness of king Noah, a history with which the people were painfully conversant. He further mentions that a wicked king causes iniquity and great destruction (v 17), carefully attributing bondage both to wickedness and to a wicked king. Mosiah then states, succinctly and prophetically, the long-term significance of his proposed change:

> Now it is not common that the voice of the people desireth anything contrary to that which is right; but it is common for the lesser part of the people to desire that which is not right; therefore this shall ye observe and make it your law—to do your business by the voice of the people. And if the time comes that the voice of the people doth choose iniquity, then is the time that the judgments of God will come upon you; yea, then is the time he will visit you with great destruction even as he has hitherto visited this land. (vv 26–27)

Following that powerful warning, he briefly outlines the proposed mechanics of a system in which lower judges would be judged of higher judges, and unrighteous higher judges would be judged by a committee of lower judges, the whole being administered "according to the voice of the people" (vv 28–29). Only then does Mosiah speak in his full authority as prophet-king, declaring:

> I command you to do these things in the fear of the Lord; and I command you . . . that ye have no king; that if these people commit sins and iniquities they shall be answered upon their own heads. For behold I say unto you, the sins of many people have been caused by the iniquities of their kings; therefore their iniquities are answered upon the heads of their kings. (vv 30–31)

In other words, if people are not free from the arbitrary force of others, they are not fully responsible for their own actions. Thus, when a wicked king uses coercion or compulsion to force his subjects to commit sin, "their iniquities are answered upon the heads of their kings" (v 31).

Mosiah declares that the opposite of this principle is also true: a righteous king, because of his position, feels a burden of responsibility for all his people's iniquities (v 33). This burden clearly weighed heavily on Mosiah, as it had on his father, Benjamin (Mosiah 2:28, 34). The last recorded words from Mosiah's proclamation express his desires for his people, phrased almost like a prayer: "I desire that this land be a land of liberty, and every man may enjoy his rights and privileges alike, so long as the Lord sees fit that we may live and inherit the land" (v 32).

The Significance of the Plan

Mosiah's proposed title, *judge*, is the same one used to denote the leaders of ancient Israel who preceded the reign of king Saul. The Old Testament judges probably held general administrative and management responsibilities rather than functioning in an exclusively judicial capacity (*Theological Dictionary of the Old Testament* 3:190). These judges were often "deliverers" or "saviors" who were chosen to deliver Israel from oppressors, often militarily (*Judges* 25; Webb 15–16; Kent 85–87). Speaking of that era, the end of the book of Judges states, "In those days there was no king in Israel: every man did that which was right in his own eyes" (21:25). This verse does not signify that people could do whatever they wished without consequence. Instead, it implies that each individual made personal choices and accepted the consequences rather than being compelled to act according to the desires of a monarch.

Likewise, Mosiah's desire that the Americas should be a land of liberty does not suggest freedom from law. On the contrary, he proposed to codify the strict laws which they had received from their fathers as the standard by which all would be judged in the future, specifically indicating that these laws were given by "the hand of the Lord" (Mosiah 29:25). The novelty of Mosiah's proposal was that those laws should be administered in the future by leaders chosen by the people.

Mosiah's proposal closely resembles Moses' plan for the governing of Israel as recorded in the book of Deuteronomy:

> How can I myself alone bear your cumbrance, and your burden, and your strife? Take you wise men, and understanding, and known among your tribes, and I will make them rulers over you. . . . And I charged your judges at that time, saying, Hear the causes between your brethren, and judge righteously between every man and his brother. (Deut 1:12–13, 16)

In ancient Israel, the judges' responsibility seemed to be to uphold the law and to judge individual matters by the standard of the established law (de Vaux 1:150–52). In codifying the laws of God, Mosiah was fully aware that for society to exist at all there must be order based on law. The history of civilization is a continual balancing act between anarchy (freedom taken to its extreme) and tyranny (order taken to its extreme), with the pendulum swinging back and forth at different times. Freedom by law to act out one's choices requires enormous self-restraint, for without self-discipline freedom is so readily abused that external controls must be imposed to maintain order and prevent chaos. The Irish political theorist Edmund Burke said it well:

> Men are qualified for civil liberty in exact proportion to their disposition to put moral chains upon their own appetites. . . . Society cannot exist, unless a controlling power upon will and appetite be placed somewhere; and the less of it there is within, the more there must be without. It is ordained in the eternal constitution of things, that men of intemperate minds cannot be free. Their passions forge their fetters. (4:51–52)

In effect, Mosiah declares that the laws of God which maintain stability and continuity in society must be obeyed, but, beyond that, the people are free to believe and do whatever they wish, to become whatever they have the potential to become. The laws will not abridge freedom of conscience, but they will, with a firm hand, punish those acts which, if continued and expanded, would prove the sure destruction of society.

Mosiah also indicates that since the law is the ultimate standard, all people must stand on equal footing before the law, with no preference for birth, wealth, or position. He desires that "every man may enjoy his rights and privileges alike" (Mosiah 29:32) and that "every man might bear his part" (Mosiah 29:34) of the burden of governing. At a later time, when Alma confronts Korihor, the anti-Christ, Mormon refers to this fundamental right of equality before the law in a discussion differentiating between punishment for criminal acts, which the law imposed, and punishment for belief, which the law forbade: "Now there was no law against a man's belief; for it was strictly contrary to the commands of God that there should be a law which should bring men on to unequal grounds. For thus saith the scripture: Choose ye this day, whom ye will serve" (Alma 30:7–8).

The Meaning of Freedom

Although the promised land was a land of liberty for the people of Nephi under the reign of the righteous kings, this liberty depended more on the people's obedience to the commandments of God than on the presence or absence of kings (2 Nephi 1:7). It is difficult to envision a people more free than those in the days of Benjamin and Mosiah. They were free to believe, worship, and act as they pleased, restrained only by the laws of justice and mercy which had been revealed "by the hand of the Lord" (Mosiah 29:25). As defined by Elder Dallin H. Oaks, "Free agency . . . means an exercise of the will, the power to choose; . . . freedom [means] the power and privilege to carry out [one's] choices" (38). The transition from kings to judges did not increase anyone's free agency, but it did give everyone an increased freedom to act, accompanied by an equal weight of responsibility. Government by the voice of the people gives the people the greatest possible latitude to act out those choices which their God-given free agency allows them to make. Not only did each Nephite have the moral duty to keep the commandments of God, but each now also assumed the additional responsibility of preserving the laws of God. The Lord holds individuals under such governments "accountable for their acts in relation to them, both in making laws and administering them, for the good and safety of society" (D&C 134:1).

People often express a desire for someone to protect and care for them, as if they were unable to care for themselves. Satan cleverly persuades them to relinquish responsibility for their lives—their innate right to exercise their agency within a free environment—to someone else, in exchange for anticipated security. Those who are thus accustomed to submissive security are often hesitant to leap into the arena of civic freedom, where they determine their future by their own choices. If they alone are responsible for their future, whom can they blame for life's frustrations? Thus Mosiah wrote at length to explain carefully to the people what they should do, and then to convince them that they really could do it. His people understood and accepted this shift of responsibility, and "therefore they relinquished their desire for a king, and became exceedingly anxious that every man should have an equal chance throughout all the land; yea, and every man expressed a willingness to answer for his own sins" (Mosiah 29:38). Clearly, the spirit of freedom was brooding over the Nephites.

Nephite History Under the Reign of the Judges

The new government had been in place only four years when a man named Amlici sought to reestablish a monarchy and have himself appointed king. The issue was put to a vote because "according to their law . . . such things must be established by the voice of the people" (Alma 2:3). Therefore, the "people assembled themselves together throughout all the land, every man according to his mind, . . . in separate bodies, . . . to cast in their voices concerning the matter; and they were laid before the judges. . . . And the voice of the people came against Amlici, that he was not made king over the people" (Alma 2:5–7).

Even though nothing in the text of Mosiah 29 delegates a specific power to the people to change the law, the impression that they could alter the law is confirmed by this experience with Amlici. Further proof of such an ability is shown later when the kingmen desired "that a few particular points of the law should be altered" (Alma 51:2, 5, 15). To change minor details of the law, as when Nephihah enacted "laws according to the laws which had been given" (Alma 4:16), would have no lasting effect. But altering the principles upon which the law was based would damage the law, and the law of God could only be damaged if the voice of the people chose iniquity.

In the case of Amlici, the people gathered to cast in their voices to make a decision. In other instances it seems that the voice of the people was also used to sustain a decision already made. In the first verse of the book of Alma, Mormon says that Mosiah "had established laws, and they were acknowledged by the people; therefore they were obliged to abide by the laws which he had made" (Alma 1:1). This acknowledgment sounds much like ratification. Later the trend toward succession in the judgeship by inheritance became common. When Nephihah, the second chief judge, died, his son Pahoran "was appointed to fill the judgment-seat, in the stead of his father" (Alma 50:39). While such an appointment may signify an open election, it is also possible that Pahoran was appointed by a select group or by revelation to Nephihah or the prophet, and that the decision was then submitted to the people in the form of a referendum for approval. Such an action by the voice of the people would be the equivalent of a sustaining voice more than of an electing voice.

Today, although men are called to positions in the priesthood "by prophecy, and by the laying on of hands" (AofF 5), the revelations direct that "all things shall be done by common consent in the church" (D&C 26:2). The Lord commanded Joseph Smith "that certain men . . . shall be appointed by the voice of the church" (D&C 38:34). Appointments in the Church require neither politicking among candidates nor an initial election. Instead they require members to sustain those chosen by revelation. By analogy, although the phrase "voice of the people" implies a voting process, as when the people "cast in their voices" to choose their original judges (Mosiah 29:39) or when there was a controversy over which of Pahoran's sons should succeed him (Hel 1:1–5), it seems probable that certain judgeships, particularly the office of chief judge, were filled by appointment, and perhaps by revelation, after the manner of kingship, and that such action was then sustained or ratified by the voice of the people.

Before the end of the first decade of the new system, Amulek declared to the inhabitants of Ammonihah that "the foundation of the destruction of this people is beginning to be laid by the unrighteousness of your lawyers and judges" (Alma 10:27). Note that the cause of threatened collapse is not some evil outside force but the wickedness of the people's own leaders. Amulek's reminding them of Mosiah's prophecy that destruction would result if the people chose iniquity (Alma 10:19; Mosiah 29:27) is a divinely pointed rebuke against the wickedness being committed by the people of Ammonihah, as evidenced by the Lord's earlier command to Alma to return to that city because "they do study at this time that they may destroy the liberty of thy people" (Alma 8:17).

The Nephites and their system of judges moved through a period of continued prophetic warnings, including Captain Moroni's dramatic defense of liberty (Alma 46:12), to a time of seeming peace and prosperity, of which Mormon says, "They had altered and trampled under their feet the law of Mosiah, or that which the Lord commanded him to give unto the people" (Hel 4:22). A few verses later, Mormon records, "For as their laws and their governments were established by the voice of the people, and they who chose evil were more numerous than they who chose good, therefore they were ripening for destruction, for the laws had become corrupted" (Hel 5:2).

The assumption of power by those who chose evil led to the rapid degeneration and final corruption of the government, as described in Helaman and 3 Nephi. When the majority chose good, the rights of the minority were protected (Alma 30:7–12); however, when those who chose evil became the majority and gained control of the government, they persecuted the minority. The leaders did "turn their backs upon the poor and the meek, and the humble followers of God" (Hel 6:39). Thus Mormon concluded, "They were in an awful state, and ripening for an everlasting destruction" (Hel 6:40).

Shocked into a realization of the desperateness of their situation by the encounter with the Gadianton robbers (3 Nephi 2:11–6:5), the people humbled themselves, returned to the fundamentals of righteous government, and "formed their laws according to equity and justice" (3 Nephi 6:4). But with amazing rapidity rampant selfishness returned, resulting in "a great inequality in all the land" (3 Nephi 6:14). As pride and wickedness reached their apogee, the people "set at defiance the law and the rights of their country" (3 Nephi 6:30), and thereby "did destroy the government of the land" (3 Nephi 7:2). The result was chaos. The prophets and saints were cast out from among the people and slain (3 Nephi 7:14; 9:10–11). (Unfortunately, the righteous have never fared well in situations of anarchy, then or now.) When fierce destruction came upon the divided Nephites in AD 34, the Lord said that the people of king Jacob had been destroyed "because of their sins and their wickedness, which was above all the wickedness of the whole earth, because of their secret murders and combinations; for it was they that did destroy the peace of my people and the government of the land" (3 Nephi 9:9).

There is no specific mention of the system of government after the marvelous visit of the risen Christ to the Nephites. But the people lived the law of consecration (3 Nephi 26:19; 4 Nephi 1:2–3), and Mormon recorded that "every man did deal justly one with another," and "they were all made free" (4 Nephi 1:2–3). Since, as Paul said, "Where the spirit of the Lord is, there is liberty" (2 Cor 3:17), the people presumably enjoyed the blessings of great freedom as they willingly obeyed the laws of their heavenly King.

While little is known about Nephite government toward the end of Nephite history, Mormon's statement that "the people of Nephi appointed me that I should be their leader" (Mormon 2:1) implies that some form of government by the voice of the people continued after the breakup of the Zion society. Sadly, that voice chose iniquity, which iniquity resulted in the tragic end of Nephite civilization in graphic fulfillment of Mosiah's prophecy (see Mosiah 29:27).

The Reasons for the Change

If this great experiment with freedom was to culminate in such an awful collapse, why did Mosiah recommend it? If this promised land was a land of liberty even under the Nephite kings, why did Mosiah propose such a radical change? The answers lie in realizing that the pinnacle of freedom comes only when the responsibility for societal and moral decisions is placed squarely on the shoulders of each individual. This responsibility includes not only making individual decisions, but also acting collectively for the good of society as a whole. This shift in responsibility was the ultimate test for the Nephites— with all power placed on the individual, they had to prove that they could be selfless, that they could subdue selfish desires for the common good.

Mosiah did not make his decision because he had read about the approach in a history book, because he was following the advice of his legal counselors, or because of pressure from the judicial arm of his cabinet; neither was it because he thought the idea was one worthy of experimentation, or even because he had exhausted all other approaches. Instead, he proposed what he did as any inspired prophet would: after much personal struggle, prayer, and fasting, he proposed a plan revealed to him by Almighty God (Hel 4:22). Thus, his proposal began by explaining, then suggesting, warning, encouraging, and finally commanding.

In our day, the Lord has said that the Constitution of the United States of America was created by "wise men whom I raised up unto this very purpose" (D&C 101:80). After the Constitutional Convention, those men stood in awe of what they had accomplished and called it a miracle. The historian Catherine Bowen wrote: "Miracles do not occur at random, nor was it the author of this book who said there was a miracle at Philadelphia in the year 1787. George Washington said it, and James Madison. They used the word in writing to their friends: Washington to Lafayette, Madison to Thomas Jefferson" (ix). The feelings of these men are easily understood by those who have completed some major accomplishment under the powerful influence of the Holy Ghost.

If the Lord could orchestrate the miracle of the Constitution in preparation for the glorious latter-day restoration so that Israel may be gathered and a people prepared for the second coming of the Savior, can there be any doubt that the same God of Heaven could direct the prophet-king Mosiah to establish a government by the voice of the people among this special branch of the house of Israel, broken off and separated from its brethren (1 Nephi 15:12), so that the full responsibility of freedom could be borne individually and equally by all the people, to prepare them for the first coming of the Savior? Each man and woman would thus be accountable to make choices and then see the consequences of those choices fulfilled—to be swallowed up in the depths of the earth in the city of Moronihah, to be burned in the great city Zarahemla, or to kneel with tear-stained cheeks midst joy inexpressible at Bountiful. Mosiah was God's prophet; this political change was God's will.

Parallels to America's Constitutional Government

Just as the Lord approved this change in Nephite affairs, he likewise placed his approval on the United States Constitution by revealing that he had suffered it to be established and that it "should be maintained for the rights and protection of all flesh, according to just and holy principles" (D&C 101:77). Why should the Constitution merit such approval? The Lord declared he established it to assure "that every man may act . . . according to the moral agency which I have given unto him" (D&C 101:78). President Ezra Taft Benson has indicated that the Constitution's genius lies in basic, eternal principles: (1) free agency is God-given; (2) the proper role of government is to secure the rights and freedoms of individuals; (3) basic human rights are God-given; (4) people are superior to the governments they form; and, therefore, (5) governments should have only limited powers (*The Constitution: A Heavenly Banner* 1–10).

The system of judges adopted by the Nephites was based on these same eternal principles, even though the mechanics of their system were substantially different. In his article "The Book of Mormon and the American Revolution," Richard L. Bushman demonstrates that the system of Nephite judges closely follows the ancient governmental traditions of the Israelites, while the American founders instead chose the path of revolution and the creation of a new governmental form. He also shows that constitutional separation of powers and checks and balances as known today were non-existent among the Nephites (189–211). While these differences clearly refute the claim that Joseph Smith authored the Book of Mormon from the perspective of American political traditions, they do not negate the similarity of underlying principles of freedom and morality which permeate the two systems.

Much like the Nephites, the American colonists sought to pattern a society after Moses' directive to "take . . . wise men, and understanding, . . . and . . . make them rulers over you" (Deut 1:13). On 31 May 1638, Thomas Hooker gave a sermon from the pulpit of the First Church of Hartford based on Deuteronomy 1:13. He indicated that the choice of public magistrates belongs to the people by God's allowance and must be exercised by the people according to His will. Eight months later this idea became the basis of the Fundamental Orders of Connecticut, a major forerunner to the Constitution (Levy 68–69). Just as Mosiah drew on inspiration and the writings of ancient Israel, so did America's Founding Fathers. A bicentennial study on the origins and nature of American political thought examined the public political writings of the Founders from 1760 to 1805. The intent of the research was to find which European political theorists were most often quoted by the Founders in order to gauge their relative influence on early American thought. Surprisingly, the most frequently cited book during the founding era was the book of Deuteronomy (Lutz 192). This study showed that 34% of all the quotations cited by the Founders were from the Bible. Can anyone doubt that such familiarity with the scriptures had a profound impact on the drafting and implementation of the Constitution?

Reference has already been made to the miracle at Philadelphia. It was followed by a second miracle, that of ratification (Nelson 60–63). In the attempt to sway public opinion toward ratification, Alexander Hamilton, John Jay, and James Madison wrote numerous persuasive essays, later known as *The Federalist Papers*. Among the many arguments proffered are several references to the guiding hand of Providence. In Federalist Paper 37, James Madison wrote:

> The real wonder is that so many difficulties should have been surmounted, and surmounted with a unanimity almost as unprecedented as it must have been unexpected. It is impossible for any man of candor to reflect on this circumstance without partaking of the astonishment. It is impossible for the man of pious reflection not to perceive in it a finger of that Almighty hand which has been so frequently and signally extended to our relief in the critical stages of the revolution. (230–31)

Just as Mosiah desired that "inequality should be no more" (Mosiah 29:32), the Constitution safeguards the same rights and immunities to all, regardless of social standing or economic strata. It "guarantees to all . . . equal, coherent, and indefeasible rights," said the Prophet Joseph Smith. "Hence we say, that the constitution of the United States is a glorious standard; it is founded in the wisdom of God" (*Teachings of the Prophet Joseph Smith* 147). Note the use of the word *standard*. The Constitution is a standard to civil law much as Nephi foresaw that the Book of Mormon would be a standard to the house of Israel (see 2 Nephi 29:2). Both are standards by which ideas and actions may be measured.

Similar to Mosiah's warning that only righteous choices could preserve liberty were the warnings of statesmen like John Adams and Daniel Webster. Adams said: "Our constitution was made only for a moral and religious people. It is wholly inadequate to the government of any other" (Howe 185). Webster predicted:

> If we, and our posterity, shall be true to the Christian religion, if we and they shall live always in the fear of God, and shall respect his commandments, . . . we may have the highest hopes of the future fortunes of our country; . . . we may be sure of one thing . . . our country . . . will go on prospering and to prosper. But, if we and our posterity reject religious instruction and authority, violate the rules of eternal justice, trifle with the injunctions of morality, and recklessly destroy the political constitution, which holds us together, no man can tell, how sudden a catastrophe may overwhelm us, that shall bury all our glory in profound obscurity. (47)

As the French historian Alexis de Tocqueville summarized in 1831, "America is great because she is good, and if America ever ceases to be good, America will cease to be great" (qtd in Benson, *God, Family, Country* 360).

Mormon Included Mosiah 29 As a Witness and a Warning

To read Mosiah 29 and its unfolding history as simply a change in Nephite government is interesting; to see in it the parallels between the reign of the judges and the American experience is fascinating. But to search it to discover why Mormon included it in his work and what its message is for these latter days is nothing less than compelling. It is imperative, as Nephi counseled, that we "liken all scriptures unto us, that it might be for our profit and learning" (1 Nephi 19:23).

The parallels in the history and development of these two systems are many. Both peoples initially acknowledged the hand of the Lord in granting them freedom, rejoiced in their liberty, and, by ratification, agreed to be bound by their new laws. Both were greatly blessed materially and spiritually. Both nations were successful in defending themselves against enemy invasion. The church of Christ was established and headquartered among both groups, and from there its truth spread to other lands and peoples, preparing them for the coming of the Savior. Unfortunately, both turned selfish. The love of liberty gave way to a desire for material security; wealth, power, and pride became their chief objects of veneration. The Nephite system collapsed into anarchy and chaos. The final verdict on the American experiment has yet to be rendered.

What has happened? The Founding Fathers' basic idea of sovereignty of the people was that people had the power to rule themselves because God had given them inalienable rights. This idea reflects Mosiah's belief that because God gives people both rights and law, people should bear personal responsibility for their choices and actions. Today the idea of sovereignty of the people appears to mean only that the majority will is supreme. Since the existence of God is largely ignored or denied, and since rights must have some source, people increasingly believe that government is the supreme grantor of rights. The unfortunate corollary of such an assumption is that if government can grant rights it can also withdraw them, meaning they are no longer inalienable. The concept of a divinely set standard is totally foreign to today's legal thinking; belief in fixed moral principles went out of favor simultaneously with belief in the existence of God. If people believe there is no God and there are no absolutes, then they begin to believe that they can choose their actions, and that they can also determine what the consequences of those actions will be. Morality becomes relative; it can be altered to fit the desires of the majority. Thus, in a democracy the will of the majority becomes supreme; it knows no external bounds or eternal laws. The result is that whoever can get the most votes is in control, regardless of what the rest of earth or heaven may think.

The Book of Mormon states that these worldly philosophies are false. It bears witness that there is a God, that God has given his children inherent rights, and that the consequences of mortal acts are based upon eternal, God-given laws. In both Mosiah's day and the era of the founding of the American republic, the people humbly and gratefully accepted the opportunity for self-government. Today, having discarded the idea of divine law and the spirit of moral restraint, many people view that same privilege as a mandatory right and use and abuse it with arrogance and impunity.

With such a small portion of the U.S. populace voting in the latter part of the 20th century, some have surmised that only a minority is currently formulating policy and making law in this nation. But since so many acquiesce to those policies and laws by their silence, the voice of the people truly is speaking. Thus, through the complacency and apathy of the majority, even a minority with unrighteous desires and designs can become the "voice of the people" choosing iniquity, with the sure consequences that such choices forebode.

While Nephi issued a prophetic promise of liberty and of absence of kings among the Gentiles in America (2 Nephi 10:10–14), the Book of Mormon is replete with prophecies that wickedness will bring bondage. But if bondage to a king is not possible, what kind of bondage is meant? If current trends continue, is it not possible that the moral segment of society could be subjected to persecution by a wicked majority? For "when the wicked rule the people mourn" (D&C 98:9). Richard Bushman has commented: "To be subject to a sovereign people which is corrupt and vicious is a more terrible situation than to be subject to a corrupt monarch. The recourse under a corrupt monarch is revolution, but what is the recourse under a corrupt democracy? A people cannot revolt against itself" ("Virtue and the Constitution" 37).

Why America Is in Peril

What is happening to the Constitution to render it seemingly ineffective in preserving those rights and freedoms it was established to protect? Why has the Supreme Court not stopped this assault against inalienable rights? The inspired Constitution provided for orderly change through amendment and for interpretation through judicial review. But while changes in constitutional structure and mechanics are periodically needed, changes in underlying constitutional principles destroy the very foundations of our system of government. Rather than reading into the Constitution only those terms, guarantees, and safeguards of fundamental principles of freedom which were written by the Framers, or those that can be clearly inferred from its language and history, many modern Supreme Court judges seem to consider themselves empowered to interpret the Constitution in a revisionary manner to reflect prevailing moral opinion. In the words of Judge Robert H. Bork:

> The values a revisionist judge enforces do not, of course, come from the law. If they did, he would not be revising. The question, then, is where such a judge finds the values he implements. . . . There is . . . strong reason to suspect that the judge absorbs those values he writes into law from the social class or elite with which he identifies. (*The Tempting of America* 16)

Can neither the president nor the Congress stop the courts from essentially creating constitutional law out of current morality? Perhaps they could, but neither the president nor the Congress is likely to try, for they are even more sensitive to the voice of the people than the courts are, and the loudest voices today refuse to be bound by what they see as an outdated and inadequate document. While people pay lip service to the Constitution, they demand that it be construed in a manner which is totally foreign to the Framers' desire to preserve liberty.

Why has this happened? The love of freedom and morality which once preserved individual liberty has given way to selfishness and complacency, with an accompanying erosion of liberty. Elder Dean L. Larsen has said, "We live in a time when . . . freedom and self-accountability are being bartered for regulation, regimentation, and programmed security" (3). The irony in this barter is that the government's very ability to provide such security is totally dependent on the preservation of individual freedom. Thus every reduction in freedom diminishes security.

The erosion of freedom today mirrors the disintegration of personal morality. Loud voices cry for more freedom in America. But what do they mean by freedom? It was Cain, encompassed with chains as he was, who coined the phrase "I am free" (Moses 5:33). Morris L. West commented:

> Without the Faith, one is free, and that is a pleasant feeling at first. There are no questions of conscience, no constraints, except the constraints of custom, convention and the law, and these are flexible enough for most purposes. It is only later that the terror comes. One is free—but free in chaos, in an unexplained and unexplainable world. One is free in a desert, from which there is no retreat but inward, toward the hollow core of oneself. (Qtd in Maxwell 4)

Today, those who yell "I am free!" are often bound by the fetters of passion, the chains of greed and the bonds of iniquity. They are at the forefront of those wanting to alter the Constitution to meet their immediate personal desires. On the one hand they want no moral restraints, and on the other hand they demand that government plan and provide for its citizens so that they are freed from personal responsibility. Their "freedom" is but another brand of slavery.

Knowing of the Lord's deep involvement in creating the Nephite system of judges (Mosiah 29) and of his anger at those who sought to destroy the liberty of his people (3 Nephi 9:9) should increase our understanding of how he feels about our actions and responsibilities toward government. Hyrum Smith once said that "to vote for wicked men . . . would be sin" (*History of the Church* 6:22). When the issues are so critical, some ask, "Why doesn't the Church tell us how to vote?" Harold B. Lee once said: "When people ask me whom to vote for, I tell them to read Mosiah 29 and section 134 of the Doctrine and Covenants, to pray about it, and then they will know whom to vote for in any given election. It is just as simple as that" (*Ye Are the Light of the World* 36). In other words, the Church and the scriptures will provide correct principles, but the Holy Ghost will dictate specific practices.

Freedom's Hope Is a Return to Righteousness

It is not too late for America, not yet. Her only hope of preservation as a nation is a return to a sense of humility and gratitude for her blessings, a return to the faith and virtue so visible in her beginnings. This will require a return to the fundamental principles of freedom and responsibility espoused by the Founding Fathers. While we may currently blame government for being unimaginably shortsighted, this shortsightedness is only a reflection of the populace that elected it. People in a free society always get the government they deserve. Therefore, convincing government to take a long-range view of America's problems, to address those problems with determination and frugality, and then to persevere in such a course is not impossible, but it will require a concerned, united, and self-sacrificing public. It requires a people willing to address the future with faith and hope, a people who have regained a vision of the future by looking back to their roots and committing to follow the example of their pilgrim forefathers, of whom one historian wrote: "They were absolutely unprepared for the conditions they actually found and brought really nothing except good constitutions, loyalty to each other, good sense, patience, forbearance, and devotion to a high religious ideal. They lacked everything but virtue" (Usher 75).

We who are members of The Church of Jesus Christ of Latter-day Saints have a unique understanding of the current dilemma, and therefore we have a special responsibility. In the words of President Harold B. Lee, "We alone know by revelation as to how the Constitution came into being, and we, alone, know by revelation the destiny of this nation" ("Faith—An Effective Weapon Against Wickedness" 912–13). To the best of our God-given ability, we must preserve the freedom we now enjoy and prevent its further erosion. Through courage and righteous determination we must seek to regain those freedoms intended for us by the Founding Fathers and the God who inspired them, that the grim fulfillment of Mosiah's ominous warning will not be reenacted in our day. President Brigham Young prophesied of our responsibility and our blessing:

> I expect to see the day when the Elders of Israel will protect and sustain civil and religious liberty and every constitutional right bequeathed to us by our fathers, and spread these rights abroad in connection with the Gospel for the salvation of all nations. I shall see this whether I live or die. (*Journal of Discourses* 11:262–63)

The parallels between the Nephite reign of the judges and the latter-day American experience suggest that Mormon included his record of the reign of the judges as a witness of what had happened with an earlier experiment with government by the voice of the people on this "land which is choice above all other lands" (2 Nephi 1:5). He also included it as a sober warning to his readers that the American experience will terminate in an equally calamitous breakdown into chaos and tragedy unless we heed the lessons taught by the Book of Mormon. These lessons revolve around one fundamental truth: the inhabitants of this land must love and "serve the God of the land, who is Jesus Christ" or prepare to be swept off when they reach the fulness of iniquity (Ether 2:9–12). The ultimate result of the freedom with which we have been blessed is that the ends we obtain will be the ones we have freely chosen. The Savior promises:

> I hold forth and deign to give unto you greater riches, even a land of promise, a land flowing with milk and honey, upon which there shall be no curse when the Lord cometh; And I will give it unto you for the land of your inheritance, if you seek it with all your hearts. And this shall be my covenant with you, ye shall have it for the land of your inheritance, and for the inheritance of your children forever, while the earth shall stand, and ye shall possess it again in eternity, no more to pass away. But, verily I say unto you that in time ye shall have no king nor ruler, for I will be your king and watch over you. Wherefore, hear my voice and follow me, and you shall be a free people, and ye shall have no laws but my laws when I come, for I am your lawgiver, and what can stay my hand? (D&C 38:18–22)

Let us seek this blessing with all our hearts. May we each exercise the faith and the courage to choose Him and Him alone.

BIBLIOGRAPHY

Benson, Ezra Taft. *The Constitution: A Heavenly Banner*. Salt Lake City: Deseret Book, 1986.

———. *God, Family, Country: Our Three Great Loyalties*. Salt Lake City: Deseret Book, 1974.

Bork, Robert H. *The Tempting of America: The Political Seduction of the Law*. New York: Free Press, 1990.

Bowen, Catherine Drinker. *Miracle at Philadelphia*. Boston: Little, 1966.

Burke, Edmund. *The Works of Edmund Burke*. 12 vols. Boston: Little, 1901.

Bushman, Richard L. "The Book of Mormon and the American Revolution." *Book of Mormon Authorship.* Ed. Noel B. Reynolds, assoc. ed. Charles D. Tate, Jr. Salt Lake City: Bookcraft, 1979. 189–211.

———. "Virtue and the Constitution." *By the Hands of Wise Men.* Ed. Ray C. Hillam. Provo, UT: Brigham Young Univ, 1979. 29–38.

de Vaux, Roland. *Ancient Israel.* 2 vols. New York: McGraw, 1961.

Hamilton, Alexander, James Madison, and John Jay. *The Federalist Papers.* Ed. Clinton Rossiter. New York: Mentor-Nal, 1961.

History of the Church. 7 vols. Salt Lake City: Deseret Book, 1965.

Howe, John R., Jr. *The Changing Political Thought of John Adams.* Princeton: Princeton Univ, 1966.

Journal of Discourses. 26 vols. 1854–86.

Judges. Trans. Robert G. Boling. The Anchor Bible, vol 6. 44 vols. Garden City, NY: Doubleday, 1975.

Kent, Dan G. *Joshua, Judges, Ruth.* Layman's Bible Book Commentary, vol 4. 24 vols. Nashville: Broadmen, 1980.

Larsen, Dean L. *Free to Act.* Salt Lake City: Bookcraft, 1989.

Lee, Harold B. "Faith—An Effective Weapon Against Wickedness in Men and Nations." *Improvement Era* (Dec 1952) 55:912–13; also in *Conference Report* (Oct 1952) 16–19.

———. *Ye Are the Light of the World.* Salt Lake City: Deseret Book, 1974.

Levy, Babette May. *Preaching in the First Half Century of New England History.* Studies in Church History, vol 6. Ed. Matthew Spinka and Robert Hastings Nichols. New York: Russell, 1945.

Lutz, Donald S. "The Relative Influence of European Writers on Late Eighteenth-Century American Political Thought." *American Political Science Review* (Mar 1984) 78:189–97.

Maxwell, Neal A. "The Simplicity of the Gospel." *Brigham Young University Speeches of the Year.* Provo, UT, 4 May 1969.

Nelson, William O. *The Charter of Liberty*. Salt Lake City: Deseret Book, 1987.

Oaks, Dallin H. "Free Agency and Freedom." *1987–1988 Devotional and Fireside Speeches*. Provo: Brigham Young Univ, 1988. 37–47.

Teachings of the Prophet Joseph Smith. Comp. Joseph Fielding Smith. Salt Lake City: Deseret Book, 1976.

Theological Dictionary of the Old Testament. 5 vols. Trans. John T. Willis, Geoffrey W. Bromiley, and David E. Greene. Ed. G. Johannes Botterweck and Helmer Ringgren. Grand Rapids, MI: Eerdmans, 1978.

Usher, Roland G. *The Pilgrims and Their History*. Williamstown, MA: Corner, 1977.

Webb, Barry G. *The Book of the Judges: An Integrated Reading*. Journal for the Study of the Old Testament Supplement Series, no. 46. Ed. David J. A. Clines and Philip R. Davies. Sheffield, England: JSOT, 1987.

Webster, Daniel. *Webster's Historical Society Address*. New York: Press of the Historical Society, 1852.

The Natural Man: An Enemy to God

9

Robert L. Millet

President Ezra Taft Benson has observed: "Just as a man does not really desire food until he is hungry, so he does not desire the salvation of Christ until he knows why he needs Christ. No one adequately and properly knows why he needs Christ until he understands and accepts the doctrine of the Fall and its effect upon all mankind. And no other book in the world explains this vital doctrine nearly as well as the Book of Mormon" (*A Witness and a Warning* 33).

Indeed, serious and careful study of the Fall in the Book of Mormon can drive people to their knees, bringing them to acknowledge their own weaknesses and thus their need for the Lord's redemption. The Atonement is necessary because of the Fall, and unless people sense the effects of Eden—both cosmologically and personally—they cannot comprehend the impact of Gethsemane and Calvary. In this article I will attend primarily to a doctrinal message about humanity that was delivered to king Benjamin by an angel of God. At the same time I will consider related passages in the Book of Mormon which bear upon and amplify this timeless truth—that the natural man is an enemy to God and a foe to all righteousness.

I am indebted to my colleague, H. Curtis Wright, professor of library science at Brigham Young University, for his assistance with many of the concepts developed in this paper.

Robert L. Millet is associate professor and department chairman of Ancient Scripture at Brigham Young University.

Throughout I use the scriptural phrase "natural man" to refer to both men and women.

The Setting

Benjamin the prophet-king had warred a good warfare, had finished his course, and was prepared to render an accounting of his earthly stewardship to his people and to God. In the strength of God, he had led his people to victory over their enemies. In the company of holy and just men, he had confounded false prophets and teachers, spoken the word of truth with power and authority, perpetuated the record of Nephi, and established peace in the land of Zarahemla (see Omni 1:25; WofM 1:12–18). His garments were clean, and his conscience was void of offense.

King Benjamin called his oldest son, Mosiah, to succeed him and asked him to summon the people to a large conference at the temple (1) to announce his retirement and the appointment of Mosiah to serve in his stead, (2) to account to his people concerning his reign and ministry, and (3) to give to them a name, "that thereby they may be distinguished above all the people which the Lord God hath brought out of the land of Jerusalem; . . . a name that never shall be blotted out, except it be through transgression" (Mosiah 1:11–12). His sermon, contained in what we know as Mosiah 2–5, is one of the most eloquent and profound in all of holy writ, a timely treatise not for slothful servants, but a dispensation of the "mysteries of God" (Mosiah 2:9) to some of the most "diligent people" whom God had led out of Jerusalem (1:11). It is also a timeless message to those in any age who have kept the commandments of God or who strive to do so. It points the way to the Master by unfolding in plainness and clarity the doctrines of the fall of man and the atonement of Christ. It sets forth the proper foundation—a theological foundation—for service, for Christian compassion, and for kindness, so that human works become the Lord's works—enduring testimonies of that Lord whose they are.

The Doctrine of the Fall

The gospel or plan of salvation is designed, according to President Brigham Young, for "the redemption of fallen beings" (*Journal of Discourses* 1:1; hereafter *JD*). The existence of a plan of deliverance indicates that there must be something from which we need to be redeemed. This is a hard doctrine, one which strikes at the heart of man-made religions and suggests the need for revealed religion. People too often attempt to temper the doctrine of the Fall, to soften its effects. Yet the Fall is a companion doctrine to the Atonement. In fact, there are no serious or extended treatments of the Atonement in the Book of Mormon that are not somehow connected, whether directly or by obvious implication, with the Fall.

We know that because Adam and Eve transgressed by partaking of the forbidden fruit, they were cast from the Garden of Eden and from the presence of the Lord, which is spiritual death. As a result came blood, sweat, toil, opposition, bodily decay, and, finally, physical death. Elder Orson F. Whitney taught that the Fall was "a step forward—a step in the eternal march of human progress" (90). Even though the Fall was a vital part of the great plan of the Eternal God—as much a foreordained act as Christ's intercession—our state, including our relationship to and contact with God, changed dramatically. Early in the Nephite record, Lehi "spake concerning the prophets, how great a number had testified of . . . [the] Redeemer of the world. Wherefore, all mankind were in a lost and in a fallen state, and ever would be save they should rely on this Redeemer" (1 Nephi 10:5–6). Again, the coming of the Messiah presupposes the need for redemption.

Joseph Smith wrote to John Wentworth, "We believe that men will be punished for their own sins, and not for Adam's transgression" (AofF 2). The Lord affirms this proclamation in his statement to Adam: "I have forgiven thee thy transgression in the Garden of Eden" (Moses 6:53). This declaration must, however, be understood in the proper doctrinal context. Although God forgave our first parents their transgression, although there is no original sin entailed upon Adam and Eve's children, and although "the Son of God hath atoned for original guilt, wherein the sins of the parents cannot be answered upon the heads of the children" (Moses 6:54), we must not conclude that all is well.

To say that we are not condemned by the fall of Adam is not to say that we are unaffected by it. Jehovah explained to Adam, "Inasmuch as thy children are conceived in sin, even so when they begin to grow up, sin conceiveth in their hearts, and they taste the bitter, that they may know to prize the good" (Moses 6:55). We do not believe, with Calvin, in the moral depravity of humanity. We do not believe, with Luther, that human beings, because of intrinsic carnality and depravity, do not even have the power to choose good over evil. And we do not believe that children are born in sin, that they inherit the so-called sin of Adam, either by sexual union or by birth. Rather, children are *conceived* in sin, meaning first, that they are conceived into a world of sin, and second, that conception is the vehicle by which the *effects* of the Fall (not the original guilt, which God has forgiven) are transmitted to Adam and Eve's posterity. To be sure, there is no sin in sexual union within the bonds of marriage, nor is conception itself sinful. Rather, through conception the flesh originates; through the process of becoming mortal one inherits the effects of the fall of Adam—both physical and spiritual.

To say that we are not punished for the transgression of Adam is not to say that we are not subject to or affected by it. In fact, Lehi taught Jacob that in the beginning God "gave commandment that all men must repent; for he showed unto all men that they were lost, because of the transgression of their parents" (2 Nephi 2:21; compare Alma 22:14). Thus we all need to repent, since we all have the ability, the propensity to sin because we inherited Adam and Eve's fallen nature. "We know that thou art holy," the brother of Jared confessed to the Almighty,

> and dwellest in the heavens, and that we are unworthy before thee; *because of the fall our natures have become evil continually*; nevertheless, O Lord, thou hast given us a commandment that we must call upon thee, that from thee we may receive according to our desires. (Ether 3:2; emphasis added)

Again, conception, which clothes us in the flesh, is the mechanism of transmission, the means by which Adam and Eve's fallen nature (both physical and spiritual death) is transferred from generation to generation. The propensity for and susceptibility to sin are implanted in our nature at conception, just as death is. Both death and sin are present only as potentialities at conception, and therefore neither is fully evident at birth. Death and sin do, however, become actual parts of our nature as we grow up. Sin comes spontaneously, just as death does. In the case of little children, the results of this fallen nature (sinful actions and dispositions) are held in abeyance by virtue of the Atonement until they reach the age of accountability. When children reach the time of accountability, however, they become subject to spiritual death and must thereafter repent and come unto Christ by covenant and through the ordinances of the gospel.

The teachings of modern apostles and prophets confirm the testimony of ancient Book of Mormon prophets. Elder Bruce R. McConkie summarized the effects of the Fall as follows:

> Adam fell. We know that this fall came because of transgression, and that Adam broke the law of God, became mortal, and was thus subject to sin and disease and all the ills of mortality. We know that the effects of his fall passed upon all his posterity; *all inherited a fallen state*, a state of mortality, a state in which spiritual and temporal death prevail. In this state all men sin. *All are lost. All are fallen.* All are cut off from the presence of God. . . . Such a way of life is inherent in this mortal existence. . . .

> Death entered the world by means of Adam's fall—death of two kinds, temporal and spiritual. Temporal death passes upon all men when they depart this mortal life. It is then that the eternal spirit steps out of its earthly tenement, to take up an abode in a realm where spirits are assigned, to await the day of their resurrection. *Spiritual death passes upon all men when they become accountable for their sins. Being thus subject to sin they die spiritually*; they die as pertaining to the things of the Spirit; they die as pertaining to the things of righteousness; they are cast out of the presence of God. It is of such men that the scriptures speak when they say that the natural man is an enemy to God. (244, 349–50; emphasis added)

"I have learned in my travels," the Prophet Joseph Smith observed, "that man is treacherous and selfish, but few excepted" (*Teachings of the Prophet Joseph Smith* 30; hereafter *TPJS*). "Men have been ever prone to apostacy," President John Taylor pointed out. "Our fallen nature is at enmity with a godly life" (197).

The Natural Man

In setting forth the doctrine of atonement, king Benjamin taught the lesson which is the focus of this paper: "The natural man is an enemy to God," he said, "and has been from the fall of Adam, and will be, forever and ever, unless he yields to the enticings of the Holy Spirit, and putteth off the natural man and becometh a saint through the atonement of Christ the Lord" (Mosiah 3:19). What is king Benjamin saying about humanity? What is the natural man, and how may he be characterized?

Simply stated, natural men and women are unregenerated beings who remain in their fallen condition, living without God and godliness in the world. They are unredeemed creatures without comfort, beings who live by their own light. On the one hand, natural men and women may be people bent on lechery and lasciviousness; they may love Satan more than God, and therefore they are "carnal, sensual, and devilish" (Moses 5:13). After having preached to and pleaded with his son Corianton and after having taught him that "wickedness never was happiness," Alma said, "And now, my son, all men that are in a state of nature, or I would say, in a carnal state, are in the gall of bitterness and in the bonds of iniquity." Now note how such persons are enemies to God: "They are without God in the world, and they have gone contrary to the nature of God; therefore, they are in a state contrary to the nature of happiness" (Alma 41:10–11).

In the same vein, Abinadi warned the priests of Noah of that day wherein natural men and women—in this case the vile and wicked—would receive their just rewards:

> And then shall the wicked be cast out, and they shall have cause to howl, and weep, and wail, and gnash their teeth; and this because they would not hearken unto the voice of the Lord; therefore the Lord redeemeth them not. For they are carnal and devilish, and the devil has power over them; yea, even that old serpent that did beguile our first parents, which was the cause of their fall. (Mosiah 16:2–3)

And then Abinadi explained how the Fall opened the way for people to reject the Spirit and choose sin: "Which [Fall] was the cause of all mankind becoming carnal, sensual, devilish, knowing evil from good, subjecting themselves to the devil. Thus all mankind were lost; and behold, they would have been endlessly lost were it not that God redeemed his people from their lost and fallen state" (Mosiah 16:3–4).

At this point we might be prone to sit back, let out a sigh of relief, and offer gratitude to God that because of the atoning work of Christ, the battle is over. But Abinadi continued his warning: "But remember that he that persists in his own carnal nature, and goes on in the ways of sin and rebellion against God, remaineth in his fallen state and the devil hath all power over him. Therefore he is as though there was no redemption made, being an enemy to God; and also is the devil an enemy to God" (Mosiah 16:5). Sons of perdition experience this exclusion to its fullest at the time of the Judgment, while all others except celestial candidates will experience much of it. We should here attend carefully to the fact that the phrase "persists in his own carnal nature" implies that individuals, in spite of the Atonement, have such a nature in which to persist.

Further, *"remaineth* in his fallen state" does not simply mean *get into* a fallen state through sin. It is true that the scriptures affirm that one becomes "carnal, sensual, and devilish" through loving Satan more than God, through willful disobedience to the commandments (Moses 5:13; 6:49). But to be a fallen being is not necessarily to be a carnal, sensual, and devilish being. One becomes fallen by coming into mortality; a fallen person becomes carnal, sensual, and devilish by defying the truth and sinning against it.

On the other hand, natural men and women need not be what we would call degenerate. They may well be moral and upright men and women, bent upon goodness and benevolence. However, they operate in and are acclimated to the present fallen world. Such persons do not enjoy the enlivening powers of the Holy Ghost: they have not received the revealed witness of the truth, and they have not enjoyed the sanctifying powers of the blood of Christ. Although their behavior is proper and appropriate according to societal standards, these natural men and women have not hearkened sufficiently to the Light of Christ to be led to the covenant gospel (Mosiah 16:2; see also D&C 84:45–48). "The whole world lieth in sin," the Savior declared in a modern revelation, "and groaneth under darkness and under the bondage of sin. And by this you may know they are under the bondage of sin, because they come not unto me" (D&C 84:49–50). More specifically, with regard to those outside the restored gospel, the Lord states: "There are none that doeth good except those who are ready to receive the fulness of my gospel, which I have sent forth unto this generation" (D&C 35:12).

And what of the members of The Church of Jesus Christ of Latter-day Saints? Are any of us natural men or women? We certainly qualify for that title if we are guilty of gross wickedness, if we have sinned against gospel light and have not thoroughly repented. And yes, we are relatively guilty, too, if we persist in a nature which leads us to exist in twilight when we might bask in the light of the Son. In 1867, President Brigham Young declared to the people of the Church:

> There is no doubt, if a person lives according to the revelations given to God's people, he may have the Spirit of the Lord to signify to him His will, and to guide and to direct him in the discharge of his duties, in his temporal as well as his spiritual exercises. I am satisfied, however, that in this respect, we live far beneath our privileges. (*JD* 12:104)

Members of the Church who refuse to climb toward greater spiritual heights, who have no inclination to further anchor themselves in the truth, who have become satisfied with their present spiritual state—these are they who are natural men and women, persons generally of good will who do not understand that through their smugness and complacency they are aiding and abetting the cause of the enemy of all righteousness. "Fallen man," C. S. Lewis perceptively observed, "is not simply an imperfect creature who needs improvement: he is a rebel who must lay down his arms" (59).

What are some broad characteristics of natural men and women? Consider the following:

1. *They are unable or unwilling to perceive spiritual realities.* Paul explained that "the natural man receiveth not the things of the Spirit of God: for they are foolishness unto him: neither *can* he know them, because they are spiritually discerned" (1 Cor 2:14; emphasis added). In exulting over the Lord's infinite mercy—in His willingness to snatch His children from evil and forgive their sins—Ammon said: "What natural man is there that knoweth these things? I say unto you, there is none that knoweth these things, save it be the penitent" (Alma 26:21). "No man has seen God at any time in the flesh, except quickened by the Spirit of God," a modern revelation teaches. "Neither can any natural man abide the presence of God, neither after the carnal mind" (D&C 67:11–12; compare Moses 1:11). "How difficult it is to teach the natural man," Brigham Young declared, "who comprehends nothing more than that

which he sees with the natural eye!" President Young went on to say:

> How hard it is for him to believe! How difficult would be the task to make the philosopher, who, for many years, has argued himself into the belief that his spirit is no more after his body sleeps in the grave, believe that his intelligence came from eternity, and is as eternal, in its nature, as the elements, or as the Gods. Such doctrine by him would be considered vanity and foolishness, it would be entirely beyond his comprehension. It is difficult, indeed, to remove an opinion or belief into which he has argued himself from the mind of the natural man. Talk to him about angels, heavens, God, immortality, and eternal lives, and it is like sounding brass, or a tinkling cymbal to his ears; it has no music to him; there is nothing in it that charms his senses, soothes his feelings, attracts his attention, or engages his affections, in the least; to him it is all vanity. (*JD* 1:2)

2. *They are fiercely independent.* Joseph Smith taught that "all men are naturally disposed to walk in their own paths as they are pointed out by their own fingers, and are not willing to consider and walk in the path which is pointed out by another, saying, This is the way, walk ye in it, although he should be an unerring director, and the Lord his God sent him" (*TPJS* 26–27). Seeking to be independent, natural men and women ironically end up conforming to the trends of the day. Natural men and women, at least those who have "the carnal mind," are "not subject to the law of God" (Rom 8:7), but are rather subject to their own whims, passions, and desires. C. S. Lewis remarked that "until you have given up yourself to [the Lord] you will not have a real self. Sameness is to be found most among the most 'natural' men, not among those who surrender to Christ. How monotonously alike all the great tyrants and conquerors have been: how gloriously different are the saints" (190).

Samuel the Lamanite expressed the tragic end of those whose natural view of reality causes them to spend their days climbing the wrong ladder:

> But behold, your days of probation are past; ye have procrastinated the day of your salvation until it is everlastingly too late, and your destruction is made sure; yea, for ye have sought all the days of your

lives for that which ye could not obtain; and ye have sought for happiness in doing iniquity, which thing is contrary to the nature of that righteousness which is in our great and Eternal Head. (Hel 13:38)

In the words of a Protestant counselor:

Fallen man has taken command of his own life, determined above all else to prove that he's adequate for the job. And like the teen who feels rich until he starts paying for his own car insurance, we remain confident of our ability to manage life until we face the reality of our own soul. . . . To put it simply, people want to run their own lives. Fallen man is both terrified of vulnerability and committed to maintaining independence. . . . The most natural thing for us to do is to develop strategies for finding life that reflect our commitment to depending on our own resources. (Crabb 15–16, 54)

3. *They are proud, overly-competitive, reactionary, and externally-driven.* Natural men and women—be they the irreverent and ungodly or the well-meaning but spiritually unregenerate—are preoccupied with self and obsessed with personal aggrandizement. Their lives are keyed to the rewards of this ephemeral sphere; their values derive solely from pragmatism and utility. They take their cues from the world and the worldly. The central feature of pride, as President Ezra Taft Benson warned the Latter-day Saints, is enmity—enmity toward God and enmity toward man. The look of natural men and women is neither up (to God) nor over (to their fellow humans), except as the horizontal glance allows them to maintain a distance from others. "Pride is essentially competitive in nature," President Benson explained. "We pit our will against God's. When we direct our pride toward God, it is in the spirit of 'my will and not thine be done.' . . . The proud cannot accept the authority of God giving direction to their lives. . . . The proud wish God would agree with them. They aren't interested in changing their opinions to agree with God's." With regard to other people, the proud "are tempted daily to elevate [themselves] above others and diminish them." There is no pleasure, as C. S. Lewis says, in "having something," only in "having more of it than the next man." In short, "Pride is the universal

sin, the great vice. . . . [It] is the great stumbling block to Zion" (Benson, "Beware of Pride" 4, 6–7).

4. *They yield themselves to the harsh and the crude.* The Spirit of the Lord has a calming and quieting influence upon those who cultivate it and enjoy its fruits. As a sanctifier, the Holy Ghost "expands, and purifies all the natural passions and affections. . . . It inspires virtue, kindness, goodness, tenderness, gentleness and charity" (Pratt 61). On the other hand, as President Spencer W. Kimball declared, the natural man—the person who lives without this divine refinement—"is the 'earthy man' who has allowed rude animal passions to overshadow his spiritual inclinations" (112).

Frequent Reactions to the Doctrine

As I indicated earlier, the doctrine of the natural man is a hard doctrine, one which is not only misunderstood but also frequently denied. Reactions to the idea that the natural man is an enemy to God are numerous. Some of these we will now consider.

1. *We all enjoy the Light of Christ.* One rejoinder to this doctrine is that every person that comes into the world is endowed by God with the Light of Christ. Although it is true that the Light of Christ is a gift and endowment from God, this is a doctrine which requires some explanation, for it is necessary to distinguish between two aspects of the Light of Christ. On the one hand, there is the natural or physical light or law by which the sun, moon, and stars operate—the light by which we see and the means by which human, animal, and plant life abound (D&C 88:6–13, 50). On the other hand, there is what might be called a redemptive dimension of the Light of Christ, a light that we must receive, a voice to which we must hearken before we are led to the higher light of the Holy Ghost, and are thereby redeemed from our fallen state. Because we have our agency, we can choose to accept or reject this light. Whether

such redemptive light takes the form of reason or judgment or conscience, we must exercise some degree of faith to enjoy its benefits. Thus, although it is true that the Spirit gives light to all of us, it only spiritually enlightens and redeems those of us who hearken to it (D&C 84:42–50).

2. *The spirit of humankind is good.* Those who contend that humans are basically good, that their inherent inclination is to choose righteousness, enjoy quoting a statement made by Brigham Young in which he seems to take quite a different view of who and what the natural man is:

> It is fully proved in all the revelations that God has ever given to mankind that they naturally love and admire righteousness, justice and truth more than they do evil. It is, however, universally received by professors of religion as a Scriptural doctrine that man is naturally opposed to God. This is not so. Paul says, in his Epistle to the Corinthians, "But the natural man receiveth not the things of God," but I say it is the unnatural "man that receiveth not the things of God." ... That which was, is, and will continue to endure is more natural than that which will pass away and be no more. The natural man is of God. (*JD* 9:305)

There is no question, in light of the belief in human depravity held by so many in the nineteenth century, that the doctrines of the Restoration were a refreshing breeze in a dry and arid spiritual climate. The revelation that God had forgiven Adam and Eve of their transgression, as well as the corollary principle that little children who die before the time of accountability are saved, served to set the Latter-day Saints apart from much of the Christian world and certainly painted a more positive and optimistic picture of human nature. The scriptures teach that we lived before we came here, that we are all the sons and daughters of God, and that our spirits literally inherited from our exalted Sire the capacity to become like him (Abr 3:22–23; D&C 76:23–24, 58–59). These are all true doctrines. When understood they can do much to lift our sights toward the glorious and the ennobling (*TPJS* 193).

Such beliefs, however, do not invalidate the burden of scripture—that there was a fall, and that the Fall takes a measured and meaningful toll upon earth's inhabitants. Obviously President Young used the phrase "natural man" differently from the way that Benjamin or Paul used it. His reference is to the spirit of man, the willing and striving eternal agent which is a child of God. His point is a good one: human beings can choose good as well as evil and can, through the proper exercise of their God-given agency, stand as spiritual beings before the Almighty. And yet our spirits can be and are influenced by our physical bodies, inasmuch as the latter are subject to our present fallen state. President Brigham Young taught:

> Now, I want to tell you that [Satan] does not hold any power over man, only so far as the body overcomes the spirit that is in a man, through yielding to the spirit of evil. The spirit that the Lord puts into a tabernacle of flesh, is under the dictation of the Lord Almighty; but the spirit and body are united in order that the spirit may have a tabernacle, and be exalted; and the spirit is influenced by the body, and the body by the spirit.

> In the first place the spirit is pure, and under the special control and influence of the Lord, but the body is of the earth, and is subject to the power of the devil, and is under the mighty influence of that fallen nature that is on the earth. If the spirit yields to the body, the devil then has power to overcome both the body and spirit of that man. (*JD* 2:255–56; compare *TPJS* 181, 187, 189, 226)

On another occasion, President Young taught that "there are no persons without evil passions to embitter their lives. Mankind are revengeful, passionate, hateful, and devilish in their dispositions. This we inherit through the fall, and the grace of God is designed to enable us to overcome it" (*JD* 8:160).

3. *Little children are innocent.* Too often, Latter-day Saints become concerned and confused about the scriptural statement that children are conceived in sin (Moses 6:55) and ask, "Are children pure?" The answer to this question is always a resounding "Yes!" No one disputes that. The real issue is *why*

children are pure. Two possibilities suggest themselves: (1) the Greek or humanistic response is that children are pure because human nature is pure, prone toward the good; while (2) the Christian gospel response is that children are pure because of the Atonement, because Jesus Christ declared them so. To paraphrase the words of Lehi, children are redeemed because of the righteousness of our Redeemer (2 Nephi 2:3). Benjamin, declaring the words of the angel, said, "And even if it were possible that little children could sin they could not be saved." That is, if Christ required children to be responsible for those actions or deeds which are ostensibly wrong and sinful, they could not be saved, had there been no atonement. "But I say unto you," Benjamin explains, "they are blessed; for behold, as in Adam, or by nature, they fall, even so the blood of Christ atoneth for their sins" (Mosiah 3:16).

The revelations state that little children "cannot sin, for power is not given unto Satan to tempt little children, until they begin to become accountable before me" (D&C 29:47). All of us know of deeds performed by little children that may only be described as evil. I am aware of a seven-year old who in an act of rage killed his brother. The act of murder is a heinous sin. But in this case the child's action is not counted as sin. Why? Because, in the words of God, "Little children are redeemed from the foundation of the world through mine Only Begotten" (D&C 29:46). Christ explained that "the curse of Adam is taken from [children] in me, that it hath no power over them" (Moroni 8:8). Little children are subject to the effects of the Fall, just as all of us are; they are not, however, held accountable for their actions. In summary, little children are saved without any preconditions—without faith, repentance, or baptism. Their innocence is decreed and declared by and through the tender mercies of an omni-loving Lord. Children are innocent through the Atonement, not because there is no sin in their nature.

4. *Joseph Smith taught that we are gods in embryo.* Some people believe that Joseph Smith and the Latter-day Saints

progressed or evolved beyond the doctrine of the Fall, that the message of the Book of Mormon was later quietly but surely superseded by the purer pronouncements in the King Follett Sermon. To me such views are groundless and misleading. It was in 1841 that the Prophet made his now-famous statement about the correctness and power of the Book of Mormon (*TPJS* 194). Only the night before the Prophet's martyrdom,

> Hyrum Smith read and commented upon extracts from the Book of Mormon, on the imprisonments and deliverance of the servants of God for the Gospel's sake. Joseph bore a powerful testimony to the guards of the divine authenticity of the Book of Mormon, the restoration of the Gospel, the administration of angels, and that the kingdom of God was again established upon the earth. (*HC* 6:600)

That scene in Carthage certainly bespeaks more than sentimental attachment on the part of the Prophet to the scriptural record—and to the doctrines it put forward—that had come to light through his instrumentality almost two decades earlier. The fact is, on some occasions Joseph Smith spoke of the nobility of humankind, and on some occasions he spoke of the carnality of humankind. (For the latter perspective, see *TPJS* 26–27, 30, 196, 249–50, 252, 258, 303, 315, 328.) To conclude that the Prophet taught only of humankind's nobility—or, for that matter, that he taught only of humankind's ignobility—is to misrepresent his broader theological view.[1]

Putting Off the Natural Man

During his speech at the temple, Benjamin explained that

> men drink damnation to their own souls except they humble themselves and become as little children, and believe that salvation was, and is, and is to come, in and through the atoning blood of Christ, the Lord Omnipotent. For the natural man is an enemy to God, and has been from the fall of Adam, and will be, forever and ever, unless he yields to the enticings of the Holy Spirit, and putteth off the natural

---

[1] For a more detailed discussion of this matter, see Robert L. Millet, "Joseph Smith and Modern Mormonism: Orthodoxy, Neoorthodoxy, Tension, and Tradition," *Brigham Young University Studies* (Sum 1989) 29:49–68.

> man and becometh a saint through the atonement of Christ the Lord, and becometh as a child, submissive, meek, humble, patient, full of love, willing to submit to all things which the Lord seeth fit to inflict upon him, even as a child doth submit to his father. (Mosiah 3:18–19)

We do not put off the natural man by living longer. We do not change our natures by simply attending meetings and being involved in the work of the Church. The Church is a divine organization. It administers the saving gospel. The transformation from the natural state to the spiritual state, however, is accomplished only through the mediation and atonement of Jesus Christ, through the power of the Holy Ghost. No one goes from death to life without that enabling power we call the grace of God. Programs to develop self-control, plans to modify human behavior, and schemes directed toward the shaping of more appropriate actions have fallen and will forever fall far short of the mark which Christ has set. These programs are at best deficient and at worst perverse. In the language of President Ezra Taft Benson:

> The Lord works from the inside out. The world works from the outside in. The world would take people out of the slums. Christ takes the slums out of people, and then they take themselves out of the slums. The world would mold men by changing their environment. Christ changes men, who then change their environment. The world would shape human behavior, but Christ can change human nature. ("Born of God" 6)

Those who are born again or born from above—who die as to the things of unrighteousness and begin to live again as pertaining to the things of the Spirit—are like little children. First and foremost, these people are, like children, clean and pure. Through the atoning blood of Christ they have had their sins remitted and have entered the realm of divine experience. Putting off the natural man involves putting on Christ. As Paul counseled the Saints in his day, those who put off the "old man" are "renewed in the spirit of [their] mind." They "put on the new man, which after God is created in righteousness and true holiness" (Eph 4:22–24), and "which is renewed in knowledge after the image of him that created him" (Col 3:10).

This renovation of the natural man may for some be dramatic and rapid. Such was the case with Enos (Enos 1:1–8) and with the people of king Benjamin who underwent a "mighty change," such that they had "no more disposition to do evil, but to do good continually" (Mosiah 5:2). It may be like the experiences of Alma the Younger or Paul, both of whom were, through the ministry of heavenly beings, redirected and reoriented (Mosiah 27; Alma 36; Acts 9). As to the miraculous conversion of king Lamoni—and thus of the unspeakable power of Christ to forge new creatures—the Nephite record attests:

> King Lamoni was under the power of God; [Ammon] knew that the dark veil of unbelief was being cast away from his mind, and the light which did light up his mind, which was the light of the glory of God, which was a marvelous light of his goodness—yea, this light had infused such joy into his soul, the cloud of darkness having been dispelled, and that the light of everlasting life was lit up in his soul, yea, he knew that this had overcome his natural frame, and he was carried away in God. (Alma 19:6)

"But we must be cautious," President Benson has warned us, "as we discuss these remarkable examples. Though they are real and powerful, they are the exception more than the rule. For every Paul, for every Enos, and for every king Lamoni, there are hundreds and thousands of people who find the process of repentance much more subtle, much more imperceptible. Day by day they move closer to the Lord, little realizing they are building a godlike life" ("A Mighty Change of Heart" 5).

Those who have put off the natural man—what Paul called the "works of the flesh" (Gal 5:19)—begin to enjoy what he also called the "fruit of the Spirit," namely "love, joy, peace, longsuffering, gentleness, goodness, faith, meekness, temperance"; they begin to "walk in the Spirit" (Gal 5:22–23, 25). As Benjamin explained, they are humble and submissive, eager to know and carry out the will of the Savior, eager to have their own wishes swallowed up in a higher will (Mosiah 3:19).

Surely the highest and grandest fruit of the Spirit is love, what the scriptures call charity, the "pure love of Christ" (Moroni 7:47). "And again I remember," Moroni stated humbly to his Master, "that thou hast said that thou hast loved the world, even unto the laying down of thy life for the world. . . . And now I know that this love which thou hast had for the children of men is charity; wherefore, except men shall have charity they cannot inherit that place which thou hast prepared in the mansions of thy Father" (Ether 12:33–34). This charity is more than an emotion, higher than a sweet feeling, more transcendent than an effort to perform good deeds. It is literally a fruit of the Spirit, a heavenly endowment which can only be granted and bestowed by an all-loving God. The true followers of Christ come to love as he loves because they have become as he is. In short, they have become saints, members of the household of faith who seek the way of holiness and have enjoyed the sublime sanctifying powers of the Holy Ghost.

Conclusion

We shall spend all our days seeking to subdue the flesh and put off the natural man; this is the challenge of mortality. "Will sin be perfectly destroyed?" Brigham Young asked. "No, it will not, for it is not so designed in the economy of Heaven."

> Do not suppose that we shall ever in the flesh be free from temptations to sin. Some suppose that they can in the flesh be sanctified body and spirit and become so pure that they will never again feel the effects of the power of the adversary of truth. Were it possible for a person to attain to this degree of perfection in the flesh, he could not die neither remain in a world where sin predominates. Sin has entered into the world, and death by sin. I think we shall more or less feel the effects of sin so long as we live, and finally have to pass the ordeals of death. (*JD* 10:173)

Zion is built "in process of time" (Moses 7:21); it is only by patience and long-suffering that the Saints of the Most High become a holy people.

There is great virtue in truth and great power in the proclamation of the truth. President Ezra Taft Benson has repeatedly warned the Saints of the condemnation, scourge, and judgment that rest upon the Church because of our neglect of the Book of Mormon (see D&C 84:54–61). He has, however, reminded us that the condemnation can be lifted through serious study and consistent application of the teachings and patterns for living provided in that sacred volume. "I am deeply concerned," he once said, "about what we are doing to teach the Saints at all levels the gospel of Jesus Christ as completely and authoritatively as do the Book of Mormon and Doctrine and Covenants. By this I mean teaching the 'great plan of the Eternal God,' to use the words of Amulek (Alma 34:9)."

> Are we using the messages and the method of teaching found in the Book of Mormon and other scriptures of the Restoration to teach this great plan of the Eternal God? . . .
> The Book of Mormon Saints knew that the plan of redemption must start with the account of the fall of Adam. In the words of Moroni, "By Adam came the fall of man. And because of the fall of man came Jesus Christ, . . . and because of Jesus Christ came the redemption of man." (Mormon 9:12.)
> We all need to take a careful inventory of our performance and also the performance of those over whom we preside to be sure that we are teaching the "great plan of the Eternal God" to the Saints.
> Are we accepting and teaching what the revelations tell us about the Creation, Adam and the fall of man, and redemption from that fall through the atonement of Christ? (*A Witness and a Warning* 32–33)

As stated earlier, just as we do not desire food until we are hungry, so the living waters can bless our lives only to the degree to which we acknowledge our fallen condition, seek diligently to put off the natural man, and receive deliverance from sin through repentance. "It requires all the atonement of Christ," Brigham Young noted, "the mercy of the Father, the pity of angels and the grace of the Lord Jesus Christ to be with us always, and then to do the very best we possibly can, to get rid of this sin within us, so that we may escape from this world into the celestial kingdom" (*JD* 11:39). In the words of C. S. Lewis, the animation and renovation of human character "is precisely what Christianity is about. This world is a great sculptor's shop. We are the statues and there is a rumor going round the shop that some of us are some day going to come to life" (140). When we do so, as individuals and as a people, to quote a modern prophet, "a new day will break and Zion will be redeemed" (*A Witness and a Warning* 66).

BIBLIOGRAPHY

Benson, Ezra Taft. "Beware of Pride." *Ensign* (May 1989) 19:4–7; also in *Conference Report* (Apr 1989) 3–7.

————."Born of God." *Ensign* (Nov 1985) 15:5–7; also in *Conference Report* (Oct 1985) 4–6.

————."A Mighty Change of Heart." *Ensign* (Oct 1989) 19:2–5.

————. *A Witness and a Warning.* Salt Lake City: Deseret Book, 1988.

Crabb, Larry. *Inside Out.* Colorado Springs, CO: NavPress, 1988.

Journal of Discourses. 26 vols. 1854–86.

Kimball, Spencer W. "Ocean Currents and Family Influences." *Ensign* (Nov 1974) 4:110–13; also in *Conference Report* (Oct 1974) 159–63.

Lewis, C. S. *Mere Christianity.* New York: Macmillan, 1960.

McConkie, Bruce R. *The Promised Messiah.* Salt Lake City: Deseret Book, 1978.

Pratt, Parley P. *Key to the Science of Theology.* Salt Lake City: Deseret Book, 1970.

Taylor, John. *Mediation and Atonement.* Salt Lake City: Deseret News, 1892.

Teachings of the Prophet Joseph Smith. Comp. Joseph Fielding Smith. Salt Lake City: Deseret Book, 1976.

Whitney, Orson F. *Conference Report* (Apr 1908) 86–93.

Abinadi's Commentary on Isaiah 10

Monte S. Nyman

About 150 BC a group of Nephites living in the land of Lehi-Nephi fell into bondage to their Lamanite neighbors. Previously the Lord had raised up a prophet named Abinadi who called the Nephites to repentance, but "they were wroth with him, and sought to take away his life; but the Lord delivered him out of their hands" (Mosiah 11:20, 26). Two years later, Abinadi returned and prophesied of their impending bondage to the Lamanites and of the fiery fate of Noah, their king. Abinadi was carried before the king and cast into prison until he could be tried before a council of the king's priests. In questioning Abinadi, the priests attempted to "find something" with which they could accuse him and either imprison or execute him. To their astonishment, he boldly confounded them in all their words (Mosiah 12:1–19).

One of the priests asked Abinadi the meaning of a passage from Isaiah, one of the greatest prophets of the Old Testament (Mosiah 12:20–24; compare Isa 52:7–10). Since the priest obviously did not understand the Isaiah text, he seemed to assume Abinadi wouldn't understand it either because Isaiah was not generally understood by the people of Nephi (2 Nephi 25:1) and was not understood particularly by those in a state of spiritual decline. But Abinadi was a prophet of the Lord, "filled with the spirit of prophecy"; he chastised the priests for

Monte S. Nyman is professor of Ancient Scripture and associate dean of Religious Education at Brigham Young University.

their lack of understanding and accused them of perverting the ways of the Lord and not applying their hearts to understanding. Then he asked them what they taught their people (Mosiah 12:25–28). To their answer, "We teach the law of Moses," he queried further, "Why do ye not keep it?" Another question probed still deeper: "Doth salvation come by the law of Moses?" (Mosiah 12:28–31). To their answer that it did, Abinadi skillfully refuted their false preaching and showed how the law of Moses was a type and shadow of Jesus Christ (Mosiah 13:27–35). He then declared that Moses and all of the prophets who had ever prophesied had testified that Jesus Christ would come into the world in the form of a man, and that he would bring to pass the resurrection of the dead (Mosiah 13:33–35). As evidence that all the prophets had testified of Christ, Abinadi quoted and commented on what is now Isaiah 53 in the King James Bible.

Abinadi's Commentary on Isaiah 53

Isaiah 53 is a well-known prophecy among Christians and Jews. Christians generally interpret it as a prophecy of the life and suffering of Jesus Christ. The Jewish interpretation is that Isaiah is describing the suffering of the entire nation of Israel, not a specific person. Abinadi's commentary sustains the Christian interpretation with details not found in the writings of other Christians. Abinadi's commentary on Isaiah 53, although sometimes confusing to Church members, amplifies the beautiful message of Isaiah. Abinadi's great doctrinal insights and explanations of the true role of Jesus Christ are textual proofs that "Jesus is the Christ, the Eternal God" (BofM title page).

After discussing the great truths of Isaiah 53, Abinadi returned to the original question raised by king Noah's priest—the meaning of the text of Isaiah 52:7–10. His answer is also a commentary on that passage. But before he interpreted those verses, Abinadi explained the messiahship of Jesus Christ and his gospel as the message of peace. Only then would the priests be prepared to understand this passage of Isaiah. In the analysis that follows, I will first quote Isaiah's words as written by Mosiah, then I will add relevant phrases from Abinadi's commentary and other interpretative helps from the New Testament and modern revelation. I will then draw conclusions from the collective commentaries.

Mosiah 14:1

> Yea, even doth not Isaiah say: Who hath believed our report, and to whom is the arm of the Lord revealed? (Compare Isa 53:1)

Although Abinadi does not comment directly on this verse, the context in which he quotes it makes his interpretation clear. He had just declared that all of the prophets since the world began testified of Christ. To support this statement, he said, "Yea, even doth not Isaiah say" and proceeded to quote the entirety of Isaiah 53. Clearly Abinadi understands this passage not to be a prophecy of suffering Israel, but a prophecy of Jesus Christ, of whom all the prophets have testified. And yet, the people were receptive neither to Isaiah's prophecies of Christ, nor to Abinadi's, nor to those of the other prophets. It was the hard hearts of the people and their lack of understanding of the law that brought Isaiah to cry, "Who hath believed our report?"

Other scriptures support Abinadi's interpretation. For example, Jacob, the brother of Nephi, had prophesied "that none of the prophets have written, nor prophesied, save they have spoken concerning this Christ" (Jacob 7:11, see also 4:4–6). The Savior himself, when he ministered in the flesh, showed how the law of Moses, the Prophets, and the Psalms, the three divisions of the Hebrew bible, had all foretold of him (Luke 24:27, 44). Paul's Epistle to the Romans confirmed that many of the people would not accept the testimony of the ancient prophets. He said, "But they have not all obeyed the gospel" (Rom 10:16), and quoted the first phrase of Isaiah 53:1 to support his statement. Thus, both the Book of Mormon and the Bible give us the correct meaning of Isaiah's words "who hath believed our report?"

Abinadi does not comment on the last half of Isaiah 53:1, "and to whom is the arm of the Lord revealed?" However, John interprets the many miracles that Jesus did among the Jews during his sojourn in the flesh as a fulfillment of Isaiah's words that the arm of the Lord would be revealed (John 12:37–38). The performance of miracles exhibited his power as the Son of God. Thus the people rejected the written testimony of their Redeemer as well as the physical evidence provided by his manifestations of miracles. Although both testimonies were rejected, the two types of witnesses established the divinity of the Messiah.

Mosiah 14:2

> For he shall grow up before him as a tender plant, and as a root out of dry ground; he hath no form nor comeliness; and when we shall see him there is no beauty that we should desire him. (Compare Isa 53:2)

This verse gives only a vague picture of Christ and his nature on earth. However, Abinadi teaches quite specifically about Christ and his nature. In Mosiah 15:1–4 Abinadi comments on the nature of Christ as both the father and the son:

> I would that ye should understand that God himself shall come down among the children of men, and shall redeem his people. And because he dwelleth in flesh he shall be called the Son of God, and having subjected the flesh to the will of the Father, being the Father and the Son. The Father, because he was conceived by the power of God; and the Son, because of the flesh; thus becoming the Father and Son. And they are one God, yea, the very Eternal Father of heaven and of earth. (Mosiah 15:1–4)

Jesus Christ attained Godhood in the premortal life (JST John 1:1–2). He was the God of Abraham, Isaac, and Jacob, and the leader of the children of Israel out of Egypt (1 Nephi 19:10; 1 Cor 10:1–4). Jesus' coming among humankind begins with his birth and childhood. Isaiah had previously foretold the

Redeemer's birth (Isa 7:14; 9:6), but in Isaiah 53 he describes his childhood. When studied in its context, Abinadi's commentary provides a beautiful explanation of the life, the nature, and the roles of our Lord and Savior as he came "down among the children of men" (Mosiah 15:1).

Abinadi's specific commentary in Mosiah 15:2 is difficult to understand on a first or even a second reading.

> And because he dwelleth in flesh he shall be called the Son of God, and having subjected the flesh to the will of the Father, being the Father and the Son. (Mosiah 15:2)

This verse refers to Jesus' mortal ministry, when he would come to earth as a mortal and be called the Son of God; however, he would subject himself while in his mortal tabernacle to do the will of his Father in Heaven. The will of the Father was that Christ "be lifted up upon the cross; and after that [he] had been lifted up upon the cross, that [he] might draw all men unto [him], that as [he had] been lifted up by men even so should men be lifted up by the Father, to stand before [him], to be judged of their works, whether they be good or whether they be evil" (3 Nephi 27:14). In other words, the Father's will was for Christ to come and atone for all humankind. Thus while he would live upon the earth as the Son of God, he would carry out the will of the Father, and through divine investiture of authority would represent the Father. Therefore, he would be the Father and the Son while living upon the earth.

The above explanation by Abinadi qualifies as a commentary on the first phrase of Isaiah 53:2: "For he shall grow up before him as a tender plant, and as a root out of dry ground." By substituting nouns for pronouns, we get a clearer picture: "For [Christ] shall grow up before [Elohim] as a tender plant." A tender plant is one that must be given special care by the gardener. It may need to be covered at night to protect it from frost, uncovered during the day to enable it to absorb the light and sunshine, and watered at frequent or regular hours. In like manner, the Father cared for his Son throughout his early childhood.

Luke records that "the child [Jesus] grew, and waxed strong in spirit, filled with wisdom: and the grace of God was upon him" (Luke 2:40). At age 12, he went with his parents on their annual passover trek to the temple. Upon their return, Jesus tarried behind—unknown to his parents. Missing him at the end of the first day's journey, they spent three days searching for him and found him conversing with the learned doctors of Judaism (vv 41–48). In response to his mother's mild chastisement he responded, "How is it that ye sought me? wist ye not that I must be about my Father's business? And they understood not the saying which he spake unto them" (vv 49–50). Even his mother seems not to have known the extent to which his Heavenly Father had tutored him. He had indeed been cared for by the Father as a tender plant.

The phrase, "root out of dry ground," may be interpreted as Christ growing up in apostate Judaism. In Revelation 22:16, Christ identifies himself as "the root and the offspring of David." Both Mary, his mother, and Joseph, his stepfather, were descendants of David and of the lineage of Judah (Matt 1:1–17; Luke 3:23–38). Judah, as a nation, was spiritually barren and could not give him the nurturing he needed to prepare him for his ministry; that nurturing was given to him instead by his Father. His nurturing was perfect and prepared Christ for his ministry in due time. Joseph Smith taught that Jesus was prepared for his ministry long before he was thirty years of age, but waited to begin his ministry until the Father directed him.

> When still a boy He had all the intelligence necessary to enable Him to rule and govern the kingdom of the Jews, and could reason with the wisest and most profound doctors of law and divinity, and make their theories and practice to appear like folly compared with the wisdom He possessed; but He was a boy only, and lacked physical strength even to defend His own person; and was subject to cold, to hunger and to death. (*Teachings of the Prophet Joseph Smith* 392)

Being thus prepared, he carried out the will of the Father when the time came for him to fulfill his ministry.

Having referred to the ministry of Jesus, Abinadi comments on the nature on the Son of God during mortality that would enable him to finalize his ministry by bringing about the Resurrection. Christ is

> the Father, because he was conceived by the power of God; and the Son, because of the flesh; thus becoming the Father and Son. (Mosiah 15:3)

Because he was conceived by an immortal being, his immortal Father in Heaven, Jesus had immortality as a part of his own nature. Because he was born of a mortal woman, he was also part mortal. Being mortal he was subject to death and had power to lay down his life; being immortal he had power to break the bands of death, or take up his life. This he clearly taught to the Jews during his earthly ministry:

> Therefore doth my Father love me, because I lay down my life, that I might take it again. No man taketh it from me, but I lay it down of myself. I have power to lay it down, and I have power to take it again. This commandment have I received of my Father. (John 10:17–18)

Possessing the power of the Father enabled him to overcome the grave and bring about the Resurrection. Through his dual nature he was the Father and Son, being immortal as well as mortal.

Abinadi's explanation of Christ's nature seems to be a commentary on the latter part of Isaiah 53:2: "He hath no form nor comeliness; and when we shall see him there is no beauty that we should desire him" (Mosiah 14:2). That Jesus had "no form nor comeliness" is the prophet Isaiah's way of saying that he looked like a normal Jewish boy and was not distinctive in his looks because he was the Son of God. People in Nazareth did not look upon him as different from his brothers and sisters or other children in the community. They referred to him as "the carpenter's son" (Matt 13:54–56) or "the son of Joseph whose father and mother we know" (John 6:42). His having "no beauty that we should desire him" is not an indication of ugliness or plainness but is poetic parallelism, a repetition of the same thought in the second line. It was another expression of the fact that he looked like any other child growing up in Nazareth. Abinadi's commentary explains how this was possible: Christ was both mortal and the divine Son of God.

After describing the dual nature of the mortal Messiah, Abinadi adds one more dimension to his description of the Savior:

> And they are one God, yea, the very Eternal Father of heaven and of earth. (Mosiah 15:4)

Verse 4 is a summation of the two previous verses. The one God referred to is Jesus Christ. The plural "they" refers to the dual roles in his ministry and to his dual nature as the Father and the Son. He is the Son of God, but by divine investiture of authority he represents the Father in his ministry; having immortality and mortality in his nature he has power over life and death. Thus he has all power in heaven and in earth. He is the divine Son of God with all the attributes of his Father to make the Atonement and bring about the Resurrection. His is the role of the Father and the Son, and he is thus one God.[1]

Abinadi's statement that Christ is "the very Eternal Father of heaven and of earth" (Mosiah 15:4) undoubtedly refers to the creative power of Christ as the Father of this earth and of other earths in the heavens. That Christ created this and other worlds is repeatedly taught in the New Testament (John 1:3, 10; Col 1:16; Heb 1:2). It is also confirmed in modern scripture (D&C 14:9; 76:24; 93:10; Moses 1:31–33). A diagram of Abinadi's teaching in Mosiah 15:2–4 would be thus:

---

[1] It should be kept in mind that Abinadi is not instructing prospective members of the Church. He is accusing, chastising, and refuting a group of apostate priests who claim to be scriptural authorities. Recall his words to them earlier: "And now Abinadi said unto them: Are you priests, and pretend to teach this people, and to understand the spirit of prophesying, and yet desire to know of me what these things mean? I say unto you, wo be unto you for perverting the ways of the Lord! For if ye understand these things ye have not taught them; therefore, ye have perverted the ways of the Lord" (Mosiah 12:25–26).

TABLE 1 *Summary of Abinadi's Commentary on Isaiah 53:2*

A. How Christ Is Both the Father and the Son		
	The Father	*The Son*
Christ's Ministry Provides the Atonement	He is the Father because he does the will of the Father (Mosiah 15:2)	He is the Son because he dwelt in the flesh (Mosiah 15:2)
Christ's Nature Provides the Resurrection	He was immortal because he was conceived by the power of God (Mosiah 15:3)	He was mortal because he was born of a mortal mother with the power to lay down life (Mosiah 15:3)
B. Christ's Dual Nature		
Christ's Role Jesus Is the Creator of Heaven and Earth	There is one God—Jesus Christ (Mosiah 15:4)	

The prophet Abinadi had masterfully shown the apostate priests the role of Christ as the Father by divine investiture of authority and the divine nature that would enable him to atone for the sins of humankind and provide for their resurrection. In addition, he testified that Christ was the Father as the Creator of heaven and earth.

The supposedly complex definition of Jesus Christ given by Abinadi is really quite simple and beautiful when seen in the light of Abinadi's commentary on Isaiah, which is supported by modern revelation. In a revelation to Joseph Smith that was at least in part originally of the record of John, the Lord proclaimed: "And that I am in the Father, and the Father in me, and the Father and I are one—The Father because he gave me of his fulness, and the Son because I was in the world and made flesh my tabernacle, and dwelt among the sons of men" (D&C 93:3–4). This shows that John, as well as Abinadi, and certainly all of the prophets, knew and appreciated the role of Jesus Christ.

Other Book of Mormon prophets also understood and taught the position of Christ as fulfilling the role of the Father as well as the Son. Nephi, son of Lehi, taught that "there is a God, and he is Christ, and he cometh in the fulness of his own time" (2 Nephi 11:7). Amulek taught the repentant lawyer Zeezrom that there is only one God who is the Son of God and that "he is the very Eternal Father of heaven and of earth, and all things which in them are; he is the beginning and the end, the first and last" (Alma 11:39; see vv 26–40).

In the meridian of time as Nephi prayed on behalf of his people concerning the coming of the sign of Christ's birth as prophesied by Samuel the Lamanite, the voice of the Lord came to Nephi saying that the sign would be given that night and that on the morrow He would come into the world to fulfill what the prophets had spoken and made known from the foundation of the world. He further testified that he would come "to do the will, both of the Father and of the Son—of the Father because of me, and of the Son because of my flesh" (3 Nephi 1:13–14). And as a last example, hundreds of years before the Nephite prophets taught these truths, the Lord appeared to the brother of Jared and identified himself as "he who was prepared from the foundation of the world to redeem [his] people. Behold, I am Jesus Christ. I am the Father and the Son. In me shall all mankind have life, and that eternally, even they who shall believe on my name" (Ether 3:14). Thus we see that this eternal truth of Christ's true position was taught throughout the history of the Nephites and among the Jaredites as well. Hopefully, as we understand the role of Jesus Christ as the Father and the Son as taught in the Book of Mormon, we will also appreciate more fully the subtitle of the Book of Mormon, "Another Testament of Jesus Christ."

A further verification of Christ's various roles as the Father was given in "A Doctrinal Exposition by the First Presidency and the Twelve" on 30 June 1916. On this occasion, the Brethren gave detailed information and scriptural evidence about the four uses of the term Father which appear in the scriptures. Their exposition is really the key to understanding Mosiah 15. Because of the length and detail of this exposition, I will just outline its four major points here and suggest further study at another time. It has been printed in *Messages of the First Presidency* by James R. Clark (5:26–34) and *The Articles of Faith* by Elder James E. Talmage (Appendix 2, pp 466–73):

1. Father as literal parent: Heb 12:9; Ether 3:14
2. Father as Creator: Ether 4:7; Mosiah 15:4; Alma 11:38–39
3. Jesus Christ, the Father of those who abide in his gospel: John 17:6–12, 20–24; D&C 9:1; 25:1; 34:3; 121:7
4. Jesus Christ, the Father by divine investiture of authority: John 14:28; Rev 22:8, 9; D&C 93:21

All the scriptural uses of the term *Father* thus refer to Jesus Christ, except our being the spirit offspring of our Father in Heaven. The title page of the Book of Mormon declares that a major purpose of the book is "the convincing of the Jew and Gentile that Jesus is the Christ, the Eternal God" (see also 2 Nephi 26:12–13). Understanding Abinadi's commentary on Isaiah helps fulfill this major purpose.

Mosiah 14:3–5

He is despised and rejected of men; a man of sorrows, and acquainted with grief; and we hid as it were our faces from him; he was despised, and we esteemed him not. Surely he hath borne our griefs, and carried our sorrows; yet we did esteem him stricken, smitten of God, and afflicted. But he was wounded for our transgressions, he was bruised for our iniquities; the chastisement of our peace was upon him; and with his stripes we are healed. (Compare Isa 53:3–5)

Abinadi gives but one verse of commentary:

And thus the flesh becoming subject to the Spirit, or the Son to the Father, being one God, suffereth temptation, and yieldeth not to the temptation, but suffereth himself to be mocked, and scourged, and cast out, and disowned by his people. (Mosiah 15:5)

Here Abinadi explains Isaiah's prophecy of Christ's ministry. Not only would Christ be rejected and humiliated, but he would also be tempted. However, he will not yield to temptation. This comment by Abinadi helps us better understand the Savior's ministry and also the perfect example he set as part of the overall Atonement for humankind. As he commanded the Nephites, we are also to be the manner of beings that he was in his ministry (3 Nephi 27:27). We must be "willing to submit to all things which the Lord seeth fit to inflict upon [us], even as a child doth submit to his father" (Mosiah 3:19), or, as Abinadi says, to submit our flesh to the Spirit as the Son had to the Father.

The writings of the New Testament Apostles also support Abinadi's commentary. Matthew paraphrased Isaiah 53:4— "Himself took our infirmities, and bare our sicknesses"—to show its fulfillment in Jesus' casting out devils and healing the sick in Capernaum (Matt 8:16–17). Paul taught the Hebrews that Jesus "was in all points tempted like as we are, yet without sin" (Heb 4:15). And Peter quotes or paraphrases parts of Isaiah 53:4–5 and equates it with Jesus' being on the cross: "Who his own self bare our sins in his own body on the tree, that we, being dead to sins, should live unto righteousness: by whose stripes ye were healed" (1 Peter 2:24). While his mission culminated on the cross, his entire life and particularly his ministry was one of temptation: being mocked, scourged, cast out, and disowned by his people. Mark records that Jesus taught his disciples "that the Son of man must suffer many things, and be rejected of the elders, and of the chief priests, and scribes, and be killed" (Mark 8:31). With the support of these scriptures, we may conclude that Abinadi gave us a briefer but very accurate commentary of the Savior's ministry.

Mosiah 14:6

> All we like sheep have gone astray; we have turned every one to his own way; and the Lord hath laid on him the iniquity of us all. (Compare Isa 53:6)

Abinadi explains the relationship between Christ and the Father after he had completed his ministry:

> Having ascended into heaven, having the bowels of mercy; being filled with compassion towards the children of men; standing betwixt them and justice; having broken the bands of death, taken upon himself their iniquity and their transgressions, having redeemed them, and satisfied the demands of justice. (Mosiah 15:9)

This commentary sheds further light on the role of Jesus Christ as the Father and the Son. Having suffered for all humankind's sins, Jesus Christ fulfilled the demands of justice in his role as the Father. His compassion to those who repent illustrates his role as the Son as his mercy satisfies the demands of justice. While the New Testament tells us that the Atonement was accomplished, we must turn to the Book of Mormon to enlarge our understanding of the roles of mercy and justice. Further sections of the Book of Mormon, such as Amulek's testimony to the apostate Zoramites (Alma 34:15–16) and Alma's instructions to his wayward son Corianton (Alma 42), are also most enlightening on these principles of mercy and justice. An analysis of these references will be left to another time.

Mosiah 14:7

Isaiah prophesies of Jesus' being judged before Pilate and Herod:

> He was oppressed, and he was afflicted, yet he opened not his mouth: he is brought as a lamb to the slaughter, and as a sheep before her shearers is dumb, so he openeth not his mouth. (Compare Isa 53:7)

Abinadi's commentary on this verse is little more than a repetition of Isaiah:

> And after all this, after working many mighty miracles among the children of men, he shall be led, yea, even as Isaiah said, as a sheep before the shearer is dumb, so he opened not his mouth. (Mosiah 15:6)

The New Testament records Jesus' appearance before Pilate and Herod. While Jesus did answer Pilate, he did so only sparingly, and on one occasion he gave him no answer (John 19:9). When Pilate sent him to Herod, Jesus answered him not a word. Herod could only retaliate by mocking him (Luke 23:8–11). Peter described the trials this way: "Who, when he was reviled, reviled not again; when he suffered, he threatened not; but committed himself to him that judgeth righteously" (1 Peter 2:23). Isaiah's prophecy was fulfilled.

Mosiah 14:8

The following verse contains the prophecy of Christ's crucifixion and death:

> He was taken from prison and from judgment: and who shall declare his generation? for he was cut off out of the land of the living: for the transgression of my people was he stricken. (Compare Isa 53:8)

In his commentary (Mosiah 15:7–13), Abinadi elaborates on the death of the Savior, speaking of the resurrection following the crucifixion and then answering Isaiah's question: "Who shall declare his generation?" Abinadi first comments on the Savior's crucifixion and death, "Yea, even so he shall be led, crucified, and slain, the flesh becoming subject even unto death, the will of the Son being swallowed up in the will of the Father" (Mosiah 15:7), and then concludes, "And thus God breaketh the bands of death, having gained the victory over death; giving the Son power to make intercession for the children of men" (v 8). Today we find the concept of breaking the bands of death and gaining a victory over death in Paul's First Epistle to the Corinthians; however, Paul is quoting what "is written" (1 Cor 15:54–55). Where was it written? Some have supposed it to be a quotation from Hosea 13:14, but if so, the Hosea text has been greatly modified. It seems more logical that this quote is a part of the plain and precious parts that have been lost from the Bible (1 Nephi 13:23–29). Nonetheless, that the resurrection of Christ would break the bands of death and gain victory over the grave was known to the Old Testament prophets. Abinadi would probably not have coined a phrase so close to what Paul was reading from the Hebrew Bible. Of course the Spirit could have dictated the same words, but it seems most logical that both Paul and Abinadi were quoting from an earlier text.

After speaking of the resurrection and atonement of Christ (Mosiah 15:8–9), Abinadi answers the question posed by Isaiah: "And now I say unto you, who shall declare his generation?"

> Behold, I say unto you, that when his soul has been made an offering for sin he shall see his seed. And now what say ye? And who shall be his seed? (Mosiah 15:10)

Abinadi combines his answer to "who shall declare his generation" with Isaiah's declaration that when Christ made "his soul an offering for sin he shall see his seed." The question and the declaration go hand in hand. Those who are spiritually begotten of Christ through being born again are adopted as his sons and daughters (Mosiah 5:7; see also Gal 4:1–7; Rom 8:14–17; and the Exposition by the First Presidency and the Twelve cited above). Thus the adopted, born-again sons and daughters of Jesus Christ will declare the message of the gospel that Jesus Christ was sent to the earth to redeem all humankind. Following his death, Christ's Apostles and others were to take this message to all the world (Mark 16:15–16). Abinadi explains at some length who these messengers will be, the prophets and those who have accepted and lived their message:

> Behold I say unto you, that whosoever has heard the words of the prophets, yea, all the holy prophets who have prophesied concerning the coming of the Lord—I say unto you, that all those who have hearkened unto their words, and believed that the Lord would redeem his people, and have looked forward to that day for a remission of their sins, I say unto you, that these are his seed, or they are the heirs of the kingdom of God. For these are they whose sins he has borne; these are they for whom he has died, to redeem them from their transgressions. And now, are they not his seed? Yea, and are not the prophets, every one that has opened his mouth to prophesy, that has not fallen into transgression, I mean all the holy prophets ever since the world began? I say unto you that they are his seed. (Mosiah 15:11–13)

Although Isaiah's prophecy continues, Abinadi has laid the groundwork and returns to the original question about the meaning of Isaiah 52:7–10, posed by Noah's apostate priest. (For Professor Nyman's analysis of the rest of Isaiah 53, see Appendix B at the end of this article.)

Abinadi's Response to the Priests

Mosiah 12:21

> How beautiful upon the mountains are the feet of him that bringeth good tidings, that publisheth peace; that bringeth good tidings of good, that publisheth salvation; that saith unto Zion, Thy God reigneth! (Compare Isa 52:7)

Abinadi's commentary on this verse is too long to quote here, but it constitutes the rest of Mosiah 15. Because of Abinadi's extensive discussion of Isaiah 53, king Noah's priests are prepared to understand not only the meaning of the verse in question but also the plan of salvation. Abinadi's commentary begins with an interpretation of Isaiah 52:7 and ends with a call to repentance. Abinadi had already established the idea that the seed of Christ are those spiritually begotten of him as their Father of eternal life. He now states that these same servants are the publishers of peace, and how beautiful upon the mountains were their feet and the feet of those who are now and who will yet publish peace (Mosiah 15:14–17). True peace comes only from the gospel, so those who travel (upon their feet) to preach the gospel upon the mountains of the earth are beautiful in the eyes of the people who accept their message.

This verse also refers to the founder of that peace—Jesus Christ. Without him there would be no peace. In Abinadi's words:

> And behold, I say unto you, this is not all. For O how beautiful upon the mountains are the feet of him that bringeth good tidings, that is the founder of peace, yea, even the Lord, who has redeemed his people; yea, him who has granted salvation unto his people; For were it not for the redemption which he hath made for his people, which was prepared from the foundation of the world, I say unto you, were it not for this, all mankind must have perished. (vv 18–19)

Christ broke the bands of death, and as the Son of God he reigns and has power over the dead that he may bring about their resurrection (v 20). The first resurrection includes those who "have been, and who are, and who shall be, even until the resurrection of Christ" (v 21). It includes the prophets and those who believed in their words and kept the commandments. They will dwell with Christ, who redeemed them, and have eternal life (vv 22–23). The first resurrection also includes those who died in ignorance before Christ came, not having had salvation declared to them (v 24). Although Abinadi does not expound upon this group, Peter and modern revelation qualify their salvation upon the condition of their accepting the gospel in the spirit world (1 Peter 3:18–20; 4:5–6; D&C 137:7–9). Abinadi also announces that little children shall have eternal life (Mosiah 15:25; see also D&C 137:10).

Abinadi closes his commentary on Isaiah 52:7 with a warning to those who rebel against Christ and die in their sins, those who have known the commandments and would not keep them. These ought to tremble and fear, for salvation does not come to such, and justice will claim them instead of mercy (Mosiah 15:26–27).

Mosiah 12:22–24

The next verses questioned by the wicked priests were:

Thy watchmen shall lift up the voice; with the voice together shall they sing: for they shall see eye to eye, when the Lord shall bring again Zion. Break forth into joy, sing together, ye waste places of Jerusalem: for the Lord hath comforted his people, he hath redeemed Jerusalem. The Lord hath made bare his holy arm in the eyes of all the nations; and all the ends of the earth shall see the salvation of our God. (Compare Isa 52:8–10)

Abinadi's commentary paraphrases Isaiah's words: "And now I say unto you that the time shall come that the salvation of the Lord shall be declared to every nation, kindred, tongue, and people" (Mosiah 15:28). Abinadi prefaced and followed his commentary on this verse with a paraphrase of Isaiah 52:10, which states that the salvation of the Lord shall be declared to every nation, kindred, tongue, and people (Mosiah 15:28–16:1). Isaiah's declaration that salvation would come when the Lord would bring again (gather) Zion and when the Lord comforted (gathered) his people in Jerusalem designates the two major gathering places of the latter days. It also sheds light upon the reference to the mountains where peace is published, or, in other words, where the gospel will be taught. Both Zion and Jerusalem are designated, in scripture, as the tops of the mountains (Isa 40:9; 1 Nephi 19:13; 2 Nephi 12:2; D&C 133:12–13). While the gospel will eventually be taught to all peoples, the major centers of administering the gospel will be from Zion (the Americas) and Jerusalem. The people who accept the gospel shall see eye to eye and confess that God's judgments are just because they will understand the gospel taught by the prophets and the missionaries.

Abinadi proceeds to warn those who have become wicked, carnal, sensual, and devilish because of the Fall (Mosiah 16:2–5). He speaks of Christ as though he had already come (v 6) and then either quotes or paraphrases the lost scripture concerning Christ's breaking the bands of death (vv 7–8). He comments further on Christ as the light and life of the world and on the power of the resurrection and judgment that is to come (vv 9–12).

Abinadi concludes his comments with a warning to Noah's wicked priests:

> And now, ought ye not to tremble and repent of your sins, and remember that only in and through Christ can ye be saved? Therefore, if ye teach the law of Moses, also teach that it is a shadow of those things which are to come—Teach them that redemption cometh through Christ the Lord, who is the very Eternal Father. Amen. (Mosiah 16:13–15)

The priests did not hearken to Abinadi's warning; rather, they put him to death because he would not recall the words he had taught about God (Mosiah 17:1–13). Sometime after Abinadi's death, Limhi, king of a group of Nephites in bondage to the

Lamanites, also witnessed that Abinadi was martyred for his testimony of Christ:

> And a prophet of the Lord have they slain; yea, a chosen man of God, who told them of their wickedness and abominations, and prophesied of many things which are to come, yea, even the coming of Christ. And because he said unto them that Christ was the God, the Father of all things, and said that he should take upon him the image of man, and it should be the image after which man was created in the beginning; or in other words, he said that man was created after the image of God, and that God should come down among the children of men, and take upon him flesh and blood, and go forth upon the face of the earth—And now, because he said this, they did put him to death; and many more things did they do which brought down the wrath of God upon them. (Mosiah 7:26–28)

Thus Abinadi was killed because he taught the truth about Christ as the God of the Nephites. The Prophet Joseph Smith was also killed because he taught the same concept of Christ and the Godhead. As members of the Church and true disciples of Jesus Christ, we have the responsibility of taking this great truth to the world. We can do this through the message given in the Book of Mormon.

The theme of this symposium is that salvation comes only through Christ. It is taken from this courageous and great defense of the Lord Jesus Christ by Abinadi. Similar testimony is borne in the book of Mosiah by king Benjamin and others. Their testimonies are just as valid and timely in this day as they were in Abinadi's. Souls are precious in the eyes of the Lord in all ages of the world. We all need to learn that there is no salvation except through Christ, who is the very Eternal Father of our salvation.

BIBLIOGRAPHY

Clark, James R. *Messages of the First Presidency*. 6 vols. Salt Lake City: Bookcraft, 1975.

McConkie, Bruce R. *Doctrinal New Testament Commentary*. 3 vols. Salt Lake City: Bookcraft, 1965.

Nyman, Monte S. *"Great are the Words of Isaiah."* Salt Lake City: Bookcraft, 1980.

Talmage, James E. *The Articles of Faith.* Salt Lake City: The Church of Jesus Christ of Latter-day Saints, 1984.

Teachings of the Prophet Joseph Smith. Comp. Joseph Fielding Smith. Salt Lake City: Deseret Book, 1976.

APPENDIX A

TABLE A-1 *Abinadi's Commentary on Isaiah*

Abinadi's Thesis: Mosiah 13:33–35		
Abinadi speaks in . . .	Commenting on . . .	Other Commentary
Mosiah 14:33–34 15:1	Isa 53:1 (Mosiah 14:1)	Rom 10:16; John 12:37–38
15:2	53:2a (14:2)	Luke 2:40–50
15:3	53:2b (14:2)	Rev 22:16; Matt 13:55–56; John 6:42
15:4	53:2 (14:2)	
15:5	53:3–5	3 Nephi 27:27; Mosiah 3:19; Matt 8:16–17; Heb 4:15; 1 Peter 2:24; Mark 8:31
15:9	53:6	Alma 34:15–16; chapter 42
15:6	53:7	
15:7–8	53:8	1 Cor 15:54–55; Mosiah 5:7
15:11–13	53:10b	
15:14–27	52:7	1 Peter 3:18–20; 4:5–6; D&C 137:7–10
15:28–16:1	52:8–10	
16:2–12	Lost Scripture?	
16:13–15	Conclusion	

APPENDIX B

Isaiah 53:9

> And he made his grave with the wicked, and with the rich in his death; because he had done no violence, neither was any deceit in his mouth. (Compare Mosiah 14:9)

Abinadi does not comment on this verse from Isaiah. Did the priests understand it? Jesus was crucified between two thieves (Matt 27:38; Mark 15:27; Luke 23:32–33; John 19:18). He was buried in the tomb of a rich man, Joseph of Arimathaea (Matt 27:57–60; Mark 15:42–46; Luke 23:50–53; John 19:38–42). Isaiah's announcement that he had done "no *evil* " (Mosiah 14:9; emphasis added) is the only word change between the text of the King James Bible and the Book of Mormon. (A capitalization difference will be discussed later.) The KJV records, "He had done no violence." "No evil" is consistent with Abinadi's earlier declaration that he yielded not to temptation (Mosiah 15:5). No "deceit in his mouth" proclaims that he spoke truth at all times. Peter varies slightly the same Isaiah passage: "Neither was *guile* found in his mouth" (1 Peter 2:23; emphasis added). The message is clear, there was no reason or basis that justified his crucifixion. However, his death was not only foreknown but was foreordained (1 Peter 1:20; Ether 3:14). Isaiah understood this clearly.

Isaiah 53:10

> Yet it pleased the Lord to bruise him; he hath put him to grief: when thou shalt make his soul an offering for sin, he shall see his seed, he shall prolong his days, and the pleasure of the Lord shall prosper in his hand. (Compare Mosiah 14:10)

The wording of the opening phrase of this verse may have two meanings depending on the interpretation of the word *Lord*, as capitalized in the Book of Mormon text. In the King James text, the word is all in capital letters, LORD. Some would interpret this to mean Jehovah, and others would interpret it to refer to Elohim. Since there are no original manuscripts, the correct interpretation can only be determined by the context. Through the years, scribes have altered the word for God back and forth to fit their own understanding.[2] If the person referred to as Lord is Elohim, then the phrase would read that it pleased Elohim to bruise Christ or allow him to suffer affliction and grief as a part of the Atonement. This interpretation was nicely summarized by John in his Gospel: "For God so loved the world, that he gave his only begotten Son, that whosoever believeth in him should not perish, but have everlasting life" (John 3:16).

If the word *Lord* is interpreted to refer to Jehovah, then it would read that it pleased Jehovah to bruise Christ. Since Jehovah is the Old Testament name for Christ, this may sound like an impossible interpretation. However, it could be interpreted to say that Christ was willing to suffer to bring about the Atonement. This interpretation is sustained in modern revelation. In a revelation to Orson Pratt, Jesus Christ identified himself as he "who so loved the world that he gave his own life, that as many as would believe might become the sons of God" (D&C 34:1–3). Perhaps both interpretations are valid. Certainly Elohim was the author of the plan of salvation that provided for a Savior (Abr 3:27–28; Moses 4:1–2), and, as revealed to Orson Pratt, Christ did make a free-will offering.

The offering of Christ's soul for sin was done in the Garden of Gethsemane. There he suffered as a God "temptations, and pain of body, hunger, thirst and fatigue, even more than man can suffer, except it be unto death; for behold, blood cometh from every pore, so great shall be his anguish for the wickedness and the abominations of his people" (Mosiah 3:7; see also 2 Nephi 9:20–21; Alma 7:11; and Luke 22:44). As he

---

[2] Illustrations of the variant use of the word *God* may be seen in a comparison of the almost identical Psalms 14 and 53, or in Psalm 110 and Matthew's quotation of it in Matthew 22:44. It seems apparent that scribes have pondered and altered these quotations to fit their private interpretations of the text.

paid this all-encompassing price for sin, he apparently had a panoramic view of all the world's experiences, past, present, and future, and, in some way beyond our comprehension, he placed himself in the position of every inhabitant of the earth, that he might satisfy the demands of justice for the punishment of every broken law of humankind. He was able to prolong his days, at least in a figurative sense, that he might pass through this agonizing ordeal for the entire period of the earth's habitation by mortal beings, from Adam to the final scene. With the payment of this eternal debt, the pleasure (will) of the Lord (Jehovah or Christ) and LORD (Elohim) was fulfilled, and Christ prospered by fulfilling the mission of his atonement. With the sacrifice of his soul and the end of his mortal life, Christ's seed became responsible for prolonging his days in another way, that of carrying on his mission. His seed, as stated above, are the prophets and teachers of the gospel and all who accept the gospel message (Mosiah 15:10–13).

Isaiah 53:11

Isaiah's prophecy continues:

> He shall see of the travail of his soul, and shall be satisfied: by his knowledge shall my righteous servant justify many; for he shall bear their iniquities. (Compare Mosiah 14:11)

An understanding of verse 11 comes by substituting nouns for the pronouns. From the context of the verse, it is clear that Elohim shall see the travail of Jesus Christ's soul and shall be satisfied. Jesus suffered in Gethsemane and had "taken upon himself [the people's] iniquity and their transgressions, having redeemed them, and satisfied the demands of justice" (Mosiah 15:9). Jesus' knowledge of the sins of all humankind (2 Nephi 9:20) and his sinlessness—a "a righteous servant"—enabled him to make an eternal sacrifice. Many people will thus be able to justify themselves and obtain salvation because Jesus paid for their sins. Some have interpreted the servant's justifying of "many" as evidence that Jesus, in his foreknowledge, only

suffered for those who he knew would repent. This interpretation is not consistent with Jacob's declaration that Jesus
"suffereth the pains of all men, yea, the pains of every living
creature, both men, women, and children, who belong to the
family of Adam" (2 Nephi 9:21); or with Jacob and Amulek's
pronouncement that the Atonement must be an infinite atonement (2 Nephi 9:7), or an infinite and eternal sacrifice (Alma
34:10). Samuel the Lamanite taught that the Atonement
brought *all* humankind back into the presence of God (Hel
14:17). However, Jacob taught that only those who repent, are
baptized, and have perfect faith in the Holy One of Israel will
be saved—and if not they will be damned (2 Nephi 9:23–24).
Therefore, although Jesus paid for the sins of all humankind,
not all will meet the criteria for obtaining those blessings in
their lives (D&C 19:16–19). Those who do meet the criteria
will be part of the fulfillment of Isaiah's further prophecy,
which follows.

Isaiah 53:12

> Therefore will I divide him a portion with the great, and he shall
> divide the spoil with the strong; because he hath poured out his soul
> unto death: and he was numbered with the transgressors; and he bare
> the sin of many, and made intercession for the transgressors. (Com-
> pare Mosiah 14:12)

The context shows that Elohim, or the Father, is still
speaking in this verse. Because Jesus had fulfilled his role
as the Redeemer of humankind, he "ascended into heaven"
(Mosiah 15:9) and took his position on the right hand of the
Father in the council of the Gods (D&C 20:24). In turn, Jesus
was willing to divide his blessings, or spoils—a term referring
to what was obtained after winning a battle—with those who
accept and remain strong in the gospel. He taught this principle
to his disciples at the end of his ministry:

> Ye are they which have continued with me in my temptations. And
> I appoint unto you a kingdom, as my Father hath appointed unto me;
> That ye may eat and drink at my table in my kingdom, and sit on
> thrones judging the twelve tribes of Israel. (Luke 22:28–30)

Jesus was able to do this because he had poured out his soul unto death, or had freely given his life that "I might take it again. No man taketh it from me, but I lay it down of myself" (John 10:17–18). In accomplishing this momentous task he was numbered with the transgressors, or suffered the most degrading of deaths at that time (McConkie 1:814–16). Prior to his death he had gone to Gethsemane and there, as Isaiah foretold, bore the sins of those who repented and also paid for those who ignorantly sinned. As explained earlier, Christ paid for the sins of all humankind, both the repentant and unrepentant, but the context of Isaiah describes only those who benefitted from the Atonement by repenting of their sins. Having completed his prophecy of Christ's suffering, Isaiah returned to prophesy of the gathering of Israel (Isa 54), the subject he had left to insert this inspiring and now well-known prophecy of Christ's mission.

Priesthood in Mosiah 11

Daniel C. Peterson

It has been correctly observed that the Book of Mormon is probably the earliest published Mormon scriptural text to discuss the structure and the nature of the priesthood. Therefore, an understanding of just what the book has to say about the priesthood is important. In this paper I intend to examine priesthood authority in the Book of Mormon in general and in the book of Mosiah specifically. I will trace the changes in the responsibility of delegating and regulating the priesthood from the familial priesthood organization during Lehi's time to the ecclesiastical priesthood organization during the time of Alma the Younger.

Familial Priesthood Organization

Our sample is perhaps too small to allow definitive judgments about how priests and priesthood are viewed in the small plates of Nephi, but it appears that the attitude of the authors of the small plates may not have been entirely positive. For example, Jacob predicts that "priestcrafts and iniquities . . . at Jerusalem" will lead to the crucifixion of the Savior (2 Nephi 10:5). Nephi defines "priestcraft" as "that men preach and set themselves up for a light unto the world, that they may get gain and praise of the world; but they seek not the welfare of Zion" and states that the Lord condemns it (2 Nephi 26:29). He also says that the latter days will be characterized by contentions

Daniel C. Peterson is assistant professor of Asian and Near Eastern Languages at Brigham Young University.

between "priests" who will "teach with their learning, and deny the Holy Ghost, which giveth utterance" (2 Nephi 28:4). Nephite prophets share these negative feelings with other prophets such as Jeremiah (Jer 1:18; 2:8, 26; 4:9; 5:30–31; 6:13; 13:13; 23:11, 33–34; 32:32; Lam 2:6; 4:13), Isaiah (Isa 24:1–6; 28:7), and Nehemiah (Neh 9:33–34). One needs to think only of Hophni and Phinehas in 1 Samuel 2–4, or of the parable of the Good Samaritan related in Luke 10, to realize how widespread the notion of the evil priest is in the scriptures.

This negative view may reflect the unpleasant experience which Lehi and his family had with the political and ecclesiastical authorities in Jerusalem. Certainly that experience would have been a frequent topic of conversation and teaching among Lehi's believing children. More likely, since Jacob had seen Jerusalem only in vision (1 Nephi 18:7; 2 Nephi 6:8–10) and since Nephi prophesied of the evils concerning priestcraft in the latter days (2 Nephi 25:7; 26:14; 28:1, 3), the unfavorable view of priestcraft was actually the Lord's, reflecting his evaluation of the corruption wrought among his people in the Old World. Nevertheless, whatever may have been the attitude of the early Nephites toward the potential abuses of priesthood authority, it is clear that their earliest records contain very little positive material—indeed, very little material of any kind—on priests and priesthood.

It is equally clear, however, that the Nephite prophets did not reject the idea of priesthood as such. I suggest that early Nephite priesthood was mediated and given structure through family and clan organization, rather than through an as yet unfounded church. Nephi himself, for example, ordained his brothers Jacob and Joseph "after the manner of [God's] holy order" (2 Nephi 6:2; compare 2 Nephi 5:26; Jacob 1:18; Alma 13:1–2, 6, 8; D&C 107:2–4). Alma 6:1 and Moroni 3 make it clear that, at least in Nephite history following the close of the book of Mosiah, priests and teachers were both clearly ordained in a manner not unlike that practiced by Latter-day Saints today. Indeed, it can be argued on the basis of Moroni

2:1 that Moroni 3 represents the instructions given by the resurrected Lord during his visit to the Nephites at the beginning of the dispensation of the meridian of times. If this is true, it is very clear that the practice of ordaining by the laying on of hands was carried across dispensations, both before and after the advent of Christ.

Governmental Priesthood Organization

By ordaining priests, Nephi functioned as a kind of king among his people—which was precisely how they viewed him (2 Nephi 5:18–19; 6:2). Indeed, while it lasted, legitimate Nephite kingship remained within the line of Nephi. For example, Mosiah's kingship was the primary kingship, and the kingship of Zeniff was derivative and subordinate. It is interesting to note that Mosiah II ruled a people who were mostly natives of Zarahemla and descendants of a colony established by Mulek; Mulek's royal prerogatives (Hel 6:10; 8:21) had been swallowed up in those of the line of Nephi (Mosiah 25:2, 13). We do not know why or how this occurred, but then we know very little about the Mulekites at all. I suspect that the explanation for this is to be found in John Sorenson's notion of the Book of Mormon as "lineage history" (50–56).

Priestly ordination is primarily a royal prerogative in the book of Mosiah as well, although Mormon documents a dramatic shift on this very issue toward the end of the book. This point must be clearly understood. I do not mean to say that Nephite kings somehow had the right to ordain simply because they held political rule; instead, I wish to suggest that kingship among the Nephites was a priesthood calling. A survey of the evidence from the book of Mosiah and elsewhere in the Book of Mormon should serve to make this suggestion plausible, if not to prove it. Indeed, at least several of the Nephite kings— Nephi (a quasi-king; 2 Nephi 6:2), Mosiah I (Omni 1:12–22), Benjamin, and Mosiah II—were also major prophets. King Benjamin appointed priests at Zarahemla (Mosiah 6:3). In the secondary Nephite kingdom which endured briefly in the land of Nephi, Zeniff exercised his right as ruler and ordained priests. These priests were then dismissed by his son and successor, Noah. In their place, Noah ordained his own priests, who were presumably more supportive of his lifestyle and more pliable in his hands (Mosiah 11:5). When Noah's priests were exiled by the Nephites and given refuge by the Lamanites, it is noteworthy that the king of the Lamanites appointed them to be teachers among his people (Mosiah 24:4–5). We must remember that Amulon and the other priests do not appear to have exercised priestly functions under the Lamanites. They were never really influenced by their religious offices, and so their teaching among the Lamanites—Nephite language, record-keeping, and a literacy program—was entirely secular. But the Amulonites' characteristically secularized view of their own offices should not blind us to their sacerdotal origins, any more than Noah's abuse of his rank should blind us to its priestly nature.

This notion of a priestly kingship is perhaps a bit jarring to modern readers, living in a society where church and state are kept separate as a matter of principle. But it should not be so disturbing to Latter-day Saints, whose aspirations for the life to come include becoming both "priests and kings" (D&C 76:56). This eschatological ideal may partially explain why the priest-king has been so frequently an earthly ideal as well. Furthermore, it seems that Christ, the true king of Israel, holds his kingship as a priesthood office. The Nephites were not modern, and we should not be surprised to see them untouched by more recent institutions. Kingship in the Book of Mormon is very much a religious affair, much as it had been (or had been intended to be) among the Israelites of the Old World (see Tvedtnes 19, n. 23). Following his famous speech, for example, Benjamin "consecrated" his son Mosiah as his successor (Mosiah 6:3) just as he had been "consecrated" by his own father (Mosiah 2:11). King Benjamin thought of kingly service to his people as precisely equivalent to service to God (Mosiah

2:16–17). Even Amlici's followers "consecrated" him king (Alma 2:9). That very same verb is used for the ordination of priests in the Book of Mormon (2 Nephi 5:26; 6:2; Jacob 1:18; Mosiah 11:5; 23:17; Alma 4:4, 7; 5:3; 15:13; 23:4). Noah Webster's 1828 *American Dictionary*, a marvelous resource for understanding the language Joseph Smith used to translate the Nephite record, defines consecration as "the act or ceremony of separating from a common to a sacred use, or of devoting and dedicating a person or thing to the service and worship of God, by certain rites or solemnities." As examples, Webster cites "the consecration of the priests among the Israelites" (see Ex 29:9) and "the consecration of a bishop."

Indeed, Mosiah, the son of Benjamin, was not merely a secular ruler but also a seer, which the Book of Mormon informs us is a more exalted title than the title of prophet (Mosiah 8:13–18; 21:28; 28:16). Seership was connected with possession of certain objects, known as "interpreters" (Mosiah 8:13). Nephite kingship was also connected with and was even symbolized or legitimized by possession of certain material objects.[1] Thus, Nephi took the brass plates with him when he abandoned the land of Nephi, perhaps in part as a token of his legitimacy. The Lamanites shared his perception of the importance of the plates; they claimed that by taking them Nephi had "robbed them," just as "they said that he had taken the ruling of the people out of their hands" (Mosiah 10:15–16; compare 2 Nephi 5:3; Alma 20:10, 13). When Benjamin transferred the kingdom to his son Mosiah, he gave Mosiah the brass plates, as well as the plates of Nephi, the sword of Laban, and the Liahona (Mosiah 1:15–16; see also 2 Nephi 5:14; Jacob 1:10;

---

[1] In the medieval Near East, the Shi'ite imams likewise preserved certain objects as emblems of their legitimacy. Ja'far al-Sadiq (d. AD 767), for example, who was the sixth imam, received not only the explicit designation, or *nass*, of his father, Muhammad al-Baqir, but, according to common report, the weapons, the book, and the scrolls of the Prophet Muhammad. These were not only valuable in their own right, but apparently were thought to contain the esoteric knowledge given by Gabriel to the Prophet, and then passed down the line of imams as their special birthright. Al-Muqtadir, one of the last 'Abbāsid caliphs to hold real political power, used the Prophet's staff and cloak as both symbols and proofs of his authority. (See, for the two cases respectively, Jafri 293 and Mottahedeh 186.)

WofM 1:13). Similarly, the sword of Goliath was preserved as a trophy for the Israelites (1 Sam 21:9; 22:10). There is undoubtedly more to the royal possession of such items than simply a claim to legitimate sovereignty. God stipulates that the Israelite king should keep a copy of the law with him at all times so he might always keep the commandments in mind (Deut 17:18–20). It should be clear that the Nephite monarch too was more than merely the supreme secular official in a secular government.

The priestly nature of Nephite kingship is evident in certain other ways as well. According to Benjamin, God appointed kings (Mosiah 2:4). However, it appears that there are several possible methods by which kings were appointed. Many believed that Nephi was chosen by God to lead his people (Mosiah 10:13). From king Benjamin's proclamation of Mosiah II as king, we see that lineage seems to have been important (Mosiah 1:10); however, there is no clear evidence that the Nephites strictly followed a rule of primogeniture (Mosiah 27:34; 28:10; 29:2–3, 6). Also, as another possibility, the people of Zarahemla conferred the kingdom upon Benjamin (Mosiah 2:11) in a kind of common consent, where the Lord reveals his choice of a king and then asks the people through his appointed servant to sustain that revelation (D&C 20:63–67; 26:2). He was "chosen by th[e] people, and consecrated by [his] father, and was suffered by the hand of the Lord that [he] should be a ruler and a king over th[e] people" (Mosiah 2:11).

Regardless of the method that God used to choose him, the king represented God on the earth, and his actions, when he was righteous and inspired, were God's actions. Joseph F. Smith defines the priesthood as "the authority given to man to act for God" (136; see also 139). Therefore, it is not inconsistent for the book of Mosiah, which repeatedly speaks of kings ordaining priests and teachers, to speak also of God as the appointer of teachers (Mosiah 2:4). Likewise, an inspired king can be said to speak for and on behalf of God, and the distinction between them means very little in this respect (Mosiah 2:31; compare D&C 1:38; 68:4). God and the king are correlatives, mirroring each other in their respective spheres (Mosiah 2:19)—God rules the universe, while the king rules subordinately over a limited portion of God's universe.[2]

The society in which the Nephite kings ruled was a temple-centered one. The king made important announcements at the temple (Mosiah 1:18; 2:5–6) both in the society at Zarahemla and in Zeniff's derivative society in the land of Nephi (Mosiah 7:17). When Jesus Christ appeared to the Nephites, he came to them at the temple in the land of Bountiful (3 Nephi 11:1–10). Even king Noah lavished money upon his temple in which his chosen priests served (Mosiah 11:10–11). The role of Nephite priests was to teach; specifically, they taught, or at least claimed to teach, the law of Moses (Mosiah 12:25, 28; 18:18; 23:17; 25:21). Abinadi attacks the priests of Noah for not having taught it well (Mosiah 13:25–26), but he does not say that they should not have taught it at all. They claimed that salvation came through the law of Moses—a proposition which Abinadi condemns as false and apostate (contrast Mosiah 12:32 with 13:28, 32). Instead, both king Benjamin and the prophet Abinadi insist that the law of Moses had been given because the Israelites had been "stiffnecked" and resistant to a higher law, and that its chief purpose was to point forward to the coming of Christ (Mosiah 3:14–15; 13:29–31; compare 2 Nephi 11:4; 25:24–30; Jacob 4:5; Alma 25:15; 34:14).

It seems striking that priests in Mosiah specifically, and in the Book of Mormon generally, only seem to teach and to preside (Mosiah 25:20). The book of Mosiah repeatedly mentions "priests and teachers." Could this be related to Joseph Smith's use of the word *priest* for the preachers of his own day?

---

[2] This idea is very common in hierarchical systems. It may be observed, for example, in the writings of Pseudo-Dionysius (ca. AD 500) among Christian thinkers, and in those of Isma'ili Shi'ism among the Muslims. Similarly, it is hardly coincidence that the various presidencies and bishoprics of The Church of Jesus Christ of Latter-day Saints seem to reflect the Godhead itself.

Webster's 1828 dictionary notes that "in the United States, the word [*priest*] denotes any licensed minister of the gospel." This is, in fact, much the way that Joseph Smith used the term. For example, the draft of his Joseph Smith-History speaks of "several learned Priests" who visited him in order to dispute his theological claims, which, in this context, would certainly refer to Protestant preachers rather than Catholic or Orthodox priests (Jessee 1:238; compare 1:298). The same usage is apparent in his account of the religious disputes which preceded his first vision (JS-H 1:6).

In other words, were the priests of Mosiah real priests, in the same sense as those of Levitical lineage in the Hebrew Bible? Surely, if they were really teachers of the law of Moses, we should see some evidence not merely that its moral precepts were discussed, but also that its sacrificial system was conveyed and put into practice. And we do. The temple was the spiritual (and perhaps literal) center of Nephite society, and we have some evidence for Mosaic sacrifice in the book of Mosiah (Mosiah 2:3–4; compare 1 Nephi 5:9; Alma 34:13–14). Furthermore, a careful reading of Mosiah 1–6 offers plausible evidence that the Nephites on at least this occasion celebrated a full-fledged Mosaic Feast of Tabernacles (see Tvedtnes, "A Nephite Feast of Tabernacles"; Welch, "King Benjamin's Speech in the Context of Ancient Israelite Festivals").

Incidentally Mosiah 1–6 also offers an interesting interpretive possibility: If king Benjamin's address coincided with a Nephite Feast of Tabernacles, then the solemn and moving celebration of the Day of Atonement would have preceded it by only a few days. Thus, when the people cried out for application of "the atoning blood of Christ" (Mosiah 4:2), it is not difficult to imagine that cry as an echo of this deeply religious season, as well as of the sacrifices characteristic of the feast in which they were at that very time engaged.

The Nephites were a pre-Christian people who understood the gospel of Jesus Christ. Their king had just proclaimed an angelically delivered message about "the atoning blood of

Christ" (Mosiah 3:18). The people understood the real significance of the ordinances and rituals laid down in the Mosaic law, which were intended to point forward to Christ (2 Nephi 11:4; 25:23–26; Jacob 4:5; Jarom 1:11; Mosiah 3:14–15; Alma 25:15–16). Their minds were thus directed to the coming of the Savior in a singularly powerful way by the rites of the Day of Atonement and the Feast of Tabernacles. "Significantly," John Tvedtnes observes, "[the] law prescribes more sacrifices for *Sukkot* [Tabernacles] than for any of the other festivals" (10). The Book of Mormon attests that before the coming of Christ the Nephites practiced the Mosaic law (2 Nephi 5:10; 25:24), and therefore the priests of the Book of Mormon were really priests and not merely a nineteenth-century farm boy's retrojection of the circuit-riding revivalist preachers of his own day into his pseudo-Biblical historical yarn.

If priests are present in Nephite society, why is the law of Moses so much less prominent in the Book of Mormon than it is in the Hebrew Bible? First of all, as Kent P. Jackson has observed, the law is really not so prominent in the Old Testament (outside of a few priestly writings) as one might think. The apostle Paul clearly talks more about it than do Lehi's contemporaries in Jerusalem, at least as they are represented in the prophetic books of the Bible. A further explanation is that Mormon edited much of the book and wrote several centuries after the coming of the Messiah had put an end to the sacrificial law. In the small plates which Mormon did not edit, there is almost no mention of priests or priesthood, a fact to which I have already alluded. Perhaps most importantly, the Book of Mormon is the record of a people who understood the subordinate and provisional role of the law of Moses, and who had among them the higher or Melchizedek priesthood (Smith, Joseph Fielding, 1:125–26).

The priests and teachers referred to throughout the Book of Mormon were often two distinct groups, even though the book often attributes teaching functions to its priests. The terms *priests* and *teachers* are mentioned in close proximity of one another twenty-two times in the Book of Mormon, and in every instance except one "teachers" are mentioned after "priests," suggesting that they might represent a subordinate priesthood office among the Nephites as they do in the Church today.[3] It is clear also from Moroni 3 that the offices were distinct, at least in later Nephite practice. This seems to be confirmed by the incident depicted in Mosiah 26:7, where the teachers are subordinate to the priests in a hierarchy consisting of teachers, priests, and Alma the Elder as "high priest." For example, Jarom knew a hierarchy of "the prophets, and the priests, and the teachers" (1:11). Alma also took the place of the king, who seems to have presided over the priests among the earlier Nephites.

According to Mosiah 11:11, even king Noah had "high priests." It may be that we are here referring to an office analogous to that of high priest in the contemporary Church (that is, a priest of the higher priesthood, as opposed to a priest of the Aaronic order), which many are able to hold simultaneously. In its many other occurrences in the Book of Mormon, the term *high priest* seems to resemble the high priest in ancient Israel, of whom there was normally only one at a time. Alma I, for instance, was the high priest over the Church, both when he and his people were in exile (Mosiah 23:16) and after they arrived in Zarahemla and experienced the subsequent expansion of the Church (Mosiah 26:7). In later periods, possibly owing to the sheer size of the Church and to difficulties of communication and centralization, regional high priests seem to have been established in Jershon and in Gideon (Alma 30:20–21), and very likely elsewhere—perhaps subordinated to the overall high priest, in this case Alma II, a resident in the capital city of Zarahemla (Alma 30:29; compare 46:6, 38;

---

[3] See 2 Nephi 5:26; Jacob 1:18; Jarom 1:11; Mosiah 23:17; 25:19, 21; 26:7; 27:5; Alma 1:3; 14:27; 15:13; 23:4; 30:31; 35:5; 45:22–23; Helaman 3:25 ("high priests" and "teachers"); Moroni 3:1, 3–4; 6:1. Only in Alma 4:7 do we find "teachers, and priests, and elders" (compare Alma 6:1 for "priests and elders"), where it is clear that the offices are simply being mentioned in reverse or ascending order.

Hel 3:25; 3 Nephi 6:21–22, 27). King Noah's employment of multiple high priests in the same location may simply have been another of his apostate and grandiloquent innovations, which tended everywhere to exchange Nephite simplicity for the lavish and the overdone.

Nephite priests served as a kind of council to which the king could go for advice. Mosiah II consulted with his priests (Mosiah 27:1), as did the king of the Anti-Nephi-Lehies (Alma 23:16). Whether the latter was carrying on Lamanite practice or simply adopting Nephite habits as he had adopted Nephite religion is unclear (Sorenson 50–56). King Noah also consulted with his priests at his own imitative court in the land of Nephi (Mosiah 12:17). It is in fact the priests of Noah who advised the king to put their former colleague Alma to death for abandoning their unrighteous ways (Mosiah 17:11–12).

The case of Alma brings up at least two interesting questions: (1) Were the priests of Noah legitimate holders of legitimate priesthood, and (2) Where did Alma get his authority? We have to assume Alma and his one-time colleagues were ordained validly by Noah (Mosiah 11:5), who was also ordained validly by his father, Zeniff. The fact that Noah was not righteous after he was ordained and that Alma himself was part of Noah's priestly group during his early ministry has nothing to do with Alma's priesthood authority. Until superior priesthood authority withdraws permission to exercise priestly functions, a legitimately ordained holder of the priesthood continues to hold valid priesthood—however unrighteous he may be, however dead to spiritual promptings, and however unlikely it may be that he will ever actually exercise his priesthood.[4]

---

[4] The ancient Christian church faced this problem in the form of the Donatist schism, which was finally declared heretical in AD 405. The Donatists held that unrighteousness in a bishop or priest invalidated any and all ordinances that he might have performed. However, the Synod of Aries determined in AD 314. that the validity of baptisms and ordinations and the like did not depend upon the worthiness or merit of the officiator. (On the Donatists, and the related Novatianist and Meletian movements, see Christie-Murray 96–97.) Granted, the

Alma, in fact, claimed to have authority from God (Mosiah 18:13), a claim which Mormon implicitly acknowledges as valid (Mosiah 18:18). Alma was a descendant of Nephi (Mosiah 17:2), a fact which may or may not be significant in discussing his priesthood authority since we do not know precisely how the priesthood functioned or was apportioned among the Nephites. Certainly most, if not in fact all, of the priests and kings of whom we know anything in the Book of Mormon up to this point were of the lineage of Nephi. Furthermore, in the power vacuum left by the absence of king Noah, the people implored Alma to assume the royal title and prerogatives (Mosiah 23:6). He turned down the title, but out of necessity, he did carry out some kingly duties. Alma ordained priests and teachers for his outcast people, among whom he was in fact the sole human source of authority (Mosiah 18:18; 23:17).

The situation involving Alma, Noah, and Abinadi also illustrates that if the king fails to exercise his responsibility, someone else may be called to assume his role. At the Lord's command, Abinadi speaks for him as the king was supposed to do (Mosiah 11:20; 12:1–2; 13:6). Because both the king and the priests failed to discharge their responsibilities, the Lord sent Abinadi to chastise them: "Have ye taught this people that they should observe to do all these things for to keep these commandments? I say unto you, Nay; for if ye had, the Lord would not have caused me to come forth and to prophesy evil concerning this people" (Mosiah 13:25–26; compare 12:29).

It is not surprising that king Noah, who does not acknowledge his own neglect of his divinely-ordained stewardship,

Christian church at this period was essentially apostate, but Latter-day Saints take basically the same position, and for good reason. If serious sin, as such, invalidated priesthood ordinances, we could never know whose marriage was legal, or who was really a member of the Church. Did the man who ordained you to the priesthood have a secret, unrepented sin? If he did, your ordination is invalid. Your mission was illegitimate, any converts you baptized are actually non-members, and you are living in adultery since you should never have been admitted to the temple. Any of your converts who served missions and baptized are similarly fraudulent, and the consequences ripple onward and outward in utterly unforeseeable ways. How could we ever be sure of anything?

demands to know, "Who is Abinadi?" Who is this unautho-
rized person trespassing upon my royal prerogatives, who has
the effrontery to declare "that I and my people should be judged
of him?" But when king Noah follows the first question with
the arrogant "Who is the Lord?" it becomes painfully clear why
the Lord sent Abinadi (Mosiah 11:27).[5] Noah broke his covenant with God, the ultimate source of his authority. Rather than
recognizing himself as the earthly analogue of the heavenly king,
he seeks to deny the authority of that heavenly king.[6] Thus,
when God sends Abinadi to Noah, he tells the prophet of the
king's impending death by fire, "For he shall know that I am
the Lord" (Mosiah 12:3).

Ecclesiastical Priesthood Organization

Noah's breach of the normal order of things in Nephite
kingship greatly affected Nephite history. First, it helped trans-
form his one-time priest, Alma, into an ardent anti-monarchist.
Drawing upon divine revelation as well as upon his own
experiences with Noah, Alma declared:

> Behold, it is not expedient that we should have a king; for thus saith
> the Lord: Ye shall not esteem one flesh above another, or one man
> shall not think himself above another; therefore I say unto you it is
> not expedient that ye should have a king. Nevertheless, if it were
> possible that ye could always have just men to be your kings it would
> be well for you to have a king. But remember the iniquity of king
> Noah and his priests. . . . Trust no man to be a king over you. (Mosiah
> 23:7–9, 13)

Later, in Zarahemla, Alma emphasized equality within the
Church, insisting that priests and teachers should labor for their
own support rather than relying upon the surplus of others

---

[5] Precisely the same question had been asked of Moses and Aaron by Pharaoh (Ex
5:2; compare Qur'an 26:23–29), and, rhetorically, by Cain (Moses 5:16). Compare too the
Rab-shakeh's speech at 2 Kgs 18:35.

[6] Compare the Pharaoh of Qur'an 26:29: Having arrogantly asked Moses and Aaron
just who the Lord is, he says (as I translate the Arabic), "If you take a god other than me, I
will have you imprisoned!"

(Mosiah 27:4–5), a clear contrast to the practice of king Noah's priests (Mosiah 11:6, 14).

Another consequence of Noah's iniquity was the establishment of a Nephite church. It is striking that the small plates of Nephi do not record a single reference to any church actually existing in the New World, while such references are quite common in and after the book of Mosiah. The small plates refer to only one actually existent church at Jerusalem with which Laban was thought to be affiliated (1 Nephi 4:26). Laban's link with that church is perhaps almost enough in itself to account for the strange neglect of the term throughout the small plates—a neglect broken only by occasional references, the majority of which are negative. Again, it is striking that no mention occurs of an actually existent New World church, despite the fact that the small plates cover nearly the first five centuries of Nephite history.

Alma founded the Church among the Nephites (Mosiah 23:16) in the sense of a separately existing organization within the larger society. It is easy to see why he did so. King Noah had rejected his part in the hierarchical social system of the Nephites, and Alma had taken his place as the spiritual leader and the earthly source of priesthood authority for those who dissented from Noah's leadership. Alma's colony thus became a secessionist group. Birth as a Nephite was no longer enough to make a man or woman one of God's people;[7] instead, a conscious and personal decision was required of anyone who wished to be numbered among the people of God.

For Alma and his followers, this decision was expressed in baptism. Alma cried out to his people:

> Now I say unto you, if this be the desire of your hearts, what have you against being baptized in the name of the Lord, as a witness before him that ye have entered into a covenant with him, that ye will

---

[7] The Qumran community of the shore of the Dead Sea existed almost simultaneously with Alma's Nephite community. Like Alma's group, they were secessionists, and birth no longer assured one place in the group. For the dating of the Qumran Essenes, see Koester 234–39.

serve him and keep his commandments, that he may pour out his Spirit more abundantly upon you? . . . And they were called the church of God, or the church of Christ, from that time forward. And it came to pass that whosoever was baptized by the power and authority of God was added to his church. (Mosiah 18:10, 17; compare 18:13–16; 25:17–18)

Even Alma was immersed as a sign of his commitment to the Lord (Mosiah 18:14).[8]

In another part of the country, king Limhi and his people also desired baptism as an expression of their commitment to do the will of God, but "they did not at that time form themselves into a church" because "there was none in the land that had authority from God" (see Mosiah 21:33–34). Alma had already fled, as had the wicked priests of Noah. Noah was dead, and under such circumstances he had obviously not managed to consecrate Limhi his successor according to Nephite practice. Ammon, the warrior from Zarahemla who had led the expedition to find them, evidently had priesthood authority, but felt himself unworthy to exercise it and declined to perform the ordinance of baptism for them (Mosiah 21:33–35). Later, when the groups led by Alma and Limhi were reunited in Zarahemla, Limhi's people were baptized by Alma: "Yea, and as many as he did baptize did belong to the church of God" (Mosiah 25:17–18).

It would be foolish to argue that baptism was unknown among the Nephites before the time of Alma. References to baptism are not uncommon in the small plates. Indeed, Moses 6:52–53, 64 informs us that the ordinance was known to Adam. Although baptism is said to "fulfil all righteousness" (Matt 3:13–15), to open the gate for salvation (2 Nephi 31:17), and to enable us to obtain a remission of sins (Mark 1:4), no text in the small plates describes baptism as an initiatory rite for entrance into a church. It is also important to bear in mind that

---

[8] The Qumran sectaries also emphasized ritual washings, which may be related to Christian baptism. On this, see LaSor, *The Dead Sea Scrolls and the New Testament* 40, 70–71, 134, 149–151; idem, *The Dead Sea Scrolls and the Christian Faith* 78–80, 203–06, 208, 214, 236–39; Bruce 50–51, 118, 128, 133–34, 136, 140, 142, 149, 151.

the Church and the priesthood are not inseparably linked. It is possible for the priesthood to exist without a church, although it is impossible for the true church to exist without priesthood. The Church today is simply the essential but temporary scaffolding which surrounds an eternal structure of family and priesthood. Until we are worthy, the priesthood is mediated through and associated with the Church. Although Nephi makes it clear that baptism is the first step on the path toward eternal life (2 Nephi 31:9, 18), it is not self-evident that baptism has always signified entrance into a church, or that entrance to a church has always been a part of that path.[9]

I propose that before the ordinance of baptism signified membership in the Church the early Nephites found their primary social and religious identification in the very fact that they were Nephites. In the earliest days of the Nephites in the New World, following Nephi required a deliberate commitment which demanded sacrifice from those who made it. Baptism was preached, and, indeed, stressed to these early Nephites as something pleasing to God and as a necessity for salvation in his kingdom—but it would be easy for unbaptized Nephites to think of themselves as members of God's people strictly because of their heritage. Eventually, however, it became apparent that being a Nephite had become merely a matter of lineage, that it involved no deliberate personal commitment to serve the Lord (Jacob 1:13–14; Omni 1:1–2; WofM 1:12–13). It was obvious that the Nephites, as such, were not "the Lord's people." A more precise definition of that phrase, and a marker for who was to be counted among the Lord's people and who was not, became necessary.

In any event, the Church maintained its separate existence in the land of Zarahemla. King Mosiah granted Alma the right to "establish churches throughout all the land of Zarahemla" and authorized him "to ordain priests and teachers over every

---

[9] By saying this I do not mean to imply that eternal life is available without the ordinances of the priesthood or that those ordinances are available or valid in this dispensation apart from The Church of Jesus Christ of Latter-day Saints.

church" (Mosiah 25:19)—a prerogative heretofore pertaining only to kingship. The overall organization was called the "church," but it was made up of subordinate local units also called "churches." There were seven of these local units in Zarahemla alone (Mosiah 25:22–23). Indeed, Mosiah gave Alma authority over the Church (Mosiah 26:8), thus effectively delegating to another man a major portion of the sacral authority which had traditionally been attached to the Nephite throne. Priests of the Church in Zarahemla taught the people as Alma directed them (Mosiah 25:21), he having been directed by God. Thus despite the separation of church and state, the pyramidal hierarchy of heavenly king, earthly king, priests, teachers, and people, so characteristic of earlier Nephite thought and practice, survived under the new order.

It is true that king Mosiah retained a council of priest-advisers even after the establishment of the Church at Zarahemla (Mosiah 27:1). This is not surprising. If the Nephites followed the universal pattern of advanced cultures in the ancient world, their priesthood represented many of their best educated and most astute men and was a natural reservoir of talented advisers for the monarch. There was no reason, even after the establishment of the Church, for king Mosiah to dismiss his council of advisers, regardless of their priestly status. And, indeed, it is noteworthy that the issues upon which they advise him are political matters transcending the Church and extending, in fact, to all subjects of the king, whether they were members of the Church or not (Mosiah 26:38–27:2). The king retained authority and responsibility for dealing with such issues.

Questions of ecclesiastical discipline, however, were now handled within the Church organization itself, without the direct involvement of the monarchy. The establishment of a church within Nephite society, membership in which was both theoretically and practically distinguishable from simple Nephite nationality, led to unprecedented problems. For one thing, some of the younger generation—those who had not experienced the great spiritual outpouring which occurred at the abdication sermon of king Benjamin—refused to be baptized or to join the Church (Mosiah 26:1–5). This fact shows that the Church in Zarahemla was meant for all of the inhabitants of that place, and not merely for the refugees from the land of Nephi. Organization of the Church by Mosiah and Alma represented a major restructuring of Zarahemlan society.[10]

The new generation's worldly influence began to take its toll on those who had already joined the Church, which was itself well into its second generation. These members of the Church began to commit "many sins," which obviously raised the issue of whether and how they were to be disciplined (Mosiah 26:6–8). In a community of intention, as the Church was, one had to ask just how seriously one could sin before it became obvious that the intention to serve God had ceased to exist. And if that intention were gone, could that person any longer be validly considered a member of that community? Such questions would not arise where simple Nephite citizenship made one a member of the people of God without personal decision. Because this was no longer the case, the dilemma of transgresson by Church members deeply affected Alma:

> Now there had not any such thing happened before in the church; therefore Alma was troubled in his spirit, and he caused that they should be brought before the king. And he said unto the king: Behold, here are many whom we have brought before thee, who are accused of their brethren; yea, and they have been taken in divers iniquities. And they do not repent of their iniquities; therefore we have brought them before thee, that thou mayest judge them according to their crimes. (Mosiah 26:10–11)

---

[10] In addition to the problem discussed in the main text, it might be noted that the only references to a historically existent priestcraft in the entire Book of Mormon occur in Alma 1:12, 16, immediately following organization of a separately existing church. As Alma II told Nehor, "Behold, this is the first time that priestcraft has been introduced among this people." 2 Nephi 26:29 defines the offense, saying that "priestcrafts are that men preach and set themselves up for a light unto the world, that they may get gain and praise of the world." Perhaps the reason that it occurred now was that, in contrast to the earlier Nephite system where kings (who, by virtue of their very rank, had no lack of glory or, presumably, of such wealth as was available to Nephites) presided over the priesthood, separation of priesthood from lineage-based leadership now opened up the "ecclesiastical" route to power, glory, and success for people who would otherwise not have had access to it.

Old habits die hard. Alma, who claimed anti-monarchical views, turned to the monarch for assistance in solving a grievous ecclesiastical problem. But he had miscalculated king Mosiah II, for he was probably Alma's greatest convert to the anti-monarchical position. And, at least in this instance, Mosiah was a more consistent partisan of that stance than was the high priest. He refused to become involved in the kind of religious-ecclesiastical issue that he had put onto Alma's shoulders. "Behold," he said, "I judge them not; therefore I deliver them into thy hands to be judged" (Mosiah 26:12).

This was extremely troubling to Alma, who now had no other option but to approach the Lord in prayer for a solution to the pressing problem facing him (Mosiah 26:13). The earthly king, who, in earlier Nephite tradition, had been the fount of religious authority and the last resort for religious questions, had definitively given up such a role. Only the Heavenly King could help him. In answer to Alma's earnest entreaties, the Lord revealed the idea of excommunication, whereby "whosoever will not repent of his sins the same shall not be numbered among my people" (Mosiah 26:32). Put into practice, this idea resulted in "blotting out" the names of a number of former adherents of the gospel. This idea of excommunication was obviously new to Alma, who had grown up under the old ideology where birth as a Nephite "numbered" one among the people of the Lord in a way which could not be "blotted out," and where one's primary ecclesiastical identity was national or genealogical rather than, as we might express it, intentional or voluntary. "And it came to pass that Alma did regulate all the affairs of the church" (Mosiah 26:36–37).

As a result of the changing responsibilities of the Nephite monarch and the fact that none of his sons would accept the kingship, Mosiah proposed the abolition of Nephite monarchy in language strongly reminiscent of Alma's own position:

> If it were possible that you could have just men to be your kings, who would establish the laws of God, and judge this people according to his commandments, yea, if ye could have men for your kings who

would do even as my father Benjamin did for this people—I say unto
you, if this could always be the case then it would be expedient that
ye should always have kings to rule over you. . . . Now I say unto
you, that because all men are not just it is not expedient that ye should
have a king or kings to rule over you. For behold, how much iniquity
doth one wicked king cause to be committed, yea, and what great
destruction! Yea, remember king Noah, his wickedness and his
abominations, and also the wickedness and abominations of his
people. Behold what great destruction did come upon them. (Mosiah
29:13, 16–18)

The example of king Noah is surely a clue that Alma's experiences in the land of Nephi had been deeply influential if
not decisive in forming Mosiah's new position.

Like Alma, Mosiah talks about monarchy from the perspective of human equality. But, although the two men may
superficially seem to be saying much the same thing, there is
a fundamental difference between their two positions. Mosiah
says,

I command you . . . that ye have no king; that if these people commit
sins and iniquities they shall be answered upon their own heads. For
behold I say unto you, the sins of many people have been caused by
the iniquities of their kings; therefore their iniquities are answered
upon the heads of their kings. And now I desire that this inequality
should be no more in this land, especially among this my people. . . .
And many more things did king Mosiah write unto them, unfolding
unto them all the trials and troubles of a righteous king, yea, all the
travails of soul for their people, and also all the murmurings of the
people to their king; and he explained it all unto them. And he told
them that these things ought not to be; but that the burden should
come upon all the people, that every man might bear his part. (Mosiah
29:30–34)

Alma expresses his anti-monarchical sentiments in much
the same terms which we today would employ, with our in-
sistence on human rights and the equality of all humanity
before God and the law. Mosiah, however, comes to the
question from the king's perspective. Mosiah worries about the
undue burden which kingship imposes even on those who con-
scientiously strive to carry out their responsibilities. Having
attempted for more than three decades to discharge his royal

duties well, Mosiah feels that the king is victimized by the inequality inherent in the Nephite monarchical system. He carries not only the responsibility for his own mistakes, but risks responsibility for the mistakes of his subjects if he has in any way, even inadvertently, misled them. Moved by Mosiah's obviously deep feelings, the people agree to his plan to abolish the monarchy: "Therefore they relinquished their desires for a king, and became exceedingly anxious that every man [even those of royal blood] should have an equal chance throughout all the land; yea, and every man expressed a willingness to answer for his own sins" (Mosiah 29:38).

So the relatively secular institution of the judgeship was introduced among and accepted by the Nephites (Mosiah 29:11, 41–42) to complement the religious office of high priest which had already been introduced. In a certain sense, this merely formalized the division of functions that Mosiah and Alma had already worked out some time before. However, the people chose Alma II as their first chief judge, who had previously received the office of high priest from his father, Alma I (Mosiah 29:42). Mosiah II had no willing heirs and gave Alma the plates of brass, the records, and the interpreters, which were sacred relics that once formed an important part of the symbolism of Nephite kingship (Mosiah 28:10, 20). Therefore, the bestowal of the chief judgeship upon Alma may be read as an attempt by the people to recombine the secular and sacred functions of the kingship in one man, who might not bear the title of king, but would nonetheless serve essentially the same role. Kingship, after all, had been a rather popular institution. Nephi's brothers thought that he coveted the title (1 Nephi 16:38), but he later refused it from his people (2 Nephi 5:18). Zeniff was made king by the voice of the people in the land of Nephi (Mosiah 7:9). Alma's people sought to persuade him to accept kingly honors, but he refused (Mosiah 23:6–7). And it was only after Mosiah's passionate appeal to his people that "they relinquished their desires for a king" (Mosiah 29:38). Furthermore, the monarchy continued to fascinate and attract

at least portions of the Nephite population long after its abolition, as is shown by repeated efforts through the years to effect
its restoration. Alma 51–62, for instance, records the struggles
Moroni had with the so-called "king-men," who sought to alter
the laws in order to reestablish a monarchical order. 3 Nephi
6:30 alludes to yet another attempt to put a king on a Nephite
throne, and 3 Nephi 7:9–10 describes a temporarily successful
effort by a Nephite splinter group to return to monarchy.
Obviously, kingship appealed to many people, not only to the
lucky one who would, if successful, gain the throne.

The apparent attempt of the Nephite people to circumvent
their king's rejection of kingship did not succeed. After only
about five years, Alma II gave up his position as chief judge to
concentrate his attention upon the high priesthood as the solution for the urgent problems which faced his people (Alma
4:15–20). Never again would a Nephite king serve as both
religious and temporal leader of his people. The relatively
secular office of the chief judgeship would continue almost to
the end of Nephite civilization, but we have no record of any
chief judge ever ordaining priests. Instead, sacerdotal ordinations were the prerogative of the high priests before the coming
of Christ (see Alma 6:1), and then, after the coming of Christ
and the apparent disappearance of that office, ordinations to
the priesthood were performed by the disciples or "elders of
the church" (Moroni 3:1). The office of high priest is not
mentioned after 3 Nephi 6:21–22, 27, by which time it had
clearly become corrupt. Priesthood functions were essentially
severed from governmental functions, and the two would never
be fully recombined in the sacral kingship with which Nephite
history had begun in the New World. The material objects
which had once pertained to the Nephite monarchy continued
to be passed down, but now along a non-royal line of high
priests and prophets (see Alma 37; 63:1–2, 10–13; 3 Nephi
1:2–3; 4 Nephi 1:47–49; Mormon 1:2–5; 4:23; 8:3–5; Moroni
10:2; JS-H).

This brief glance at the question of priesthood and authority in the book of Mosiah has revealed an intricately complex and remarkably consistent system underlying the many incidental details of its already highly involved narrative. We should be impressed with what the book of Mosiah discloses about the nuanced richness of the Book of Mormon.

BIBLIOGRAPHY

Bruce, F. F. *Second Thoughts on the Dead Sea Scrolls*. 2nd ed. Grand Rapids, MI: Eerdmans, 1961.

Christie-Murray, David. *A History of Heresy*. London: New English, 1976.

Jafri, S. H. M. *Origins and Early Development of the Shi'a Islam*. London: Longman, 1979.

Jessee, Dean C., ed. *The Papers of Joseph Smith*. 1 vol to date. Salt Lake City: Deseret Book, 1989–.

Koester, Helmut. *History, Culture, and Religion of the Hellenistic Age*. Philadelphia: Fortress, 1982.

LaSor, William Sanford. *The Dead Sea Scrolls and Christian Faith*. Chicago: Moody, 1976.

———. *The Dead Sea Scrolls and the New Testament*. Grand Rapids, MI: Eerdmans, 1972.

Mottahedeh, Roy P. *Loyalty and Leadership in an Early Islamic Society*. Princeton: Princeton Univ, 1980.

Smith, Joseph F. *Gospel Doctrine*. 8th ed. Salt Lake City: Deseret Book, 1949.

Smith, Joseph Fielding. *Answers to Gospel Questions*. 5 vols. Salt Lake City: Deseret Book, 1957.

Sorenson, John L. *An Ancient American Setting for the Book of Mormon*. Salt Lake City: Deseret Book, 1985.

Tvedtnes, John A. "A Nephite Feast of Tabernacles." Preliminary Report. TVE-78. Provo: F.A.R.M.S., 1978.

Webster's 1828 American Dictionary. Facsimile. San Francisco: Foundation for American Christian Education, 1967.

Welch, John W. "King Benjamin's Speech in the Context of Ancient Israelite Festivals." Working Paper. WEL-85c. Provo: F.A.R.M.S., 1985.

Church Discipline in the Book of Mosiah

12

H. Donl Peterson

The Church of Jesus Christ of Latter-day Saints is the kingdom of God on earth (D&C 65), presided over by divinely called apostles and prophets. Its thousands of wards and branches are made up of baptized believers who have accepted Jesus Christ as their Savior and Exemplar. Members of the Church are committed to holy principles and ideals and to a oneness in purpose that will lead them to eternal life in the presence of our Heavenly Father. Among the many things the Church provides are the teachings of Christ, a group of supportive and caring friends, and assistance in time of need. Its priesthood representatives administer the holy ordinances necessary for salvation, and its members are entitled to the gifts of the Holy Ghost.

In light of what the Church is and what it provides for its members, it is important to ask how it responds to those members who do not live the commandments of the Lord. How should Church leaders and members respond when fellow members break their sacred commitments? Throughout history religious organizations have addressed the issue of discipline in a multitude of ways, including toleration, recrimination, ostracism, lampooning, physical punishment, financial reprisals, and even death. These are not, however, the Lord's way.

The Book of Mormon provides some excellent insights into the Lord's method of handling transgression among

H. Donl Peterson is professor of Ancient Scripture at Brigham Young University.

Church members. In Mosiah 26 the Lord reveals to the prophet Alma his pattern of discipline, which is still used in the Church today.

The Setting

We read that during the reign of Mosiah II, king Benjamin's son, many of the younger generation "did not believe in the traditions of their fathers. . . . They could not understand the word of God; and their hearts were hardened" (Mosiah 26:1, 3). They did not believe in the resurrection of the dead or the coming of Christ. They would not be baptized into nor would they affiliate with the Church. Lacking the Spirit in their lives and rejecting the teachings and mores of their parents, they were in a "carnal and sinful state" (v 4). Early in Mosiah's reign, these wicked people, who had not been "half so numerous" as the faithful, became more numerous "because of the dissensions among the brethren" (v 5). With flattering words the wicked enticed many Church members to abandon their standards and join with them in their sins.

These errant members of the Church needed to be admonished by their leaders, so they were brought before the priests. The priests, apparently concerned by the magnitude of the problem, brought the unfaithful members before Alma, the high priest, whom Mosiah had authorized to administer all the affairs of the Church. Many witnessed against the sins of the accused members (Mosiah 26:9).

With numerous members involved in various iniquities, Alma was "troubled in his spirit," for "there had not any such thing happened before in the church" (Mosiah 26:10). He brought the matter before king Mosiah and explained: "Behold, here are many whom we have brought before thee, who are accused of their brethren; yea, and they have been taken in divers iniquities. And they do not repent of their iniquities; therefore we have brought them before thee, that thou mayest judge them according to their crimes" (v 11). Alma received little direction or consolation from Mosiah because it was a religious, not a civil matter: "Behold I judge them not; therefore I deliver them into thy hands to be judged" (v 12). Mosiah apparently was reminding Alma that, as the high priest, he had the stewardship over the Church and was therefore the person entitled to receive revelation for this dilemma.

Having this heavy burden of responsibility caused Alma to turn to the Lord in prayer, "for he feared that he should do wrong in the sight of God" (Mosiah 26:13). After Alma "had poured out his whole soul to God" (v 14), the Lord answered his faithful servant's pleadings. The revelation Alma received, recorded in Mosiah 26:15–32, contains the divine paradigm for Church disciplinary action. Because of the eternal nature of the gospel plan, we know that the principles revealed to Alma are as relevant now as they were then.

Only Converts Should Be Baptized

After commending Alma for his "exceeding faith" and devotion to the work of the ministry, the Lord taught him that prevention is the best way to handle transgression. The best prevention comes from baptizing only those who are converted. The Lord explained: "He that will hear my voice shall be my sheep; and him shall ye receive into the Church, and him will I also receive. This is my church; whosoever is baptized shall be baptized unto repentance. And whomsoever ye receive shall believe in my name; and him will I freely forgive" (Mosiah 26:21–22). Only repentant converts who had accepted Jesus as the Christ were to be baptized into the Church of Jesus Christ. Alma had to judge whether or not the prospective member was truly a repentant believer committed to a Christlike life.

The Savior explained to Alma why repentance and faith in the Lord Jesus Christ are essential prerequisites to membership in the Church:

> For it is I that taketh upon me the sins of the world; for it is I that hath created them; and it is I that granteth unto him that believeth unto the end a place at my right hand. For behold, in my name are they called; and if they know me they shall come forth, and shall have a place eternally at my right hand. And it shall come to pass that when the second trump shall sound then shall they that never knew me come forth and shall stand before me. And then shall they know that I am the Lord their God, that I am their Redeemer; but they would not be redeemed. And then I will confess unto them that I never knew them; and they shall depart into everlasting fire prepared for the devil and his angels. Therefore I say unto you, that he that will not hear my voice, the same shall ye not receive into my church, for him I will not receive at the last day. (Mosiah 26:23–28)

If people are truly committed to the Savior's ideals when they join the Church and then become wayward, reactivation is primarily a matter of "re-membering" the peace, hope, and purpose they once knew. But if people are baptized without conversion, they will not have that sacred time to reflect upon—that time when the Holy Spirit whispered peace to their souls and spoke of eternal life through the atonement and teachings of the Savior. Alma was reminded that conversion must precede baptism into the Church of Jesus Christ.

The Judgment Must Be Commensurate with the Violation

Next, the Lord told Alma that "whosoever transgresseth against me, him shall ye judge according to the sins which he has committed" (Mosiah 26:29). Church officers today—bishops, stake presidents, mission presidents, and general authorities—are appointed to be judges in Israel. The scriptures clearly establish guidelines for them to follow. For instance, Doctrine and Covenants 134:10 states:

> We believe that all religious societies have a right to deal with their members for disorderly conduct, according to the rules and regulations of such societies; provided that such dealings be for fellowship and good standing; but we do not believe that any religious society has authority to try men on the right of property or life, to take from them this world's goods, or to put them in jeopardy of either life or

limb, or to inflict any physical punishment upon them. They can only excommunicate them from their society, and withdraw from them their fellowship.

These guidelines leave Church officers today with several options in judging "according to the sins which [a member] has committed." The present *General Handbook of Instructions* mentions two alternative forms of discipline—informal and formal (10:2–5).

In informal circumstances, a bishop, stake president, or mission president may feel a need to initiate counsel with a member who could potentially face unusually strong temptations. This is called "preventative action," part of the "Private Counsel and Caution" approach mentioned in the *General Handbook* (10:3).

When appropriate, a Church officer may "restrict a member's privileges" or place him or her on "informal probation." "Such restrictions may include suspending the right to partake of the sacrament," function in a church calling, or enjoy temple privileges. When the member makes sufficient progress, the informal probation is lifted. If the member does not adhere to the guidelines given, further action may be required (*General Handbook* 10:3).

In present Church practice, formal discipline is necessary only for more grievous infractions. A disciplinary council (formerly called a Church Court) *must* be held when a member is accused of murder, incest, or apostasy (*General Handbook* 10:3–4). Likewise, when a prominent Church leader commits a "major offense against morality," when the transgressor is a "predator," when one has habitual patterns of improper conduct, or when the misconduct is widely known, a disciplinary council *must* be held (10:4). It may also be necessary for Church leaders to convene a disciplinary council for other conduct unbecoming a member of the Church (10:4). Judicially, a disciplinary council has four options: (1) no action, (2) formal probation, (3) disfellowshipment, or (4) excommunication (10:5). The objective of the council is not to expel members, but to help them become Saints. Saving souls is the Church's primary aim. Only under extreme circumstances are members excommunicated from the Church. In fact, discipline is not just intended to protect the Church, but to help sinners in the healing process. In a powerful general conference address on this subject, Elder Robert L. Simpson stated: "Priesthood courts of the Church are not courts of retribution. They are courts of love" (32).

Confession—A Necessary Step

The Lord further instructed Alma: "As often as my people repent will I forgive them their trespasses against me" (Mosiah 26:30). The Lord wants to forgive. However, Alma was explicitly told under what circumstances he was to forgive those who had transgressed the commandments of God: "If he confess his sins before thee and me, and repenteth in the sincerity of his heart, him shall ye forgive, and I will forgive him also" (v 29). Thus, although the Lord is very willing to forgive, the sinner must meet certain conditions. Transgressors must confess before God and, when appropriate, before a Church leader.

When transgressors have truly had a change of heart, the Lord, who knows all things, once again bestows the Holy Spirit. But repentant members need, in addition to blessings from the Lord, the blessing of the Church. The judges in Israel have been commissioned by the Lord to judge members' personal worthiness before extending various Church callings to them, allowing them to receive their endowments, be sealed in the temple, go on a mission, or receive a patriarchal blessing. Thus, confession is in harmony with the biblical statement wherein the Apostle James counsels, "Confess your faults one to another, and pray one for another" (James 5:16).

It seems easier for most people to confess their sins to God, whom they do not see, than to confess them face to face to a Church leader. Some members reason that they have sincerely repented because they have taken the matter to God. But

Mosiah 26:29 refutes that reasoning and says that confession to a Church leader may also be necessary. President Spencer W. Kimball explains that

> many offenders in their shame and pride have satisfied their consciences, temporarily at least, with a few silent prayers to the Lord and rationalized that this was sufficient confession of their sins. "But I have confessed my sins to my Heavenly Father," they will insist, "and that is all that is necessary." This is not true where a major sin is involved. Then two sets of forgiveness are required to bring peace to the transgressor—one from the proper authorities of the Lord's Church, and one from the Lord himself. (*The Miracle of Forgiveness* 179; hereafter *Miracle*)

The Lord reemphasized the importance of confession when he told the Prophet Joseph Smith, "By this ye may know if a man repenteth of his sins—behold, he will confess them and forsake them" (D&C 58:43). The Lord further revealed to Joseph Smith the importance of members' confessing their "sins unto [their] brethren, and before the Lord" (D&C 59:12). In *Faith Precedes the Miracle*, President Kimball explained how confession to the bishop can help the confessor:

> The bishop may be one's best earthly friend. He will hear the problems, judge the seriousness thereof, determine the degree of adjustment, and decide if it warrants an eventual forgiveness. He does this as the earthly representative of God, who is the master physician, the master psychologist, the master psychiatrist. If repentance is sufficient, he may waive penalties, which is tantamount to forgiveness so far as the church organization is concerned. The bishop claims no authority to absolve sins, but he does share the burden, waive penalties, relieve tension and strain, and he may assure a continuation of church activity. He will keep the whole matter most confidential. (182)

The Importance of Honesty in Confessing Sins

Because confession before Church leaders is an essential step in the repentance process, it is important that members be open and honest in confession. President Kimball wrote that when "they are in sweet attunement, Church leaders are entitled '. . . to have it given unto them to discern . . . lest there shall be any among you professing and yet be not of God' (D&C 46:27.)" (*Miracle* 184). He also explained the seriousness of lying to an authorized servant of the Lord:

> Those who lie to Church leaders forget or ignore an important rule and truth the Lord has set down: that when he has called men to high places in his kingdom and has placed on them the mantle of authority, a lie to them is tantamount to a lie to the Lord; a half-truth to his officials is like a half-truth to the Lord; a rebellion against his servants is comparable with a rebellion against the Lord; and any infraction against the Brethren who hold the gospel keys is a thought or an act against the Lord. As he expressed it: "For he that receiveth my servants receiveth me; and he that receiveth me receiveth my Father." (D&C 84:36–37.)

> And he made it explicit again when he said: "What I the Lord have spoken, I have spoken, and I excuse not myself; and though the heavens and the earth pass away, my word shall not pass away, but shall all be fulfilled, *whether by mine own voice or by the voice of my servants, it is the same.*" (D&C 1:38. Italics added. See also 3 Nephi 28:34.) (*Miracle* 183)

What Repentant Sinners Must Confess to Church Leaders

Sometimes those desiring to repent ask what they must confess to their Church leader. Must they confess that they are lazy in their employment, or that they are not as friendly as they ought to be, or that they have not shared equally in responsibilities around the home? President Marion G. Romney stated that we need only confess those sins to our Church leaders that may affect our standing in the Church. He explained:

> Where one's transgressions are of such a nature as would, unrepented of, put in jeopardy his right to membership or fellowship in the Church of Jesus Christ, full and effective confession would, in my judgment, require confession by the repentant sinner to his bishop or other proper presiding Church officer—not that the Church officer could forgive the sin (this power rests in the Lord himself and those only to whom he specifically delegates it) but rather that the Church, acting through its duly appointed officers, might with full knowledge of the facts take such action with respect to Church discipline as the circumstances merit. (125)

President Brigham Young stated:

> I believe in coming out and being plain and honest, with that which should be made public, and in keeping to yourselves that which should be kept. . . . If you have sinned against the people, confess to them. If you have sinned against a family or a neighbourhood, go to them and confess. If you have sinned against your Ward, confess to your Ward. If you have sinned against one individual, take that person by yourselves and make your confession to him. And if you have sinned against your God, or against yourselves, confess to God, and keep the matter to yourselves, for I do not want to know anything about it. . . .
>
> For the sins you commit against yourselves and your God, unless repented of and forgiven, the Lord will hold his private council and judge you according to the degree of guilt that is upon you; and if you sin against others, he will make that public, and you will have to hear it. . . .
>
> Keep your follies that do not concern others to yourselves, and keep your private wickedness as still as possible. . . .
>
> We wish to see people honestly confess as they should and what they should. (*Journal of Discourses* 8:362)

Another reason to be open and honest in confessing sins is to help Church leaders make proper judgments. Before a judge in Israel can make a wise judgment he must first have all the facts. Members who withhold information or misrepresent the facts are doing themselves a disservice by prolonging and compounding the repentance process and causing judgments to be inaccurate. The Prophet Joseph Smith said, "Let the Twelve and all Saints be willing to confess all their sins, and not keep back a part" (*Teachings of the Prophet Joseph Smith* 155).

Confession to Those Who Are Offended

Often when members sin they not only offend God and jeopardize their standing in the Church, but they also offend other people. To repent fully, people must face those whom they have offended and confess their transgressions. The one who was offended may initiate the contact since the offender may not always know that he or she has caused an offense.

Jesus, during his Palestinian ministry, taught, "Moreover if thy brother shall trespass against thee, go and tell his fault between thee and him alone: if he shall hear thee, thou hast gained thy brother" (Matt 18:15). The Doctrine and Covenants likewise explains, "And if thy brother or sister offend thee, thou shalt take him or her between him or her and thee alone; and if he or she confess thou shalt be reconciled" (D&C 42:88).

Voluntary vs. Involuntary Confession

Voluntary confession is initiated by offenders who desire to put their lives in order; involuntary confession follows after a transgressor is confronted with inquiries and accusations. When members confess their sins, they "cast [their] burden upon the Lord" (Ps 55:22), and bring upon themselves his forgiveness. The Lord pleads with us to benefit from his atoning sacrifice: "Come unto me, all ye that labour and are heavy laden, and I will give you rest" (Matt 11:88). Voluntary confession helps lift the grievous burdens of sin from our shoulders and enables the Savior, who is both willing and able, to assist us. In a similar manner, confession to a Church leader helps lift the burden to be shared by one with strong and willing shoulders. Some of the sweetest expressions in the English language are "I'm sorry," "Please forgive me," "I was wrong," "I made a mistake," and "I will do better." These voluntary confessions are spiritually therapeutic for both speaker and listener. They are often found at the conclusion of the sorrowful chapters in one's life story, but they allow subsequent chapters to be more positive and optimistic.

Just as voluntary humility is better than compelled humility, so is voluntary confession preferable to involuntary confession. But involuntary confession is still better than living in sin. "For a man sometimes, if he is compelled to be humble, seeketh repentance; and . . . whosoever repenteth shall find mercy; and he that findeth mercy and endureth to the end the same shall be saved" (Alma 32:13). So it is with confession. President Kimball stated:

> Even making the admission upon confrontation is better than continuing to lie and evade the truth. In fact, many of those forced sooner or later to admit their sins do come to a full, sincere repentance and a humble desire to receive forgiveness. This again involves the same steps to repentance, with conviction, abandonment of sins, and confession, as fundamental to the process. (*Miracle* 182)

After Corianton had grievously sinned while serving as a missionary, Alma the Younger sent him back to the Church members who knew of his sins, with the admonition to "acknowledge your faults and that wrong which ye have done" (Alma 39:13). Even though his confession was stipulated, it surely had a positive effect upon the repentant Corianton as well as upon the members of the Church who may have assumed that the offense was being concealed or ignored.

The Lord said to Alma the Elder, "If he [a sinner] confess his sins before thee and me, and repenteth in the sincerity of his heart, him shall ye forgive, and I will forgive him also" (Mosiah 26:29). A present-day bishop who holds the keys to temple privileges, as well as to Church callings and membership itself, has, as did Alma, two things to consider about forgiveness: (1) Has the transgressor confessed and made restitution as far as possible to all offended parties? and (2) Has the transgressor sincerely restructured his or her life upon the gospel foundation? If the answer is yes to these questions, the repentant member can be forgiven.

Forgiving Each Other's Trespasses

After the Lord explained under what circumstances the prophet Alma was to forgive transgressors in behalf of the Church (Mosiah 26:29), he explained that members should forgive each other's sins unconditionally. The commandment reads, "And ye shall also forgive one another your trespasses; for verily I say unto you, he that forgiveth not his neighbor's trespasses when he says that he repents, the same hath brought himself under condemnation" (v 31).

The Savior said it well when he gave us a pattern for prayer: "Forgive us our debts, as we forgive our debtors" (Matt 6:12; 3 Nephi 13:11). He continued, "For if ye forgive men their trespasses, your heavenly Father will also forgive you: But if ye forgive not men their trespasses, neither will your Father forgive your trespasses" (Matt 6:14–15; 3 Nephi 13:14–15). In the Doctrine and Covenants the Lord explained the importance of forgiving each other unconditionally this way: "Wherefore, I say unto you, that ye ought to forgive one another; for he that forgiveth not his brother his trespasses, standeth condemned before the Lord; for there remaineth in him the greater sin. I, the Lord, will forgive whom I will forgive, but of you it is required to forgive all men" (D&C 64:9–10).

It is inconceivable that one whose heart is full of hatred or revenge or jealousy—or any other unholy passion—could live in God's presence. President Kimball stated, "To be in the right we must forgive, and we must do so without regard to whether or not our antagonist repents, or how sincere is his transformation, or whether or not he asks our forgiveness" (*Miracle* 283).

It is not always easy to forgive, but it is always possible. Many stories have been told about people who have been grievously wronged, maligned, maimed, abused, or tortured, but who have applied the Lord's teachings on forgiveness and have once again felt peace and contentment in their lives.

In the book of Moses, Enoch explained "that . . . all men, everywhere, must repent, or they can in nowise inherit the kingdom of God, for no unclean thing can dwell there, or dwell in his presence; for, in the language of Adam, Man of Holiness is his name" (Moses 6:57). Unfortunately, those who refuse to forgive others destroy their own opportunities for peace and happiness, as well as adversely affecting the lives of many others.

Excommunication

The Lord explained to Alma that when all attempts to reclaim an erring member have failed, he was to remove that person from the Church: "Now I say unto you, Go; and whosoever will not repent of his sins the same shall not be numbered among my people; and this shall be observed from this time forward" (Mosiah 26:32). The Book of Mormon explains that under Alma's leadership "those that would not confess their sins and repent of their iniquity, the same were not numbered among the people of the church, and their names were blotted out" (v 36).

The Savior further explained that those who were excommunicated were not to be cast out of the Nephite synagogues or their "places of worship; for unto such shall ye continue to minister; for ye know not but what they shall return and repent, and come unto me with full purpose of heart, and I shall heal them; and ye shall be the means of bringing salvation unto them" (3 Nephi 18:32). Moroni, writing to the modern Saints, reiterated the same policy over three hundred years later: if erring members "repented not, and confessed not, their names were blotted out, and they were not numbered among the people of Christ. But, as oft as they repented and sought forgiveness, with real intent, they were forgiven" (Moroni 6:7–8).

Conclusion

Alma recorded the Lord's words on Church discipline so that "he might have them, and that he might judge the people of that church according to the commandments of God" (Mosiah 26:33). Then Alma "regulate[d] all the affairs of the Church" (v 37) according to the revealed pattern. As a consequence, "they began again to have peace and to prosper exceedingly in the affairs of the church, walking circumspectly before God, receiving many, and baptizing many" (v 37).

Continuing with the Lord's revealed pattern, Alma and his fellow laborers "did admonish their brethren; and they were also admonished, every one by the word of God, according to his sins, or to the sins which he had committed, being commanded to pray without ceasing, and to give thanks in all things" (Mosiah 26:39). It is noteworthy that both the leaders and the other members of the Church were "admonished . . . according to [their] sins." In the wisdom of God, all members of the Church, regardless of their callings, are accountable to God, and also to the Church, for serious misconduct. Today even members of the First Presidency may be tried for their membership.

Thus the principles explained in Mosiah 26, together with interpretive statements by Latter-day prophets, help us understand the Lord's way of handling Church disciplinary action:

1.   Only true believers in the Lord Jesus Christ, meaning those who have repented of all past sins, should be baptized into the Church of Jesus Christ (vv 18–28).

2.   If members transgress the commandments of Jesus Christ, Church leaders must see that the judgments they receive fit their violations. Church leaders can discipline disorderly members by excommunication, withdrawing fellowship, or limiting privileges, but they cannot impose penalties affecting life, physical well-being, or property (v 29).

3.   Church leaders are to forgive transgressors, as far as the Church is concerned, if they confess their sins and repent in the sincerity of their hearts (vv 29–30).

4.   Honest and open confession is a necessary step in the repentance process. Confessors must face all whom they have offended: the Lord, Church leaders (if their violations could affect their Church standing), and all others who have been adversely affected by their transgressions. Though voluntary confession is the ideal, there is some merit in involuntary confession (v 29).

5.   Members of the Church are to forgive everyone, without any qualifications (v 31).

6.   Although it is sometimes necessary to excommunicate transgressors, they should not be treated unkindly. Church members are to welcome into their public meetings those who are excommunicated, disfellowshipped, or placed on probation with the hope that they will repent and return to full fellowship with the Saints (vv 26–39).

7.   All members of the Church, regardless of their callings, are subject to Church discipline (v 39).

The more I ponder the great truths in the Book of Mormon, the more I stand in awe of its divine message and importance. Although Church discipline is not a major theme in the Book of Mormon, it is sufficiently explained in chapter 26 of the book of Mosiah to establish parameters for Church leaders responsible for reclaiming transgressors while protecting the sanctity and purposes of the Church. Mosiah also explains to the transgressor what he or she must do in order to return to the fold of God. Disciplinary councils, then as now, were designed to be "courts of love."

BIBLIOGRAPHY

General Handbook of Instructions. Salt Lake City: The Church of Jesus Christ of Latter-day Saints, 1989.

Journal of Discourses. 26 vols. 1854–86.

Kimball, Spencer W. *Faith Precedes the Miracle.* Salt Lake City: Deseret Book, 1972.

———. *The Miracle of Forgiveness.* Salt Lake City: Bookcraft, 1969.

Romney, Marion G. "Repentance Worketh Salvation." *Improvement Era* (Dec 1955) 58:962, 964; also in *Conference Report* (Oct 1955) 123–25.

Simpson, Robert L. "Courts of Love." *Ensign* (July 1972) 2:48–49; also in *Conference Report* (Apr 1972) 30–33.

Teachings of the Prophet Joseph Smith. Comp. Joseph Fielding Smith. Salt Lake City: Deseret Book, 1976.

For the Sake of Retaining a Remission of Your Sins

13

W. Ralph Pew

In his concluding comments during the Second Annual Book of Mormon Symposium, President Jeffrey R. Holland said, "We have an everlastingly rich source of doctrinal ore here to mine, especially in the Book of Mormon, and I encourage all of us to participate in that task" (316). This metaphor implies that we must diligently explore and excavate the scriptural terrain of the Book of Mormon in our search for the doctrinal gems of eternal life and exaltation. King Benjamin's speech in Mosiah chapters 2 through 5 is a crowning jewel of doctrine and counsel. In that speech, Benjamin prophesies with divine power and conviction concerning the life and mission of Jesus Christ, and he explains how the application of the Atonement brings a remission of sins. His teachings and testimony tie retaining a remission of sins to our caring for the spiritually and temporally poor. He awakens us to this truth by boldly stating the purpose of his sermon:

> And now, for the sake of these things which I have spoken unto you—that is, for the sake of retaining a remission of your sins from day to day, that ye may walk guiltless before God—I would that ye should impart of your substance to the poor, every man according to that which he hath, such as feeding the hungry, clothing the naked, visiting the sick and administering to their relief, both spiritually and temporally, according to their wants. (Mosiah 4:26)

W. Ralph Pew is an attorney in Mesa, Arizona.

The principles, truths, and counsel contained in Benjamin's sermon teach that the Atonement is only as effective in our lives as our daily actions and conduct allow it to be.

If the keystone of all the doctrines of salvation is the Atonement, then the capstone of our earthly probation is our diligent effort to walk guiltless before God through serving others (Mosiah 2:17) and performing good works (D&C 58:26–28). Transforming the natural man into a saint (Mosiah 3:19) is a journey that begins with the cleansing and purifying experience of obtaining an initial remission of sins through faith, repentance, and baptism. Throughout the remainder of that journey we must press forward along the strait and narrow path that leads to eternal life. We must receive the endowments of enabling grace as well as provide a determined personal effort. King Benjamin taught that our Creator supports and sustains us from one moment to another (Mosiah 2:21), that he expects us to emulate him by reaching out to serve others, and that by serving we will retain a remission of our sins (Mosiah 4:26). Jesus promises, "You shall receive grace for grace" (D&C 93:20). By pressing forward along the narrow path we bring the abundant blessings of the Atonement into our lives.

To comprehend the critical nature of this post-baptismal journey, we will first review the stated purposes of king Benjamin's address and its doctrinal context. This will help us appreciate his reasons for addressing his people and show us that his listeners had been baptized and had a basic understanding of the principles of repentance, baptism, and forgiveness. We will focus principally on king Benjamin's entreaty that we retain a remission of our sins by caring for the spiritually and temporally poor. We will conclude by examining his admonition that we remain spiritually pure as we endure to the end of our mortal probation.

Having been instructed by an angel (Mosiah 3:2; 4:1; 5:5) and recognizing he was soon to die (Mosiah 2:28), king Benjamin requested that his son Mosiah gather the righteous Nephites at the temple in Zarahemla so he could counsel and instruct them (Mosiah 2:1). King Benjamin identified two reasons for gathering the people: first, to declare the divine mandate that Mosiah be a king and ruler over the people (Mosiah 2:29, 30); and second, to give unto them the name of Christ (Mosiah 1:11; 5:7–9). In his address he reported on his regal stewardship, he taught of Jesus Christ, and he directed the people to serve their Heavenly King. He also testified of the coming of Jesus Christ, the Son of God (Mosiah 3:1–5, 8). Feeling the tremendous responsibility that accompanied both his ecclesiastical and civil stewardships, king Benjamin additionally declared that one of his reasons for addressing the people was to rid his garments of their blood (Mosiah 2:27–28). For the salvation of his own soul, king Benjamin did not want to be held responsible to God for not teaching his people the plain and precious truths concerning the mission of Jesus Christ and the eternal consequences of sin (Mosiah 2:27, 38–41).

King Benjamin's desires concerning the awesome responsibility of declaring the word of God in truth and soberness to all people parallel those of prophets before and after him. The great prophet Jacob said:

> O, my beloved brethren, remember my words. Behold, I take off my garments, and I shake them before you; I pray the God of my salvation that he view me with his all-searching eye; wherefore, ye shall know at the last day, when all men shall be judged of their works, that the God of Israel did witness that I shook your iniquities from my soul, and that I stand with brightness before him, and am rid of your blood. (2 Nephi 9:44; see also Jacob 1:18–19; Mormon 9:35)

The only way king Benjamin could rid himself of the blood and sins of his people was by teaching them the word of God with diligence and exactness and by bearing strong, pure testimony (see Alma 4:19) concerning the doctrines he had learned through prayer, meditation, and revelation. He commanded them not to trifle with his words, but to open their ears to hear and their hearts to understand (Mosiah 2:9; see also D&C 6:12; 133:57; 136:32–33).

Prophets throughout all ages have been instructed by the Lord to teach repentance and baptism. The resurrected Savior carefully declared this mandate during his appearance to the Nephites: "Now this is the commandment: Repent, all ye ends of the earth, and come unto me and be baptized in my name, that ye may be sanctified by the reception of the Holy Ghost, that ye may stand spotless before me at the last day" (3 Nephi 27:20). To the eleven apostles in Jerusalem the Savior said, "Go ye therefore, and teach all nations, baptizing them in the name of the Father, and of the Son, and of the Holy Ghost" (Matt 28:19). Alma taught, "Come and be baptized unto repentance, that ye also may be partakers of the fruit of the tree of life" (Alma 5:62).

King Benjamin understood that the celestial course to eternal life requires baptism. If the gathered multitudes had not been baptized, he surely would have taught a much different sermon by focusing on the fundamentals of faith, repentance, and baptism for the remission of sins. Instead, he elected to teach them that they could retain the remission of sins they had received at baptism if they would diligently care for the spiritual and temporal needs of others.

To place king Benjamin's address in its proper doctrinal context, we need to remember that the Nephites must have had a fundamental understanding of repentance, baptism, and forgiveness. So it is with us. To comprehend fully the eternal significance of retaining a remission of our sins, we must first understand and appreciate the fundamental truths concerning these principles.

Repentance

The LDS Bible Dictionary provides a clear and precise definition of repentance:

> The Greek word of which [repentance] is the translation denotes a change of mind, i.e., a fresh view about God, about oneself, and about the world. Since we are born into conditions of mortality, repentance

comes to mean a turning of the heart and will to God, and a renunciation of sin to which we are naturally inclined. Without this there can be no progress in the things of the soul's salvation, for all accountable persons are stained by sin, and must be cleansed in order to enter the kingdom of heaven. (S.v. "Repentance")

Knowing that sin is a malady afflicting all men, the Savior says: "For, behold, the Lord your Redeemer suffered death in the flesh; wherefore he suffered the pain of all men, that all men might repent and come unto him. And he hath risen again from the dead, that he might bring all men unto him, on conditions of repentance. And how great is his joy in the soul that repenteth!" (D&C 18:11–13).

Baptism for the Remission of Sins

Baptism is an outward ordinance symbolizing an inward resurrection into spiritual life (see Moses 6:65). During Adam and Eve's time in the Garden of Eden they enjoyed personal communion with God. But as a result of their transgression, Adam and Eve were driven from the Garden and separated from him. This separation is known as spiritual death (Alma 12:16, 32; see also Hel 14:18). Baptism cleanses us from sin, gives us victory over death, provides us with a promise of constant intimate fellowship with God through faith and obedience, and starts the soul on a celestial course toward sanctification.

Forgiveness of Sins

The miracle of forgiveness as declared in the scriptures and lovingly taught by President Spencer W. Kimball brings great joy and peace to us. This infinite miracle is a direct result of the great mediation and atonement of Jesus Christ. The Atonement, when accepted and applied through repentance, sanctifies and purifies us. This propitiation, wherein Jesus Christ voluntarily paid the debt demanded by justice for the

sins of the entire world, is truly the miracle of all miracles.
Elder Bruce R. McConkie taught:

> *Forgiveness*, which includes divine pardon and complete remis-
> sion of sins, is available, on conditions of repentance, for all men
> except those who have sinned unto death. . . . To accountable persons
> in the world, remission of sins comes by repentance and baptism of
> water and of the Spirit. For those who have once been cleansed in this
> way and who thereafter commit sin—but not unto death—(and all
> members of the Church are guilty of sin, in either greater or lesser
> degree) *the law of forgiveness* embraces the following requirements:
> (1) Godly sorrow for sin. . . .
> (2) Abandonment of sin. . . .
> (3) Confession of sin. . . .
> (4) Restitution for sin. . . .
> (5) Obedience to all law. . . .
> At what times and under what circumstances do men gain forgive-
> ness of their sins? Manifestly, they attain this reward at any time when
> they are in complete harmony with the divine will, that is at any time
> when they have complied with the Lord's law whereunder they are able
> to become pure and spotless before him. (S.v. "Forgiveness")

Retaining a Remission of Your Sins

King Benjamin's imperatives for retaining a remission of
sins logically imply that a remission of sins, once *obtained*,
cannot be *retained* without a lifetime of additional effort
through charitable conduct. A return to iniquity after an initial
remission of sins is analogous to the return of leukemic blood
cells after an initial remission of the disease. The *Nelson
Textbook of Pediatrics* explains that "leukemia is a malignant
disease due to uncontrolled [growth] of leukocyte precursors
in blood, bone marrow and [certain bodily] tissues" (1143). But
proper treatment can often bring this life-threatening disease
into remission, eliminating the cancerous, malignant blood
cells.

So it is with spiritual leukemia. The spread of unrighteous
behavior in our lives is brought into remission at baptism.
Maintaining this state of spiritual well-being requires that we
forsake iniquity and embrace righteousness. As diffusion of

leukemic blood cells destroys the body, so sin destroys the soul.

Spiritual leukemia may be correctly characterized as a form of pride. Elder Neal A. Maxwell has said, "Just as meekness is in all our virtues, so pride is in all our sins" (50). The insightful Christian writer C. S. Lewis has commented, "For pride is spiritual cancer: It eats up every possibility of love, or contentment or even common sense" (112). President Ezra Taft Benson has counseled: "Pride is the universal sin, the great vice. . . . Pride is the great stumbling block to Zion" (6–7). The Book of Mormon prophet Jacob admonished: "O that he would rid you from this iniquity and abomination. And, O that ye would listen unto the word of his commands, and let not this pride of your hearts destroy your souls!" (Jacob 2:16).

The insidious encroachment of pride into our lives impairs our desire to impart of our spiritual and temporal substance to those in need, thereby preventing us from retaining a remission of our sins. This spiritual cancer can only be brought into remission and effectively eliminated from our souls through faith, repentance, baptism, and sanctification by the Holy Ghost. In the process of obtaining sanctification, which comes after experiencing spiritual rebirth and a mighty change of heart at baptism, we can keep the diffusion of cancerous pride and sin in remission.

Scriptural references to retaining a remission of sin are found only in Mosiah 4:11–12 and 26, and in Alma 4:13–14. The pivotal nexus between imparting of our substance to those in need and retaining a remission of our sins is found in Mosiah 4:26 and Alma 4:13–14. Living by the teachings contained in these verses will place the saint (see Mosiah 3:19) on a secure course to eternal life.

In Mosiah 4:26, part of king Benjamin's final address to his people, Benjamin teaches us that to retain a remission of sins we must "impart of [our] substance to the poor, every man according to that which he hath, such as feeding the hungry, clothing the naked, visiting the sick and administering to their relief, both spiritually and temporally, according to their wants." In Mosiah 4:11–12, king Benjamin implores us to retain a remission of our sins by remembering the greatness of our God, praying daily, and standing steadfast in the faith of Jesus Christ.

Long after king Benjamin's address, Mormon comments on the concept of retaining a remission of sins in his abridgment of the events of the ninth year of the reign of the judges. In describing Alma's experience, Mormon indicates that the wickedness of Church members began to lead those who were unbelievers from one iniquity to another, thereby bringing destruction upon the people (Alma 4:11). Then Mormon reports:

> Yea, he [Alma] saw great inequality among the people, some lifting themselves up with their pride, despising others, turning their backs upon the needy and the naked and those who were hungry, and those who were athirst, and those who were sick and afflicted. Now this was a great cause for lamentations among the people, while others were abasing themselves, succoring those who stood in need of their succor, such as imparting their substance to the poor and the needy, feeding the hungry, and suffering all manner of afflictions, for Christ's sake, who should come according to the spirit of prophecy. (Alma 4:12–13)

In contrast to the wickedness of the time, Mormon identifies the charitable characteristics exemplified by those who had obtained a remission of their sins through baptism and who had continued in faith concerning the coming of Christ. He says they were "looking forward to that day, thus retaining a remission of their sins; being filled with great joy because of the resurrection of the dead, according to the will and power and deliverance of Jesus Christ from the bands of death" (Alma 4:14).

These verses in Mosiah and Alma are the only references in scripture that use any form of the word *retain* in connection with a remission of sins. Although few in number, these three scriptural references testify that retaining a remission of sins is as vital to spiritual life as retaining a remission of cancerous leukemic blood cells is to physical life.

Although king Benjamin's counsel to retain a remission of sins seems very simple and straightforward, its eternal consequences are of paramount importance. Obtaining an initial remission of sins results from complying with the laws of the preparatory gospel by exercising faith, repenting, and being baptized. But it was never intended that we should linger at the gate of the path that leads to eternal life. Jesus expects us to progress along this path (see 2 Nephi 31:17–20). However, he knows the tender nature of the covenant and that our fledgling steps will be halting and unsure. After all, "He marked the path and led the way" ("How Great the Wisdom and the Love," *Hymns* #195). Indeed, Christ condescended in that he descended below all things so that he could ascend above all things and declare, "I am the way" (John 14:6). His declaration assures us that we need not walk alone, but walk we must. In this context, a restatement of king Benjamin's message could be formulated in these simple terms: retaining a remission of sins depends upon our following the Lord along the strait and narrow way.

If we too follow king Benjamin's plain and precious teachings concerning retaining a remission of sins, we facilitate our progression along the path that leads to sanctification. The purification and sanctification of our souls occurs as we yield our hearts unto God (Hel 3:35). The word most commonly used to describe the actions of people pursuing this path is *charity*, the pure love of Christ that never fails (1 Cor 13:8; Moroni 7:46–47).

A contemporary author, Robert Fulghum, described the following event which took place in Oslo, Norway, on the tenth of December, 1980:

> A small, stooped woman in a faded blue sari and worn sandals received an award. From the hand of a king. An award funded from the will of the inventor of dynamite. In a great glittering hall of velvet and gold and crystal. Surrounded by the noble and famous in formal

black and in elegant gowns. The rich, the powerful, the brilliant, the talented of the world in attendance. And there at the center of it all—a little old lady in sari and sandals. Mother Teresa, of India. Servant of the poor and sick and dying. To her, the Nobel Peace Prize.

No shah or president or king or general or scientist or pope; no banker or merchant or cartel or oil company or ayatollah holds the key to as much power as she has. None is as rich. For hers is the invincible weapon against the evils of this earth: the caring heart. And hers are the everlasting riches of this life: the wealth of the compassionate spirit. (190)

I witnessed pure desire of the heart in an experience that occurred in the fall of 1989. On one of the few cool nights in Mesa, Arizona, I attended the annual banquet for the Sunshine Acres Children's Home, a center for abandoned and orphaned children. I sat in the small chapel located in the desert of northeast Mesa and listened to the Home's annual report. Then I watched as several professional and civic leaders in the community were recognized for the volunteer service they had rendered to this marvelous organization. As I traveled home that evening, my mind was full of king Benjamin's speech, and my heart was swollen by the influence of the Spirit. I contemplated the power of pure and selfless service, not that of the volunteer professionals I had just seen being recognized, but that of Vera Dingman, the Home's founder. Mrs. Dingman and her late husband, Jim, created Sunshine Acres in 1954. Since Jim's death, she has directed the nurturing of over 900 children who would have otherwise had little chance for success in this life. Vera Dingman imparts her spiritual substance to others, a substance which she derives from a source within the pure love of Christ. Imparting of our substance to those in need is a precept that should permeate all religions. It emanates from the Spirit of Christ which is given to all who come into this world (see Moroni 7:16).

An example of Christlike service from within the Church is found in the life of a friend, a mother of four. This young woman, temporarily raising her family alone, personally cares for the physical needs of a couple whom she has been assigned to visit teach. She feeds them, helps to clean their house, and does many other chores associated with the daily life of the couple. She also provides transportation for a handicapped member of her ward so that traveling to and from Church meetings will not be a burden. Her financial contributions truly represent the "widow's mite." Her attitude of giving can best be characterized by her comment concerning the new local unit budget program: "I still need to finish paying this year's budget amounts before the new program becomes effective." Her obedient spirit and cooperative attitude make her the topic of discussion anytime the need arises for a dependable individual to fill an assignment. Her heart is full of the desire to do good as she imparts of her temporal and spiritual substance.

Nephi taught that temporal and spiritual acts of service are necessary to remain on the path that leads to life:

> And now, my beloved brethren, after ye have gotten into this strait and narrow path, I would ask if all is done? Behold, I say unto you, Nay; for ye have not come thus far save it were by the word of Christ with unshaken faith in him, relying wholly upon the merits of him who is mighty to save. Wherefore, ye must press forward with a steadfastness in Christ, having a perfect brightness of hope, and a love of God and of all men. Wherefore, if ye shall press forward, feasting upon the word of Christ, and endure to the end, behold, thus saith the Father: Ye shall have eternal life. (2 Nephi 31:19–20)

King Benjamin's vital directive to retain a remission of sins by remaining faithful after baptism and continuing in the path of service to others confirms Nephi's teachings.

Addressing the welfare session of general conference in October of 1980, President Marion G. Romney quoted Mosiah 4:26 and queried:

> Is there any question, brothers and sisters, about our obligation in this program? Is there any doubt that retaining a remission of sins depends upon our caring for one another? If we believe these teachings, if we profess to follow the Savior and his prophets, if we want to be true to our covenants and have the Spirit of the Lord in our lives, then we must do the things that the Savior said and did. He it was who said: "Verily, verily, I say unto you, He that believeth on me, the works that I do shall he do also" (John 14:12). ("Welfare Services: The Savior's Program" 92)

Providing for others both spiritually and physically necessarily requires that we have "substance" to share. President Romney taught: "How can we give if there is nothing there? Food for the hungry cannot come from empty shelves. Money to assist the needy cannot come from an empty purse. Support and understanding cannot come from the emotionally starved. Teaching cannot come from the unlearned. And most important of all, spiritual guidance cannot come from the spiritually weak" ("The Celestial Nature of Self-Reliance" 93).

Caring for the Poor—A Covenant Obligation

Paul taught that inheritance of the promises of the Abrahamic covenant was not determined by genealogical descent (see Rom 9:6), but by acceptance and faithful adherence to the covenant of baptism (see Gal 3:27–29). That the baptismal covenant includes the obligation to minister to others is apparent from Alma's instruction to the conscientious followers of Christ at the waters of Mormon: "And now, as ye are desirous to come into the fold of God, and to be called his people, and are willing to bear one another's burdens, that they may be light; Yea, and are willing to mourn with those that mourn; yea, and comfort those that stand in need of comfort, . . . what have you against being baptized in the name of the Lord?" (Mosiah 18:8–10). James reminded meridian Church members that part of pure religion was a continuing ministry "to visit the fatherless and widows in their affliction" (James 1:27). In this dispensation the Lord counseled Frederick G. Williams through the Prophet Joseph to "succor the weak, lift up the hands which hang down, and strengthen the feeble knees" (D&C 81:5).

In a parable concerning the Final Judgment, Jesus clearly identifies the importance of administering relief to those in need:

> For I was an hungred, and ye gave me meat: I was thirsty, and ye gave me drink: I was a stranger, and ye took me in: naked, and ye

clothed me: I was sick, and ye visited me: I was in prison, and ye came unto me. Then shall the righteous answer him, saying, Lord, when saw we thee an hungred, and fed thee? or thirsty, and gave thee drink? When saw we thee a stranger, and took thee in? or naked, and clothed thee? Or when saw we thee sick, or in prison, and came unto thee? And the King shall answer and say unto them, Verily I say unto you, Inasmuch as ye have done it unto one of the least of these my brethren, ye have done it unto me. (Matt 25:35–40)

Failure to care for the poor according to the baptismal covenant is spiritually fatal; we lose remission of sins and forfeit our victory over spiritual death. A spiritual autopsy in this case would reveal the cause of death to be an uncontrolled diffusion of carcinogenic pride and selfishness (see Prov 3:27; Ezek 16:49; Alma 5:28). Moroni warns that pride is hazardous to our spiritual health and will prevent us from imparting of our substance to those in need:

And I know that ye do walk in the pride of your hearts; and there are none save a few only who do not lift themselves up in the pride of their hearts, unto the wearing of very fine apparel, unto envying, and strifes, and malice, and persecutions, and all manner of iniquities; and your churches, yea, even every one, have become polluted because of the pride of your hearts. For behold, ye do love money, and your substance, and your fine apparel, and the adorning of your churches, more than ye love the poor and the needy, the sick and the afflicted. O ye pollutions, ye hypocrites, ye teachers, who sell yourselves for that which will canker, why have ye polluted the holy church of God? Why are ye ashamed to take upon you the name of Christ? Why do ye not think that greater is the value of an endless happiness than that misery which never dies—because of the praise of the world? Why do ye adorn yourselves with that which hath no life, and yet suffer the hungry, and the needy, and the naked, and the sick and the afflicted to pass by you, and notice them not? (Mormon 8:36–39)

Caring for the temporal needs of the poor is not sufficient by itself. All things are spiritual unto the Lord, and at no time has he given us a temporal law (D&C 29:34). President Joseph F. Smith said: "You must continue to bear in mind that the temporal and the spiritual are blended. They are not separate. One cannot be carried on without the other, so long as we are here in mortality" (208).

King Benjamin also taught us to impart our *spiritual* substance to those in need. Before we can share of our spiritual substance with others, we must first become spiritually self-reliant and build a spiritual reservoir of strength within our own souls. Elder Dallin H. Oaks has said:

> We seek spirituality through faith, repentance, and baptism; through forgiveness of one another; through fasting and prayer; through righteous desires and pure thoughts and actions. We seek spirituality through service to our fellowmen; through worship; through feasting on the word of God, in the scriptures and in the teachings of the living prophets. We attain spirituality through making and keeping covenants with the Lord, through conscientiously trying to keep all the commandments of God. Spirituality is not acquired suddenly. It is the consequence of a succession of right choices. It is the harvest of a righteous life. (144)

Developing a source of spiritual strength within our own hearts and souls will lead us to meet with compassion the spiritual and temporal needs of those around us. The Prophet Joseph Smith, addressing the Nauvoo Relief Society on 9 June 1842, said, "The nearer we get to our heavenly Father the more we are disposed to look with compassion on perishing souls to take them upon our shoulders and cast their sins behind our back" (Ehat and Cook 123).

In Mine Own Way

Administering relief to others must be accomplished in the Lord's way. King Benjamin said, "See that these things are done in wisdom and order; for it is not requisite that a man should run faster than he has strength" (Mosiah 4:27). Through modern-day revelation the Lord has established a program to provide for his Saints (D&C 104:15):

> But it must needs be done in mine own way; and behold this is the way that I, the Lord, have decreed to provide for my saints, that the poor shall be exalted, in that the rich are made low. For the earth is full, and there is enough and to spare; yea, I prepared all things, and have given unto the children of men to be agents unto themselves. Therefore, if any man shall take of the abundance which I have made,

and impart not his portion, according the law of my gospel, unto the poor and the needy, he shall, with the wicked, lift up his eyes in hell, being in torment. (D&C 104:16–18)

President Romney has taught that present-day Church programs provide the Lord's way for assisting others:

Full implementation of the united order must, according to the revelation, await the redemption of Zion (D&C 104:34). In the meantime—while we are being more perfectly taught and are gaining experience—we should be strictly living the principles of the united order insofar as they are embodied in present Church requirements, such as tithing, fast offerings, welfare projects, storehouses, and other principles and practices. Through these programs we should, as individuals, implement in our own lives the basis of the united order. ("The Purpose of Church Welfare Services" 94–95)

How does living these principles exalt the poor and humble the rich so this great work can be accomplished in the Lord's own way? President Marion G. Romney provides a clear answer to this question:

In the process both are sanctified. The poor, released from the bondage and humiliating limitations of poverty, are enabled as free men to rise to their full potential, both temporally and spiritually. The rich, by consecration and by imparting of their surplus for the benefit of the poor, not by constraint, but willingly as an act of free will, evidence that charity for their fellowmen characterized by Mormon as "the pure love of Christ" (Moroni 7:47). In this way, they qualify to "become the sons of God" (Moroni 7:48). ("The Purpose of Church Welfare Services" 94)

Paying an abundant fast offering is one way of assisting others. One of President Kimball's statements at the April 1974 welfare session of general conference describes the attitude we should have when we impart of our substance through fast offerings:

Sometimes we have been a bit penurious and figured that we had for breakfast one egg and that costs so many cents and then we give that to the Lord. I think that when we are affluent, as many of us are, that we ought to be very, very generous.

. . . I think we should be very generous and give, instead of the amount we saved by our two meals of fasting, perhaps much, much more—ten times more where we are in a position to do it. I know there are some who couldn't. (184)

Does rendering charitable service in the Lord's way to those who stand in need require that we limit our assistance only to those of the Church? The answer is clearly no. Our willingness to share with others should extend to all our Father's children. In restating the history of the Nephites during the first five years of the reign of judges, Mormon said:

> And thus, in their prosperous circumstances, they did not send away any who were naked, or that were hungry, or that were athirst, or that were sick, or that had not been nourished; and they did not set their hearts upon riches; therefore they were liberal to all, both old and young, both bond and free, both male and female, whether out of the church or in the church, having no respect to persons as to those who stood in need. (Alma 1:30)

In the April 1989 general conference, President Gordon B. Hinckley spoke of the assistance that was given by Church members to the suffering people in Africa:

> As we look across the broad spectrum of humanity at the masses who walk in hunger and poverty and in whose lives are the constant afflictions of disease or misery, let us be generous with our substance to assist. We did a significant thing back in 1985 when we held two special fast days. In a great outpouring of love, our people contributed on those two days more than ten and one-half million dollars to help bridge the gap between life and death for uncounted starving and underprivileged people. The Church continues to have a program, a Hunger Fund, to which we may contribute with love-filled hearts to assist those not of our faith who are in misery in many parts of the world. (66)

In imparting of our substance to those who stand in need and in administering to their relief, we must always keep in mind that to do so in the Lord's way requires that we give to the poor with a pure heart, a good conscience, faith unfeigned (1 Tim 1:5), and with an eye single to the glory of God (D&C 88:67).

Endure to the End

Although we sometimes sporadically try to do the things which the Lord has commanded, we must strive consistently to perform good works until the end of our mortal probation. The scriptures teach the importance of enduring to the end with great clarity. While teaching the Nephites, the resurrected Savior said:

> And it shall come to pass, that whoso repenteth and is baptized in my name shall be filled; and if he endureth to the end, behold, him will I hold guiltless before my Father at that day when I shall stand to judge the world. And he that endureth not unto the end, the same is he that is also hewn down and cast into the fire, from whence they can no more return, because of the justice of the Father. (3 Nephi 27:16–17)

The natural man or woman thinks of enduring to the end as simply withstanding the march of time, or just "hanging in there." This attitude is not enough. *Webster's Ninth New Collegiate Dictionary* defines the word *endure* as "to continue in the same state." Therefore, enduring to the end requires that we continue in the state that we acquired when we came forth out of the waters of baptism with our sin-stained souls purged through the baptism of fire and the reception of the Holy Ghost. At that moment our lives were cleansed before the Lord, our hearts were purified, and we embarked upon a course of obtaining sanctification through righteous conduct. We must therefore consider the phrase *endure to the end* to mean more than passively marking days off the calendar of our earthly probation; we must endure by persisting in the state of cleanliness and purity obtained at the time of our baptism. We must retain a remission of our sins.

The scriptures are replete with examples of how we are to endure to the end. The adverbs used in the scriptures to describe the nature and quality of our enduring include enduring "well" (D&C 121:8), enduring "in faith" (D&C 20:25; 63:20; 101:35), enduring valiantly (D&C 121:29), enduring happily (James

5:11), enduring with our "whole souls" (Omni 1:26), enduring worthily (Mormon 9:29), enduring patiently (2 Thes 1:4; Heb 6:15; D&C 24:8), and enduring "as a good soldier" (2 Tim 2:3). To obtain the ultimate gift of Christ, the blessing of eternal life wrought through the cleansing power of forgiveness, we must endure to the end by following "the example of the Son of the living God" (2 Nephi 31:16).

The indescribable blessings of eternal life come to those who, through faith, repentance, and baptism for the remission of sins, endure to the end and are cleansed of all unrighteousness (see Alma 7:14). However, our repentance and good works are subordinate to the grace of God. All of our good works will never be sufficient to bring us back into the presence of the Father without the application of divine mercy through the Atonement.

King Benjamin's concluding admonition to his people is to "be steadfast and immovable, always abounding in good works" (Mosiah 5:15). So it is with us in these latter days. Our faith in Jesus Christ must be steadfast and immovable. With a pure heart we should impart of our substance, both spiritual and temporal, to those in need. By so doing we will preserve and retain the remission of sins we received at baptism, and we will obtain forgiveness for sins we commit as we faithfully, though less than perfectly, endure to the end.

BIBLIOGRAPHY

Benson, Ezra Taft. "Beware of Pride." *Ensign* (May 1989) 19:4–7; also in *Conference Report* (Apr 1989) 3–7.

Ehat, Andrew F., and Lyndon W. Cook, comps. and eds. *The Words of Joseph Smith.* Salt Lake City: Bookcraft, 1980.

Fulghum, Robert. *All I Really Need to Know I Learned in Kindergarten.* New York: Villard, 1989.

Hinckley, Gordon B. "Let Love Be the Lodestar of Your Life." *Ensign* (May 1989) 19:65–67; also in *Conference Report* (Apr 1989) 80–84.

Holland, Jeffery R. "Conclusion and Charge." *The Book of Mormon: First Nephi, The Doctrinal Foundation.* Ed. Monte S. Nyman and Charles D. Tate, Jr. Salt Lake City: Bookcraft, 1988. 315–23.

Hymns. Salt Lake City: The Church of Jesus Christ of Latter-day Saints, 1985.

Kimball, Spencer W. *Conference Report* (Apr 1974) 183–85.

Lewis, C. S. *Mere Christianity.* New York: Macmillan, 1960.

Maxwell, Neal A. *Meek and Lowly.* Salt Lake City: Deseret Book, 1987.

McConkie, Bruce R. *Mormon Doctrine.* 2nd ed. Salt Lake City: Bookcraft, 1966.

Nelson Textbook of Pediatrics. 10th ed. Ed. Victor C. Vaughn III, R. James McKay, and Waldo E. Nelson. Philadelphia: Saunders, 1975.

Oaks, Dallin H. *Pure in Heart.* Salt Lake City: Bookcraft, 1988.

Romney, Marion G. "The Celestial Nature of Self-Reliance." *Ensign* (Nov 1982) 12:91–93; also in *Conference Report* (Oct 1982) 132–36.

————. "The Purpose of Church Welfare Services." *Ensign* (May 1977) 7:92–95; also in *Conference Report* (Apr 1977) 117–21.

————. "Welfare Services: The Savior's Program." *Ensign* (Nov 1980) 10:92–93; also in *Conference Report* (Oct 1980) 135–37.

Smith, Joseph F. *Gospel Doctrine.* Salt Lake City: Deseret Book, 1975.

Webster's Ninth New Collegiate Dictionary. 1990 ed.

Spiritual Rebirth   14

S. Michael Wilcox

We are taught in the Doctrine and Covenants that the Light of Christ is given to every individual born into the world. If we heed that light, it will direct us to our Father (D&C 84:45–47), to eternal life. However, there is an obstacle which can block or hinder us from following the light of Christ back to the Father. This obstacle is an integral part of our mortal natures. It must be eliminated, or we will eventually be enslaved by the adversary. That which hinders us from responding more fully to the Light of Christ has several names in scripture, but most often it is called "the natural man," "nature," or "the flesh." In order to overcome the natural man we must be born again through the atonement of Jesus Christ, and thereafter continue to progress spiritually through our faith and our actions.

The Natural Man

Some believe the natural man is identical to the physical body and thus falsely condemn our earthly tabernacles. It is important to distinguish between the two. At the end of the Creation, God declared, "All things which I had made were very good" (Moses 2:31). Our physical body was included in that declaration. The Lord has also taught that "the elements are eternal, and spirit and element, inseparably connected, receive a fulness of joy; and when separated, man cannot

S. Michael Wilcox is assistant professor of Ancient Scripture at Brigham Young University.

receive a fulness of joy" (D&C 93:33–34). Since we cannot obtain this fulness of joy without the physical element, that element is not evil. It is the carnal, untamed desires of the natural man that bring evil.

King Benjamin stated that "the natural man is an enemy to God, and has been from the fall of Adam" (Mosiah 3:19). Because the Fall introduced good and evil into the world, we are able to exercise free agency in partaking of either good or evil (Mosiah 16:3). Recognizing this fact, the Lord explained to Adam, "Inasmuch as thy children are conceived in sin, even so when they begin to grow up, sin conceiveth in their hearts, and they taste the bitter, that they may know to prize the good. And it is given unto them to know good from evil; wherefore they are agents unto themselves" (Moses 6:55–56). The Pearl of Great Price teaches that after the Fall some of Adam and Eve's children did indeed "[love] Satan more than God. And men began from that time forth to be carnal, sensual, and devilish" (Moses 5:13).

If the natural man continually yields to worldly enticings, he will continually be an enemy to God. As already indicated, we are all conceived in sin, and, therefore, as we grow up, sin is conceived in our hearts (Moses 6:55). From this we learn that the natural man is partially centered in the heart. In his letter to the Ephesians, Paul states that humanity fulfills "the desires of the flesh and of the mind" (2:2–3), thereby indicating that the natural man is also closely associated with the mind. In truth, the heart and mind are in all probability the real seat of the natural man. Do not the scriptures testify that "as [a man] thinketh in his heart, so is he" (Prov 23:7)?

If we do not "put off" the natural man, we become "carnal, sensual, and devilish, by nature" (Alma 42:10). Alma taught that "all men that are in a state of nature . . . are in the gall of bitterness, . . . [and are] contrary to the nature of God" (Alma 41:11; see also Hel 13:38). Those who remain in a natural or carnal state degenerate until they reach a state called the "fulness of iniquity" (Ether 2:10) and consequently suffer final captivity by the devil. It was this thought that caused Lehi to exhort Laman and Lemuel to choose righteousness and its resulting liberty, rather than choose evil with its resulting captivity. He pleaded with his sons "not [to] choose eternal death, according to the will of the flesh and the evil which is therein, which giveth the spirit of the devil power to captivate, to bring you down to hell, that he may reign over you in his own kingdom" (2 Nephi 2:29). Abinadi spoke to the wicked priests of king Noah and warned them of their own "carnal and devilish" nature (Mosiah 16:3). He then warned the priests of the consequences of having a carnal nature: "Remember that he that persists in his own carnal nature, and goes on in the ways of sin and rebellion against God, remaineth in his fallen state and the devil hath all power over him. Therefore he is as though there was no redemption made, being an enemy to God; and also is the devil an enemy to God" (Mosiah 16:5).

A few illustrations will give us insight into the natural man. Many people do not perceive the beginnings of a carnal nature. Almost any action which is rationalized by the phrase, "Oh, that's natural," will find its true source in the natural man. If a novel or a movie portrays a suggestive scene, is it not the natural reaction to dwell on it and feed the lust? If one person has more material possessions than another, is it not natural for one to be proud and the other envious? When one is injured by another, is it not the natural reaction to seek revenge? Illustrations could be given of anger, sloth, gluttony, violence, selfishness, profanity, and other natural behavior. Even the Lord warns men who hold the priesthood that it is "the nature of almost all men, as soon as they get a little authority, . . . to exercise unrighteous dominion" (D&C 121:39).

We often personify our natures as entities which are separate from ourselves. "It's not my nature to be patient." We say, "I naturally tend to fly off the handle at times," or, "I'm overly aggressive by nature." We cannot justify these statements; our goal is not to maintain our own carnal nature. It is the Savior's nature the Book of Mormon prophets declare all must seek.

King Benjamin states that if one "yields to the enticings of the Holy Spirit," one will be able to "[put] off the natural man and [become] a saint through the atonement of Christ the Lord." He then defines a saint as someone who is "submissive, meek, humble, patient, full of love, willing to submit to all things which the Lord seeth fit to inflict upon him, even as a child doth submit to his father" (Mosiah 3:19).

Through the Holy Spirit we can develop the qualities of a saint. Paul taught the Galatians to "walk in the Spirit, and ye shall not fulfil the lust of the flesh. For the flesh lusteth against the Spirit, and the Spirit against the flesh: and these are contrary the one to the other" (5:16–17). Through the Spirit, we must seek to conform our natures to the Savior's nature. This requires us to experience a mighty change, a spiritual rebirth (Alma 5:14).

Becoming Born Again

The scriptures call the process of relinquishing the natural man and becoming a saint being "born again." The Christian world discusses this doctrine at length, leading many to believe that salvation comes through the simple acceptance of Christ as one's personal Savior without requiring much effort on the part of the believer. However, the teachings of Benjamin, Abinadi, and Alma in the Book of Mormon reveal that the process requires more than accepting Christ.

Experiencing a "Mighty Change"

Being born again involves both death and birth; it is a transition or a "mighty change" (Mosiah 5:2). To be born again implies the death of the natural man, which is a figurative death that occurs in the heart. Remember, the Lord told Adam that people conceive sin in their hearts while they are yet children (Moses 6:55). The Atonement plays a key role in changing a person's heart; it is the love of the Savior, faith in his atonement, and hope in his merciful forgiveness that provide the power and motivation to change.

At the end of his address, Benjamin asked his people if they believed his words. Their reply is one of the best descriptions of the process of spiritual rebirth in all scripture:

> And they all cried with one voice, saying: Yea, we believe all the words which thou hast spoken unto us; and also, we know of their surety and truth, because of the Spirit of the Lord Omnipotent, which has wrought a mighty change in us, or in our hearts, that we have no more disposition to do evil, but to do good continually. (Mosiah 5:2)

Born again persons have experienced this mighty change of heart. They do not desire or glory in evil, but glory in good. They are eager to listen to the voice of the Spirit, the Light of Christ, the prophets, and the scriptures, rather than to hold to the inclinations of the natural man. Lust, greed, selfishness, and anger may continue to tempt them, but they will seek to control those feelings and thoughts by bending their wills to the will of the Savior. This "mighty change" will be evidenced by a "broken heart and a contrite spirit," which betoken humility, not pride, in being "saved."

A broken heart is not just a sad or mournful heart; it is a submissive one. Just as "broken" horses follow the slightest commands of their master, so too are spiritually reborn individuals "willing to submit to all things which the Lord seeth fit to inflict upon [them]" (Mosiah 3:19). Christ provided the supreme example of submitting to the will of the Father. As Christ atoned for the sins of the world he pleaded, "O my Father, if it be possible, let this cup pass from me," but said, "Nevertheless not as I will, but as thou wilt" (Matt 26:39). To bring the Atonement to pass, even the Savior humbly submitted to his Father.

Whenever the Book of Mormon speaks of being born again, the heart is the center of the altered state. A few examples may help illustrate this truth. The converted Lamanites "did all declare unto the people the self-same thing—that their hearts had been changed; that they had no more desire to do evil"

(Alma 19:33). Alma the Younger spoke often of these truths, which he learned by his own experience, as related in Mosiah 27 and Alma 36. He reminded the people of Zarahemla of his father's experience after he listened to Abinadi: "There was a mighty change wrought in his heart. . . . He preached the word unto your fathers, and a mighty change was also wrought in their hearts, and they humbled themselves. . . . They were faithful until the end; therefore they were saved." He then asked the crucial question: "And now behold, I ask of you, my brethren of the church, have ye spiritually been born of God? Have ye received his image in your countenances? Have ye experienced this mighty change in your hearts?" (Alma 5:11–14).

It is important to realize that not all people undergo as mighty a change of heart as did king Benjamin's subjects, the converted Lamanites, and Alma the Younger. In fact, most do not. Degrees of change vary because people vary in degrees of iniquity. Some need more change than others. Obviously there would be a difference between one who has lived a proper life based on the light he or she had received and one who has given in totally to carnal tendencies. Both must be born again, but the change will necessarily be different.

Obtaining Forgiveness of Sins

After king Benjamin explained the atonement of Christ to his people, they were overcome by the Spirit. They were not a sinful or rebellious people; they had "been a diligent people in keeping the commandments of the Lord" (Mosiah 1:11). Yet, after hearing of the natural man and the Atonement they "viewed themselves in their own carnal state, even less than the dust of the earth." They prayed for the cleansing mercy of the Atonement that they might "receive forgiveness of [their] sins, and have [their] hearts . . . purified." Their prayers were answered and they were "filled with joy, having received a remission of their sins, and having peace of conscience, because of the exceeding faith which they had in Jesus Christ" (Mosiah 4:2–3).

Many truths emerge from these two verses. First, even "diligent people" need to recognize "their own carnal state." This is not so much a recognition of specific sinful acts as of a sinfulness that results from the desires of one's heart. We begin to realize that the specific sin of snapping at a spouse or child is really the result of impatience; arguing with a neighbor is the result of pride or anger; adultery or fornication is the result of lust. We begin, through the Light of Christ, to see the roots of sin. As long as we concentrate on the outward acts and not on the heart, we will never be truly born again. As Lamoni's father prayed, so must all pray and ask, "What shall I do that I may be born of God, having this wicked spirit rooted out of my breast, and receive his Spirit?" (Alma 22:15).

We learn another truth from Benjamin's people. When they recognized their sinfulness they asked for Christ to apply his atoning blood in their behalf, that they might receive forgiveness of their sins, and that their hearts might be purified. They asked for this purification because of their faith in Christ. This is one of the finest examples in scripture of the practical results of having faith in the Savior's atonement. That faith will lead us to seek the death of the natural man through purification of the heart. Faith in the Lord Jesus Christ is the only power equal to the task of overcoming the natural man.

Benjamin's people immediately received the joy and "peace of conscience" that comes with a remission of sins. Mormon reminds his readers that this miracle was wrought because of the people's "exceeding faith . . . in Jesus Christ" (Mosiah 4:3).

Receiving the Image of Christ

Alma adds an important truth relative to the process of spiritual rebirth. The death of the natural man is but the beginning. We must then receive "[Christ's] image in [our] countenances" (Alma 5:14). Remember, Benjamin's counsel was not only to put off the natural man; a saint had to be born. Saints have the image of Christ engraved on their countenances as a result of their acceptance of the Atonement and their subsequent lives of obedience and righteousness. As they continue to refine their characters in accordance with the Savior's character, they reflect his image more and more. Alma revealed this truth the moment he awoke from his three-day sojourn in hell: "I have repented of my sins," he told the people who prayed for his recovery, "and have been redeemed of the Lord; behold I am born of the Spirit" (Mosiah 27:24). Alma testified that his experience must be applied to all people:

> Marvel not that all mankind, yea, men and women, all nations, kindreds, tongues and people, must be born again; yea, born of God, changed from their carnal and fallen state, to a state of righteousness, being redeemed of God, becoming his sons and daughters; and thus they become new creatures; and unless they do this, they can in nowise inherit the kingdom of God. (Mosiah 27:25–26)

Alma calls the spiritually reborn person a "new creature" (v 26), a "son" or "daughter" of God (v 25). The father of this son or daughter is Jesus Christ. No father wants his children to remain infants forever; a father wants his children to progress, grow, and improve in every worthy way. Christ is a righteous, perfect father. He desires his children to progress and become like him. To do so they must follow his example and acquire all the traits and qualities he possesses, just as he followed the Father and attained his qualities and perfection by growing from grace to grace. These reborn sons and daughters of Christ, having entered into a state of grace through the Atonement, then progress from grace to grace until they have reached perfection, or to use Paul's words, until they reach a "knowledge of the Son of God, unto a perfect man, unto the measure of the stature of the fulness of Christ" (Eph 4:13). This progression brings the fruit of the tree of life which the Book of Mormon describes as white, sweet, desirable, precious, beautiful, pure, and most joyous to the soul (see 1 Nephi 8:11–12;

11:8–9, 22–23; Alma 32:42). To know this fruit by our own experience is the whole purpose of mortality.

The Process of Being Born Again: Alma the Younger

The process of being born again and becoming a son or daughter of Christ is dramatically portrayed in the life of Alma the Younger. Before the Atonement wrought a mighty change in him, he was a "very wicked and an idolatrous man" (Mosiah 27:8). He used his power of speech to lead people away from God into all manner of iniquities. He caused "much dissension" and gave "the enemy of God . . . power over" the people (Mosiah 27:9). He sought to "destroy the church of God" (Mosiah 27:10). He rebelled against God until the appearance of an angel helped him to see his sinful life. While speaking of this experience in later years to his son Helaman, Alma described the agonies of a damned soul: "The very thought of coming into the presence of my God did rack my soul with inexpressible horror. Oh, thought I, that I could be banished and become extinct both soul and body, that I might not be brought to stand in the presence of my God, to be judged of my deeds" (Alma 36:14–15).

He described the pain and bitterness as he was "harrowed up to the greatest degree . . . with all [his] sins" (Alma 36:12). In the midst of this agony he cried within his heart, "O Jesus, thou Son of God, have mercy on me" (Alma 36:18). In the moment of his plea, the power of the Atonement took hold of Alma, and he was born again. The mighty change took place. It was a change that had immediate and long-term effects:

> I could remember my pains no more; yea, I was harrowed up by the memory of my sins no more. And oh, what joy, and what marvelous light I did behold; yea, my soul was filled with joy as exceeding as was my pain! Yea, I say unto you, my son, that there could be nothing so exquisite and so bitter as were my pains. Yea, and again I say unto you, my son, that on the other hand, there can be nothing so exquisite and sweet as was my joy. (Alma 36:19–21)

Before the mercy of the Atonement was extended, the thought of coming before God filled Alma with horror. After the change Alma "saw . . . God sitting upon his throne, surrounded with numberless concourses of angels, in the attitude of singing and praising their God; yea, and [his] soul did long to be there" (Alma 36:22). Before his acceptance of the Savior, Alma fought the Church; afterwards, he sought to build it up. Before, he was filled with wickedness and iniquity; afterwards, his life was patterned according to the Savior's perfect example. Before, he rebelled; afterwards, he obeyed. In every aspect of his life Alma was a new creature. This is the power of the Atonement and the result of being born again. As he awoke, Alma invited all to experience this healing change. He testified that Christ "remembereth every creature of his creating, he will make himself manifest unto all" (Mosiah 27:30).

The Fruits of Spiritual Rebirth

We have discussed several aspects of spiritual rebirth and how it relates to the natural man and to the Atonement. The Book of Mormon also provides an excellent description of the born again individual. That description can be gleaned from many scriptures (see Col 3:9–10, 12, 14; Alma 5:14–31), but Mosiah 4 and 5 provide an ideal example. Mosiah 4 shows us that in detailing these traits we must remember that they are characteristics which the spiritually reborn individual seeks to acquire; they do not appear in their fullest expression at the moment of change. According to Benjamin, if we "have come to the knowledge of the glory of God, . . . have known of his goodness and have tasted of his love, . . . have received a remission of [our] sins," and if we remember him, and remain humble and steadfast in our faith, we will (1) "always rejoice"; (2) "be filled with the love of God"; (3) "retain a remission of [our] sins"; (4) grow in the knowledge of God and of that which is "just and true"; (5) "not have a mind to injure one another, but to live peaceably"; (6) "render to every man according to that which is his due"; (7) teach our children "to walk in the ways of truth and soberness, . . . [and] to love one another, and to serve one another"; and (8) "succor those that stand in need of [our] succor . . . [and] administer of [our] substance unto him that standeth in need" (Mosiah 4:11–16). So that his people would not be discouraged or overly guilt-ridden by such a high ideal, Benjamin counseled them to "see that all these things are done in wisdom and order, for it is not requisite that a man should run faster than he has strength" (Mosiah 4:27).

Mosiah 5 expounds upon the qualities of people who have been spiritually reborn. Through "the manifestations of [the] Spirit," these born again individuals have "great views of that which is to come; and were it expedient, [they] could prophesy of all things" (Mosiah 5:3). The Prophet Joseph Smith alluded to this "great view" when he taught that "we must have a change of heart to see the kingdom of God" (*Teachings of the Prophet Joseph Smith* 328). Born again people are "willing to enter into a covenant with God . . . to be obedient to his com- mandments in all things . . . all the remainder of [their] days" (Mosiah 5:5). They are willing to "take upon [themselves] the name of Christ" because they are now his children, "his sons and daughters" (Mosiah 5:7–8). They will keep Christ's name "written always in [their] hearts" (Mosiah 5:12). To do that, the Savior must be close to "the thoughts and intents of [their] hearts" (Mosiah 5:13). Lastly, they will be "steadfast and immovable, always abounding in good works" (Mosiah 5:15).

Often people wonder if they have been born again. If they have a desire to do good, are willing to covenant with the Lord to be obedient, are trying to refine their characters in the image of Christ by constantly thinking of him and doing the works he did, they can feel secure that they truly have been born again. However, it will be a long time before they progress to the full measure of Christ, the father who leads them into eternal life.

Baptism—The Covenant of Rebirth

The ordinance that symbolizes the mighty change of heart or spiritual rebirth is baptism. The old natural man of sin is buried in the water. The new son or daughter of Christ is resurrected from that burial. Old sins are washed away, and the new son or daughter is clothed with the Holy Ghost.

Through baptism certain covenants are made which, if honored, will lead the new son or daughter to a fulness of light and truth. These covenants are renewed each time we partake of the sacrament, which symbolizes our continual recommitment to the mighty change and the development of Christlike qualities by our (1) taking upon ourselves the name of Christ, (2) remembering him, and (3) keeping his commandments. These covenants parallel the baptismal covenants.

As we have seen, king Benjamin's people were "willing to enter into a covenant with . . . God to do his will, and to be obedient to his commandments in all things . . . all the remainder of [their] days" (Mosiah 5:5). They were also willing to "be called the children of Christ, his sons, and his daughters," and to "take upon [themselves] the name of Christ" (Mosiah 5:7–8). Benjamin then exhorted them to "remember to retain the name written always in your hearts, that ye are not found on the left hand of God, but that ye hear and know the voice by which ye shall be called, and also, the name by which he shall call you. For how knoweth a man the master whom he has not served, and who is a stranger unto him, and is far from the thoughts and intents of his heart?" (Mosiah 5:12–13). Benjamin's people entered into all three sacramental covenants.

We keep the commandments of God because they will help us develop a Christlike character. We remember the Atonement because it helps us maintain the humility and broken heart necessary to retain a remission of sins. We remember the Savior because his life is the perfect example all must follow to become like the Father and attain exaltation. A constant recommitment to take on the name of Christ is a necessary reminder that one has covenanted to become like him. Spiritually newborn sons and daughters of Christ promise to walk in their father's footsteps.

Many people have been given names of righteous people from scriptures or righteous ancestors. Often parents name their children after righteous people in the hope and expectation that they will grow up to be like their namesake. In a simple manner this is part of the power behind taking the name of Christ. Through baptism, we promise to become like Jesus Christ, whose name we now bear.

Conclusion

The doctrine of Christ is simple. We need not be great scholars of the scriptures to understand it; it was never intended to be difficult or mysterious. Having faith in Christ brings the fulness of light and truth which leads to a mighty change of heart and to spiritual rebirth. This change destroys the natural man and creates a newborn son or daughter of Christ. Through constant faith and repentance, and through keeping and renewing the covenants made at baptism, we become worthy of the companionship of the Holy Ghost, who, as a being of light and truth, refines, purifies, and sanctifies us by teaching us truth and by showing us "all things" necessary for exaltation (see 2 Nephi 32:5). Thus we grow from grace to grace. If we lovingly and diligently try to obey every principle, law, commandment, and counsel of God, we will receive the fulness of God's glory. Benjamin promised his people, if they were

> steadfast and immovable, always abounding in good works, that Christ, the Lord God Omnipotent, may seal you his, that you may be brought to heaven, that ye may have everlasting salvation and eternal life, through the wisdom, and power, and justice, and mercy of him who created all things, in heaven and in earth, who is God above all. (Mosiah 5:15)

Abinadi gave the same assuring promise that those with faith in Christ "are raised to dwell with God who has redeemed them" (Mosiah 15:23). Alma the Younger bore his testimony that he knew Christ would "raise [him] up at the last day to dwell with him in glory" (Alma 36:28). Spiritual rebirth is not the equivalent of exaltation, but it does place the individual on the path to eternal life. The sealing of an individual to eternal life comes later, but without these first steps salvation cannot come. Through these simple principles, gods are developed, and individuals walk a pathway opposite to that of the natural man.

BIBLIOGRAPHY

Teachings of the Prophet Joseph Smith. Comp. Joseph Fielding Smith. Salt Lake City: Deseret Book, 1976.

Deliverance from Bondage

15

Clyde J. Williams

Two of the most frequently overlooked portions of the Book of Mormon are found in Mosiah chapters 7–8 and chapters 19–24. These scriptures record the experiences Limhi and Alma had with bondage. For many, the stories of intrigue found in these chapters are perceived as mere side-trips from the main message of Abinadi and his efforts to persuade Noah and his people to come unto Christ. However, I am convinced that each part of the Book of Mormon, including this one, was written for the latter days with one or more purposes in mind.

President Benson, speaking of the ancient Book of Mormon writers, declared:

> If they saw our day and chose those things which would be of greatest worth to us, is not that how we should study the Book of Mormon? We should constantly ask ourselves, "Why did the Lord inspire Mormon (or Moroni or Alma) to include that in his record? What lesson can I learn from that to help me live in this day and age?" ("Book of Mormon" 6)

Because of these questions, I searched for reasons why the prophet Mormon included the story of Limhi in the Book of Mormon. While I do not pretend to know the mind of Mormon, I am certain that one of the main reasons for including Limhi's story in the Book of Mormon is for the lessons it teaches about bondage—the steps leading to it, its different types, what we

---

Clyde J. Williams is assistant professor of Ancient Scripture at Brigham Young University.

must do to be delivered from it, and the different degrees of help the Lord gives us in dealing with it.

To appreciate fully the message of Limhi and his people, we must understand how they came to be in bondage to the Lamanites. Mosiah, the father of king Benjamin, had been warned by the Lord to take those among the Nephites who would "hearken unto the voice of the Lord" and leave the land of Nephi (Omni 1:12). They were led by the power of God to the land of Zarahemla where they discovered the descendants of Mulek, whose ancestors had fled Jerusalem at the time of its destruction (see Omni 1:13–15; Mosiah 25:2). The people of Zarahemla accepted the Nephites and made Mosiah their king (Omni 1:19).

Following Mosiah's death, his son Benjamin was made king (Omni 1:23). During Benjamin's reign, Zeniff and a considerable number of Nephites returned to the land of Nephi and settled there (Omni 1:27–30; Mosiah 9). Zeniff's son, Noah, later became king but ruled unrighteously (see Mosiah 11). For deserting his people as they were being attacked by the Lamanites, Noah was later put to death by some of the men when he commanded further desertion (Mosiah 19:8–9, 20). Following king Noah's death, his son Limhi, who was a "just man" (Mosiah 19:17), became king.

The Steps Leading to Bondage

A careful examination of the narrative of Zeniff, Noah, and Limhi reveals at least four major steps that led them into bondage: they were over-zealous; they embraced wickedness; they failed to follow the living prophet; and they lacked spiritual knowledge. Limhi identified the first step as he spoke to his people:

> And ye all are witnesses this day, that Zeniff, who was made king over this people, he being *over-zealous* to inherit the land of his fathers, therefore being deceived by the cunning and craftiness of king Laman, who having entered into a treaty with king Zeniff, and having yielded up into his hands the possessions of a part of the land.

> ... And all this he [king Laman] did, for the sole purpose of bringing this people into subjection or into bondage. (Mosiah 7:21–22; emphasis added)

Zeniff's over-zealousness led him to make an unwise agreement with one whose ultimate purpose was to bring these Nephites into bondage.

While we question the wisdom of Zeniff, we could ask if the same kind of zeal causes people today to make agreements or sign contracts that will ultimately place them in political or financial bondage. Individuals can be over-zealous for material possessions, or they can become so involved in a cause or in their work that they begin to neglect the weightier matters that are most important, such as family, church, and service to others.

Over-zealousness is an exercise of free agency that can have serious consequences. President Marion G. Romney voiced his concern about our use of free agency in these words: "Free agency, however, precious as it is, is not of itself the perfect liberty we seek, nor does it necessarily lead thereto. As a matter of fact, through the exercise of their agency more people have come to political, economic, and personal bondage than to liberty" (43).

The Nephites who exercised their agency by following Zeniff were not immediately placed in physical bondage, but that decision certainly moved them much closer to that possibility. The same could be said of those of us today who risk our homes or savings in speculative financial ventures. It is important to remember that such people, like Zeniff, may be over-zealous, yet they are not necessarily wicked people. They may be a humble God-fearing people who have become trapped in their quest for financial success.

The second step leading Zeniff's group toward bondage was their gradual embracing of wickedness. Zeniff's son Noah was not like his father; rather, he was guilty of three major sins—winebibbing, adultery, and greed (Mosiah 11:3–4, 14–15). Noah's bad example led his people to adopt his sinful ways

(11:2, 15). In later years, Noah's son Limhi would lament: "Yea, I say unto you, great are the reasons which we have to mourn; for behold how many of our brethren have been slain, and their blood has been spilt in vain, and all because of iniquity. For if this people had not fallen into transgression the Lord would not have suffered that this great evil should come upon them" (Mosiah 7:24–25).

Sin of any kind leads one into bondage—some sins more rapidly than others. Until the murder of the prophet Abinadi, the most serious of Noah's sins was adultery. Immorality has a tremendous tendency to lead one into bondage. Concerning this point President Spencer W. Kimball gave the following warning:

> In the area of one of Satan's most destructive evils, we strongly warn all our people from childhood to old age to beware of the chains of bondage, suffering, and remorse which come from improper use of the body.
>
> The human body is the sacred home of the spirit child of God, and unwarranted tampering with or defilement of this sacred tabernacle can bring only remorse and regret. We urge: stay clean, uncontaminated, undefiled. (*Teachings of Spencer W. Kimball* 7; hereafter *TSWK*)

The third step on the road to bondage was the failure of Noah and his people to heed the warnings of the prophet Abinadi. In his first visit to Noah's people, Abinadi warned that "except they repent[ed] and turn[ed] to the Lord their God, . . . they [would] be brought into bondage" (Mosiah 11:21). After his warning was rejected and his life threatened, Abinadi fled. Two years later the Lord sent him to warn Noah and his people once more, but the nature of his warning had changed; he now told the people that they would be put into bondage because of their iniquities (Mosiah 12:2). At this point there was no way to avoid bondage. What now remained in question was their final fate, for Abinadi solemnly warned that unless they repented they would be "utterly destroy[ed] from off the face of the earth" (Mosiah 12:8).

Their rejection of Abinadi's testimony culminated in his martyrdom. In this dispensation modern prophets have been and are still being rejected by many. The Prophet Joseph Smith was slain because he taught the truth about God, and there are those today who "trample [the Lord's prophets] under their feet" (1 Nephi 19:7) by failing to hearken to their counsel.

The fourth step that allowed Noah to lead his people toward bondage was their lack of spiritual knowledge. While speaking to the priests of king Noah, Abinadi said, "Ye have not applied your hearts to understanding; therefore, ye have not been wise" (Mosiah 12:27). These people were in a condition of mental slavery because they had not read and understood the scriptures. Their condition resembles President Kimball's description of the condition of those who lived before the Protestant Reformation: "For hundreds of years before [Martin] Luther, there had been mental slavery. People did not read their Bibles, they listened only to the priest. They were in spiritual bondage. But beginning with this break of Martin Luther from the church of which he had been a member, freedom of thought and freedom of religion began to be a nearer reality" (*TSWK* 426–27).

Likewise, when Alma the Elder's heart was penetrated by Abinadi's message, he was led by the power of God to bring spiritual knowledge to the people and to establish the Church anew among those who would believe. His efforts led 450 souls out of the bondage of sin and ignorance (Mosiah 18:35).

Types of Bondage

The Nephites in the land of Nephi experienced several different kinds of bondage, which may be categorized into four types: intellectual, financial, spiritual, and physical. Intellectual or mental bondage results from ignorance of spiritual things. When people do not understand the purpose of life or their ultimate potential, they are in bondage to ignorance and cannot be saved (D&C 131:6). President Benson's declaration that the Church is still under condemnation for neglecting the Book of Mormon ("A Sacred Responsibility" 78) would seem to indicate that many of the Saints today are suffering the effects of some degree of mental bondage. To the extent that we allow ourselves to accept false political, social, and educational ideas we move toward a bondage that would deprive us of our God-given freedoms.

Financial bondage occurs when selfishness, greed, and materialism take over. Such was the case when king Noah laid a 20 percent tax on his people to support his riotous life (Mosiah 11:3–15). This materialism and greed ultimately led Noah's people into financial bondage, paying 50 percent of all they possessed to the Lamanites (Mosiah 7:22; 19:15). Financial bondage in modern times may differ from that of king Noah's people; nevertheless, the negative effects are still the same. Unfortunately, in our society there is a trend toward increased debt to support a more opulent lifestyle. The desire to possess material things is a plague of wide proportions. In 1987, 21.2 percent of Americans' disposable income went to pay debts (U.S. Bureau of the Census, table 829). By August 1989 the consumer installment debt had risen to nearly 704 billion dollars (U.S. Department of Commerce, S–14). Certainly financial bondage is a serious problem today.

Spiritual bondage, or the bondage of sin, is referred to by President Romney as "the most awful bondage" (45). Although physical bondage is the most recognizable form of bondage— the Lord often uses it to persuade people to repent—the eternal effects of spiritual bondage are of greater consequence. It was the bondage of sin that ultimately led king Noah's people into physical bondage. Their neglect of the scriptures and their refusal to heed the warning voice of the prophets made it easier for them to rationalize and commit sin. They used their finances to support their lifestyle of leisure and licentiousness. This addiction to sin became so powerful that in the face of possible death many fathers deserted their wives and children to save their own lives (Mosiah 19:11). Who could imagine accepting such distorted values?

The degree of spiritual bondage among the people in the land of Nephi differed from person to person, much as it does in today's society. The vast majority of people today (72%) are unconditionally opposed to the idea of extramarital sex ("Morality" 53). However, if statistics were available showing how many people are entertained annually by videos and movies which condone extramarital affairs, the picture would be much less encouraging. Spiritual bondage begins not while physically committing sin, but intellectually when we begin to accept sin. These oft-repeated words of Alexander Pope's "An Essay on Man" summarize well the process that leads to spiritual bondage:

> Vice is a monster of so frightful mien,
> As, to be hated, needs but to be seen;
> Yet seen too oft, familiar with her face,
> We first endure, then pity, then embrace.
> (Epistle 2, ll. 217–20)

One of the most dramatic examples of our society's movement from enduring and pitying immorality to embracing it was revealed in a survey reported in the 9 December 1985 issue of *U.S. News & World Report* ("Morality" 52–53). In 1969 a Gallup poll indicated that 68 percent of all adults and 49 percent of young adults thought that premarital sex was wrong ("Morality" 52). The 1985 *U.S. News* poll indicated that a tremendous shift in attitude had occurred: 61 percent of all adults and 78 percent of all young adults now felt that premarital sex was not wrong ("Morality" 52). This change represents a 30 percent shift in moral values in a 16-year period. It would appear that with the sin of premarital sex we have arrived at the stage which Pope called "embrace." This pattern of increasing acceptance of sin was also the pattern of king Noah and his people.

The final type of bondage which the Nephites in the land of Nephi experienced was physical bondage, or slavery. While physical bondage could refer to those who are subject to bad habits or appetites, in this paper the term physical bondage is applied only to those who are prisoners or slaves to another person or nation. It is difficult to find a time in history when there were not at least some of our Heavenly Father's children in physical bondage. In the Book of Mormon, this bondage often comes as a result of people's failure to follow the principles of the gospel or to give heed to the warnings of the prophets. Intellectual and spiritual bondage are generally precursors to physical bondage, which was the case with the Nephites in the land of Nephi.

One additional point applies to both physical and intellectual bondage: everyone is born with the Light of Christ, and that Light eventually causes all who are in bondage to seek their God-given freedoms. Concerning this principle President Ezra Taft Benson affirmed:

> There is a God in heaven who is the sovereign power of the universe, and we are His literal offspring. He has endowed us with inalienable rights, among which are life, liberty, and the pursuit of happiness. This He has implanted in the human breast. This is why men cannot be driven indefinitely or led by despotic rulers to intellectual or physical slavery and bondage. Fear and despotism may rule for a generation or two, or three, but in time the human spirit rebels, the spirit of liberty manifests itself, and its tyrannous hand is overthrown. (*This Nation Shall Endure* 69)

Perhaps never in known history has a more dramatic example of this principle occurred than in the events which have recently taken place in eastern Europe. People who have been long deprived of personal freedoms have finally stepped forward and said, in essence, "I want to have freedom to vote, to speak, and to worship according to the dictates of my own conscience." These events are a great evidence of the Light of Christ that influences all humankind to desire freedom.

What Delivers a People from Bondage?

Having examined the different types of bondage and the steps that lead people into bondage, we need to examine the process that leads people out of bondage. On the subject of deliverance from bondage, the stories of Limhi and his people and that of Alma the Elder and his people present some unique insights.

In fulfillment of Abinadi's prophecy (Mosiah 11:21–23), Limhi and the Nephites in the city of Nephi were placed in bondage by the Lamanites after being led astray by the poor example of king Noah. Upon experiencing the hardships associated with bondage, these Nephites determined to go to battle against the Lamanites (21:6). They were soundly defeated three times (21:12). Only after being defeated for the third time did they begin the process that would enable them to escape from bondage.

The first step outlined in the Book of Mormon for removing the chains of bondage is to be humble before the Lord. Because of heartache and the heavy yoke of bondage, Limhi and his people humbled themselves before the Lord (Mosiah 21:13), "turn[ing] to the Lord with full purpose of heart" as Limhi had instructed (7:33). Notice that the command to turn to the Lord is not to be half-hearted, but rather requires one's "*full* purpose of heart." This process of being humbled requires a changing or "turning" that must occur in individual lives if they are to be spared or delivered from bondage. President N. Eldon Tanner declared: "A person who is guilty of a serious transgression cannot progress, and he is not happy while the guilt is upon him. Until he has confessed and repented he is in bondage" (78). Limhi's people acknowledged their guilt and turned to the Lord for his help.

The second step that leads away from bondage is for people to engage in mighty prayer. Prayer should automatically accompany being humbled before the Lord. In Mosiah 21 we read that the people of Limhi "did humble themselves even in the depths of humility; and they did cry mightily to God; yea, even all the day long did they cry unto their God that he would deliver them out of their afflictions" (v 14). These Nephites learned to put their trust in the Lord as Limhi had encouraged them to do (Mosiah 7:33). Even though they sincerely and humbly relied on the Lord, "the Lord was slow to hear their cry" (Mosiah 21:15) because they had been slow to hear and respond to his word.

The third step of Limhi's people toward deliverance from bondage was their willingness to covenant with the Lord to keep his commandments (Mosiah 21:32). Their obedience not only moved them toward freedom from physical bondage, it also enabled them to begin to enjoy a release from spiritual bondage before they had actually escaped from the hands of the Lamanites. In the words of President Marion G. Romney:

> Freedom thus obtained—that is, by obedience to the law of Christ—is freedom of the soul, the highest form of liberty. And the most glorious thing about it is that it is within the reach of every one of us, regardless of what people about us, or even nations, do. All we have to do is learn the law of Christ and obey it. To learn it and obey it is the primary purpose of every soul's mortal life. (45)

The fourth and final step in escaping bondage is to serve the Lord with all diligence (see Mosiah 7:33; 21:32). To both the Nephites and the Jaredites the Lord declared that freedom from bondage would continue for those who inhabit this choice land as long as they "serve the God of the land, who is Jesus Christ" (Ether 2:12; compare 2 Nephi 1:7). Once Limhi and his people had covenanted with God to serve him and keep his commandments, they were able to devise a plan of escape from their Lamanite captors (Mosiah 22). That Limhi and his people began to witness the hand of the Lord helping them in their time of bondage confirms the promise of the Lord "that he [would] pour out his Spirit more abundantly" upon those who would serve him and keep his commandments (Mosiah 18:10).

Different Degrees of Help from the Lord

A subtle yet important lesson to be learned from Mosiah 21–24 pertains to the differing degrees of bondage which Limhi's and Alma's people experienced and the reasons for those differences. The following chart contrasts the bondage of Limhi's and Alma's people.

TABLE 1 *Degrees of Bondage*

Limhi's Group	Alma's Group
Limhi's group was placed in bondage with much bloodshed (21:5–12).	Alma's group was placed in bondage with no bloodshed (23:35–38; 24:9).
The Lord was slow to hear their cries because they had been slow to hear Him (21:15).	The Lord was not slow to hear their cries (24:10–13).
The Lord softened the Lamanites' hearts so they eased the burdens of Limhi's group (21:15).	The Lord physically eased the burdens of Alma's group (24:14–15).
They prospered by degrees as their faith increased (21:16).	The Lord visited them in their afflictions (24:14).
Gideon devised a plan of escape (22:9).	The Lord said, "I will deliver you" (24:16).
They got the guards drunk (22:7, 10).	The Lord put the guards to sleep (24:19).
They needed to have Ammon lead them to Zarahemla (22:11).	The Lord led them to Zarahemla (24:23–25).

As this chart shows, because Alma and his people had been humbled by the word of God rather than being compelled to be humble by their bondage as Limhi's group had been, the Lord made the bondage of Alma and his people much easier to endure. The message for us is that it is better to repent sooner than later. The slower we are to hearken to the Lord, the slower he must be in responding to our needs. How reassuring it must have been to Alma's people to experience the miracle of not feeling the burdens which were placed upon their backs. They could have no question in their minds about whose power it was that delivered them and led them back to the land of Zarahemla.

The question may be asked why Alma's group was put into bondage since they had repented, had made covenants, and had served the Lord for some time. The answer seems to go back to Abinadi's prophecy. When he first came to the Nephites in the land of Nephi, he warned that they would be brought into bondage if they did not repent (see Mosiah 11:21). This warning went unheeded until Abinadi returned two years later. His warning then proclaimed that they *would* be brought into bondage, and if they still refused to repent they would be destroyed (see Mosiah 12:2, 8). It was at this time that Alma was converted and began to teach the words of Abinadi secretly to those Nephites who would listen. Thus, even though Alma and his people had repented, it was still necessary that Abinadi's first prophecy be fulfilled.

A great principle we can learn from this portion of the book of Mosiah (chapters 19–24) is that the longer we wait to repent and forsake our sins, the more serious the consequences will be. Elder Melvin J. Ballard reiterated this principle: "Every man and woman who is putting off until the next life the task of correcting and overcoming the weakness of the flesh are sentencing themselves to years of bondage, for no man or woman will come forth in the resurrection until he has completed his work, until he has overcome, until he has done as much as he can do" (242).

Sadly, for many this bondage has already begun in this life. As with Limhi and his people, if we are slow to hearken to the counsel of the Lord, we only make our transformation to freedom more difficult and increase the degree of our bondage.

Conclusion

I have explained the steps that lead people along the road to bondage and examined the types of bondage we can encounter, the most serious and far-reaching of which is spiritual bondage. Furthermore, I have outlined the process by which one can escape from the hold of bondage. Significantly, the degree of bondage we experience is directly related to the timing of our repentance. The best time to repent is now.

Finally, we should understand that the Lord never intended or desired that his children should be in bondage. In the words of Elder Mark E. Petersen, "Let us remember that it is against the will of God that any one of us should be in bondage—in any way—neither to sin nor to addiction nor to debt" (63).

Lehi taught his son Jacob that we have all been created by God to experience joy and to be free (2 Nephi 2:25, 27). However, when we experience bondage of any kind and therefore seek relief through applying divine principles, we must remember that deliverance will finally come "according to [the Lord's] own will and pleasure" (Mosiah 7:33). May we thus be blessed with the patience and wisdom to understand, avoid, and overcome bondage in our lives.

BIBLIOGRAPHY

Ballard, Melvin J. *Sermons and Missionary Services.* Ed. Bryant S. Hinckley. Salt Lake City: Deseret Book, 1949.

Benson, Ezra Taft. "The Book of Mormon—Keystone of Our Religion." *Ensign* (Nov 1986) 16:4–7; also in *Conference Report* (Oct 1986) 4–7.

———. "A Sacred Responsibility." *Ensign* (May 1986) 16:77–78; also in *Conference Report* (Apr 1986) 98–100.

———. *This Nation Shall Endure.* Salt Lake City: Deseret Book, 1977.

Kimball, Spencer W. "Guidelines to Carry Forth the Work of God in Cleanliness." *Ensign* (May 1974) 4:4–8; also in *Conference Report* (Apr 1974) 4–9.

————. *Teachings of Spencer W. Kimball*. Ed. Edward L. Kimball. Salt Lake City: Bookcraft, 1982.

"Morality." *U.S. News and World Report* (9 Dec 1985) 99:52–53.

Petersen, Mark E. "Blessings in Self-Reliance." *Ensign* (May 1981) 11:61–63; also in *Conference Report* (Apr 1981) 80–84.

Pope, Alexander. "An Essay on Man." *The Poems of Alexander Pope*. Ed. John Butt. New Haven: Yale, 1963. 501–47.

Romney, Marion G. "The Perfect Law of Liberty." *Ensign* (Nov 1981) 11:43–45; also in *Conference Report* (Oct 1981) 60–64.

Tanner, N. Eldon. "Our Responsibility to the Transgressor." *Ensign* (Nov 1974) 4:76–79; also in *Conference Report* (Oct 1974) 107–11.

U.S. Bureau of the Census. *Statistical Abstract of the United States 1990: The National Data Book*. 110th ed. Washington, DC: GPO, Jan 1990.

U.S. Department of Commerce. Bureau of Economic Analysis. *Survey of Current Business*. Washington, DC: GPO, Oct 1989.

Subject Index

covenant defined, 258
Sacrifice, 3, 41, 42, 51
Saint, defined, 250
Salvation, only through Jesus, 3, 4
Samuel the Lamanite, on Atonement, 185
   on procrastination, 148
Sanctification, 157, 231, 233, 235, 243
Scripture, other books to come forth, 1
Scriptures of the Restoration, 6–7
Security, 120
Seed of Christ, 175–76, 184
Seer, 191
Sermons, of King Benjamin and Abinadi,
   54–55
Service, 39, 238–39
   leads to eternal life, 237
Sexual union, 142
Slavery, 75
   See also Mental slavery
Smith, Hyrum, 133
Smith, Joseph, killed for concept of Christ,
   179
   on confession of sins, 219
   on importance of parents' testimonies, 25
   on Jesus' ministry, 166
   on qualifying to see kingdom of God, 257
   testimony of Book of Mormon, 154
   unschooled, 2
Smith, Joseph F., on ministering to the poor,
   239
   on priesthood, 192
Sons of perdition, 145
Sorcery, 105
Spirituality, 240
Spiritual leukemia, 232–33
Stewardship, King Benjamin reports, 40
Sunshine Acres Children's Home, 236
Synagogues, 223

— T —

Tanner, N. Eldon, on confession, 269
Taxes, levied by King Noah, 94
Temple, contrast between King Benjamin's
   and King Noah's, 51–52
   of Nephites, 193
   religious center of ancient and modern Israel, 50
   worship in, 51
Ten Commandments, 99
Testimony, importance of parents', 25
   of King Benjamin, 229
Tocqueville, Alexis de, on America's greatness, 128–29

Transgression, 46, 61, 66, 67, 204
Tree of life, 254
Tyranny, 118

— U —

United Order, 241
Unprofitable servants, 80–81

— V —

Vanity, 102
Vice, 267

— W —

Walls around Jerusalem, 2
Welfare program, 237
Wentworth, John, 141
Whoredoms, condemned by Abinadi, 95
Williams, Frederick G., counseled to succor
   the poor, 238
Witchcraft, 105
Wives and concubines, of King Noah, 95

— Y —

Young, Brigham, on confession of sins, 219
   on government of the United States, 134
   on natural man, 148, 151–52

— Z —

Zion (the Americas), 178

Scripture Index

BOOK OF MORMON

12:32	98, 193	15:8	108, 174
12:37	98	15:8–9	5, 175
13:1	98	15:9	173, 181, 184, 185
13:3–10	99		
13:6	198	15:10	175
13:9	9	15:10–13	184
13:11	99	15:11–13	175, 181
13:25	99	15:14–17	176
13:25–26	193, 198	15:14–27	181
13:26	99	15:18–19	176
13:27, 34	7	15:20	28, 109, 177
13:27–35	162	15:21	177
13:28	108	15:21–23	109
13:28, 32	106, 193	15:22	110
13:28, 32, 33, 34–35	107	15:22–23	177
13:29–30	106	15:23	108, 260
13:29–31	193	15:24	109, 110, 111, 177
13:29–35	7		
13:31	106	15:25	109, 177
13:32	108	15:26–27	177
13:32–35	101	15:28	177
13:33	5, 108	15:28 to 16:1	178, 181
13:33–35	162, 181	16:1	16
13:34–35	108	16:2	146
14–16	100	16:2–3	145
14:1	163	16:2–5	178
14:2	164, 167, 181	16:2–12	181
14:6	172	16:3	248, 249
14:7	173	16:3–4	145
14:8	174	16:4	108
14:9	182	16:4, 15	108
14:10	182	16:5	145, 249
14:11	184	16:6	178
14:12	185	16:6–7	4
14:33–34	181	16:6–8	109
15	176	16:7–8	178
15:1	108, 165, 181	16:9–10	109
15:1, 2–4, 5–7, 8, 23	108	16:9–12	178
15:1–4	164	16:11	109
15:1–5	6	16:13–15	101, 178, 181
15:2	35, 165, 169, 181	16:14	7
		16:15	108
15:2–4	108, 168	17:1–4	104
15:3	35, 167, 169, 181	17:1–13	178
		17:2	198
15:4	168, 169, 171, 181	17:5	101
		17:7	101
15:5	12, 35, 171, 181, 182	17:7–8	108
		17:8	101
15:5–7	108	17:11–12	197
15:6	173, 181	17:12	102
15:7	174	17:13	102
15:7–8	181	17:18	103
15:7–13	174	17:20	102, 103

18:8	32
18:8–10	238
18:9	32
18:10	32, 270
18:10, 17	201
18:13	198
18:13–16	201
18:14	61, 201
18:18	193, 198
18:19	26
18:35	265
19–24	261, 272
19:5–9	52
19:8–9, 20	262
19:11	52, 267
19:12–15	53
19:15	266
19:17	262
19:20	103
19:26	53
20:21	111
21–24	271
21:5–12	271
21:6	269
21:12	269
21:13	269
21:14	270
21:15	270, 271
21:16	271
21:28	191
21:32	270
21:33–34	201
21:33–35	201
22	270
22:7, 10	271
22:9	271
22:11	271
23:6	198
23:6–7	207
23:7–9, 13	199
23:8	114
23:16	196, 200
23:17	191, 193, 196, 198
23:21	12
23:35–38	271
24:4–5	190
24:4–7	56
24:5–7	27
24:9	271
24:10–13	271
24:14	271
24:14–15	271
24:16	271

24:19	271
24:23–25	271
25–27	59, 60, 61, 70
25:2	262
25:2, 13	189
25:5	59
25:15–18	61
25:17–18	201
25:18	61
25:18, 23	61
25:19	203
25:19, 21	196
25:20	193
25:21	193, 203
25:21–22	61
25:22	64
25:22–23	203
26	212, 225
26:1–2	14
26:1, 3	212
26:1–5	204
26:2	192
26:3	63
26:4	63, 212
26:5	212
26:6	61, 62, 66
26:6–8	204
26:6, 35–39	11
26:7	196
26:9	212
26:9, 10	67
26:10	212
26:10–11	204
26:11	212
26:12	205, 213
26:13	205, 213
26:13–32	61, 67
26:15–16	16
26:15–32	213
26:18	1
26:18–28	224
26:20	13
26:21–22	213
26:22	61
26:23–25, 27	66
26:23–28	214
26:25–27	66
26:26–39	225
26:28–29, 32	67
26:29	214, 216, 217, 221, 224
26:29–30	224
26:30	216
26:31	222, 225

DOCTRINE AND COVENANTS

PEARL OF GREAT PRICE